POETRY AND FILM

POETRY AND FILM:
ARTISTIC KINSHIP BETWEEN
ARSENII AND ANDREI
TARKOVSKY

Compiled by Kitty Hunter Blair

Tate Publishing

First published 2014 by order of the Tate Trustees
by Tate Publishing, a division of Tate Enterprises Ltd,
Millbank, London SW1P 4RG
www.tate.org.uk/publishing

A catalogue record for this book is available from the British Library

ISBN 978 1 84976 249 6

Distributed in the United States and Canada by ABRAMS, New York

Library of Congress Control Number applied for

Designed by Andrew Shoolbred
Printed in Hong Kong by Printing Express

Front cover: Detail from Pieter Breughel the Elder, *Hunters in the Snow*
1565. The camera focuses on this detail in *Solaris*, where a series of
Breughel paintings hang in the space station library.
Back cover: Still from *Solaris*, showing a spread from Cervantes's
Don Quixote
Frontispiece: Arsenii Tarkovsky as a young man

It has been granted me to live with you,
To make my way into your nightly dreams,
And to be reflected in your mirror.
                    Arsenii Tarkovsky, from 'Testament', 1934–7

When I was little I was a fire-worshipper ...
    The knife would grow brighter and brighter with a silvery-blue
iridescence as the wheel in its narrow belt whirled faster and faster.
The knife-grinder pressed the knife against the magical carborundum
stone and there came a shower of golden rain, wonderful golden rain,
and I would put my hand out to catch it. The sparks felt warm but
didn't burn at all.
    I could watch for hours on end. Nothing on earth could distract
me from my prayerful contemplation.
    Sparks flew from twenty knives at once, from twenty whirling
grindstones. Open-mouthed, seeing nothing but fire, I moved from
one knife-grinder to another. They were wizards and magicians, the
bearers of my mystery, and their machines flung out feathery tassels
of fire. I was like one possessed. I was too small to think about what
was happening to me, I was dissolving into fire ...
    The butcher's knife, smeared with sticky blood, grows clean,
starts to shine, sparks surge out from under it, and the magic stone
whirls and whirls, and the sparks go on raining and raining, and all
you have to do is put your hand underneath.
                    Arsenii Tarkovsky, from 'The Knife-grinders', 16 July 1945

Contents

Acknowledgements and credits

My warm thanks are due to many generous friends who commented on my work while this book was taking shape, in particular to Julia Dale, herself a fine poet and verse translator, for her perceptive criticism and suggestions, and Galya Scott for scrupulously vetting my translations and pointing out misreadings of the original Russian (any remaining errors are my responsibility alone); both gave unstintingly of their time and expertise. Sasha Jennings gave me some felicitous renderings; Imogen Stidworthy was an invaluable sounding-board. Marina Tarkovskaia shared her knowledge of her father's work with great generosity. I am immensely grateful to everyone at Tate Publishing who has been involved in the book's production, particularly to Rebecca Fortey, and above all to Roger Thorp for welcoming the project and giving it his enthusiastic support.

IMAGE CREDITS

The Tarkovsky family photographs and the shot of the River Sugakleia were kindly provided by Marina Tarkovskaia.

The frontispiece and the family group on p.80 are by Lev Gornung, a close friend of the family and godfather to both Andrei and Marina. He took dozens of pictures of them, many of which were used by the film-maker in *Mirror*. He was also a poet. He left a rich legacy of photographs of Russian writers and artists, including Anna Akhmatova. The portrait of the poet on p.175 is by A. Krivomazov.

The photograph of Bagrati Cathedral on p.145 is by Vakhtang Tsintsadze and is reproduced here by gracious permission of his daughter, Nana Tsintsadze.

Mos Films generously consented to the reproduction of stills from Andrei Tarkovsky's *Mirror*, *Ivan's Childhood*, *Solaris*, *Andrei Rublëv* and *Stalker*.

Note on transliteration and pronunciation

Generally the Library of Congress transliteration system has been followed. However, surname endings have been rendered -oy and -sky (rather than -oi, -skii); and in quotations from poems, since sound is all-important, the system has been discarded in favour of phonetic transliteration. Stressed vowels are indicated in bold print. The word *iurodivy* occurs several times and I have simplified the ending to -*y*, regardless of number and gender.

Ë is pronounced *yo* as in yonder. A single apostrophe ' represents the Russian soft sign, which palatalises the preceding consonant, i.e. a slight hint that it is followed by a *y* as in yes.

The bell in
the crypt
*Ivan's
Childhood*

Introduction

I
Affinities

Arsenii Tarkovsky's first collection of poems appeared in 1962, the year his son Andrei was awarded the Golden Lion at the Venice Film Festival for his first feature film, *Ivan's Childhood*. Although the poet had been writing for three decades, he was renowned only as a translator of verse, much of it from the languages of the Caucasus and Central Asia. His own poetry was read by a fairly narrow circle of cognoscenti; for more than half his career he was writing 'for the desk drawer', as the saying went in Soviet times, because his work did not fit into parameters acceptable to the censors. For the first audiences of Andrei Tarkovsky's films his father's poems were very important, but to many people they were new.[1] Now, close on half a century later, when his son's place in film history is firmly established and his influence acknowledged worldwide, the poet is still little known outside Russia beyond the lines recited in three of Andrei Tarkovsky's films: a total of seven poems out of some six or seven hundred.

Most of us come to the poems after seeing the films, where they counterpoint and penetrate the filmic world, interacting with the visual images and becoming part of an already complex meditation on time, nature, art, family and individual fate. As the viewer hears them they seem utterly natural, despite the originality of such an interweaving of poetry and cinematic image. Even for the viewer who takes them in from subtitles while hearing the recitation without understanding it, the impression left is of an alluring terrain, unknown and harmonious, lying beyond the immediate experience of the film. When the filmgoer first reads the poems in printed form, he or she seems to be arriving in familiar country, for so many of the images and themes that we associate with Andrei's work are to be found in his father's verse. The poetic world of the father accords with that of his son to a remarkable degree; furthermore, the poet's vision takes over the reader's imagination rather as the intense gaze of the film-maker becomes that of the viewer.

Many of Arsenii Tarkovsky's key images have their counterparts in Andrei's films. Water often acts as a medium. Its contemplation can lead into the poet's and reader's interior world: the moments preceding dreams, and recollections of earliest childhood self-awareness, as in 'On the Riverbank' (p.123). In 'After the War' (p.100) rapids show the poet his double, and his future together with his past; the rushing water has taken him out of his space and time. Water can unify different eras, as in 'When the bathing woman with heavy braided hair' (p.81), where, through the immediacy of the brook's dazzling surface, the present sunlit midday becomes one with a mythical past of nature gods. Tears and rain merge in mourning ('Just like forty years ago' [2], p.117), rather as they do when Maria, in *Mirror*, weeps as she reads her husband's poems while gazing out at the rain. Rivers and bridges speak of separation and loss ('Song', 'The Wind' (pp.112–13), or of death ('Ivan's Willow', p.100). In 'Life, Life' (p.142) an affirmation of immortality is set against a background of the sea:

> Already each of us is by the sea,
> And I am one who hauls the nets ashore
> When shoals of immortality sweep in.

Sea pictures are relatively rare, and they take poet and reader beyond the rivers and lakes of the Russian countryside on to vaster, unchartered waters.

The cine camera has a unique capacity for resting on water, bringing the spectator's gaze into its fluidity; the contemplation of water, on screen as in nature, awakens a sense of time's flow, of its going on forever – an intuition of timelessness. This is one of the most recognisable and recurring traits of Tarkovsky's films. Moments of artistic or spiritual discovery are often accompanied by water or rain, as when Rublëv has understood how he must paint the Last Judgement and walks out of the church into a downpour. In *Stalker* heavy rain falls suddenly at the threshold to the Room when the Writer has decided not to go in, when the Professor is dismantling his bomb and when Stalker speaks of bringing his family to live in the Zone. The Russian Crucifixion sequence in *Andrei Rublëv*, a series of meticulously composed, painterly set pieces, emerges from a shot of white cloth moving in the current of the stream, and is followed by flecks of white paint on the water's surface. The water brings together the words just spoken (Theophanes's declaration, with which the monk concurs, that if Christ were to reappear he would be crucified again, which seems to echo Fëdor Dostoievsky's 'The Grand Inquisitor' from *The Brothers Karamazov*), ikon-painting tradition, its tools (brushes and paint), the present reality of an event that happened fourteen centuries before the action recounted in the film or two millennia ago. The water becomes a medium in which art, nature and history merge.[2]

Fire images recur in the poems as often as water, from the delicate intensity of the early poem 'Its yellow flame twinkling' (p.107), where the candle represents love, to the late 'Sight is fading – my power' (p.175), where the poet compares himself to a candle. All through his work the poet equates words and light. Fire images range from the fragile, lucent candle flame to bonfires, campfires and the destructive conflagrations of warfare or cataclysm. They are inseparable from the searing heat in which the work of art is forged, and which consumes the poet in the process of creation ('You who lived in this world before me', p.87). The poet is sometimes a prophet, whose words burn 'with fiery light' ('To a Notebook of Poems', p.196); Joan of Arc burns to death, her prophecy fulfilled ('Joan of Arc's Tree', p.85). The poet identifies himself with Prometheus, who gave humanity fire and the arts ('Aeschylus', p.126). If water associates with the totality of time, fire emphasises change; even the steadiest candle flame is patently bound for extinction. There is nothing in the poems to match the countless candles blazing in the church in the opening episode of *Nostalghia*, yet candles in the poems can be extraordinarily intense in their connotations, as in the cycle of poems 'In Memory of Anna Akhmatova' (p.160). The poet is aware of an 'outlandish' word on the dead poet's lips:

> But its sense could not be fathomed,
> And if grasped would not be held,
> So dim it might have been unreal
> But for the fitful play of light
> Cast by guttering candles.

It is impossible not to think of Gorchakov's progress across the baths, shielding the candle which seems to hold another (or the same?) truth.[3]

Water and fire can be seen simultaneously in film, and almost physically felt by the viewer; in the poems they are experienced by evocation, together with the metaphors contained, as Arsenii suggests,[4] in most words and certainly in all elemental words.

Nature is observed by father and son reflectively and minutely, with delight, often as if their vantage point were from within. When the poet gazes closely at the ground he can see 'scales all shining with rainbows' ('There was nothing you would not do', p.94): the tiny facets of leaves, moss or grass are radiant with dew or raindrops; similarly the film-maker can focus on a patch of ground or water so that it seems to reveal another world or a new way of seeing. The trope of man's sacred bond with the earth – Mother Earth or damp earth – with its roots in folk song and verse, runs all through Russian literature, and time and again the poet talks of himself as part of the natural world: leaves are his 'brothers'; he wants to dwell among the roots of Titania's kingdom; he sings for the sake of the earth into which he will eventually pass. In 'Damp, earthy smells were borne through the window' (p.174) he is one with the cycle of nature:

> Sleep in your mother's home, wearied with winter,
> Sleep like a grain of rye in black earth,
> And do not fret that the end may be death.

It is as if the poet, like English poets of the seventeenth century in T.S. Eliot's analysis, 'possessed a mechanism of sensibility which could devour any kind of experience', unaffected by the 'dissociation of sensibility' which loses the link between sensation and thought.[5] In 'Transformation' he merges physically by Ovidian metamorphosis with the landscape that has captivated him, and there is a sense of liberation in the escape from armour into the roots of the elder tree.

Beyond the earth, the poet had a lifelong interest in astronomy, of which he had expert knowledge. In 'The Bull, Orion and the Great Dog' (p.140) he writes:

> I can go on waiting
> For Orion, unimaginable wonder,
> To rise behind the sacrificial Bull,
> Taking on the shape of a crazed butterfly,
> With the font where Earth and Sun were christened
> Held between its scraping, wiry feet.

It is typical of the poet to bring together far distant skies and the tactile butterfly – tiny, fragile and weird. Earlier in the poem he sees the skies in terms of earthly architecture; 'dark voids' are compared to an 'ancient church' and one is reminded of the ruined churches of the films.

Poetry itself becomes part of nature, and the poet and nature are engaged in constant exchange:

> I have loved this earth,
> I have lived on this earth.
> When I wanted to drink
> I would look for a spring,
> I learned to sing from birds ...
> May my voice teach song
> To the very stones. ('The Olive Grove', p.184)

Arsenii looks at nature not only as a poet but also as a scientist and a philosopher, considering 'the connection between sound and colour', the working of the compound eye, the exchanges between emotion and intellect, and he can compare language to spectrum analysis ('Opening my notebook I studied the grass', p.82). Nature contains an 'alphabet', at the same time the sky is 'Wide open to reason's wings' ('Grigorii Skovoroda', p.170), as if the poet's contemplation meets with an answering receptivity in nature; Adam – or the poet – breathes the gift of 'reasonable speech' into the roots of the grass ('The Steppe', p.83).

When Andrei made *Solaris*, ostensibly a film about space exploration, he imbued almost every scene with nostalgia for the earth; both Natalia Bondarchuk, the heroine, and Vadim Iusov, the cameraman, spoke in interview about the 'sensuousness' of Andrei's treatment of the landscape around the hero's father's house. The film-maker said that nature, rather than people, was the real protagonist of his films: 'Nature always gives us a sensation of truth.'[6] On occasion he would have leaves painted to achieve a particular visual impact; film allows nature to be modified. In the *kinoroman* of *Andrei Rublëv* the film-maker raises a philosophical question about the tangled branches at which his artist hero is gazing: 'Tender shoots bursting open to throw out garlands of buds and leaves, black branches entangled reasonably, naturally – supple, free, bearing their own rustling, recurring destiny.'[7] His observation of nature is as attentive and thoughtful as that of his father. Unsurprisingly, the *kinoroman* has many instances of the sense of geometrical composition so often seen in the films: 'The long, solitary trail of a bivalve was suddenly intersected by another, identical to it, and then stretched on into the shining warmth of the sun, to the spot where the sand bank almost touched the trembling surface of the lake.'[8]

Houses in the poems have their own character and presence: a betrayed and abandoned 'simulacrum' in 'A ghost, an empty sound' (p.154); coldly dispassionate in 'To Youth' (p.194), where 'native granite' evokes deadlock in a relationship:

> The house is like a face with soulless eyes,
> Native granite; I enter, you're not there,
> But from the mirror, as if in a pit,
> Stares the sleepless face of futile toil

The house in 'Rooms were low-ceilinged' (p.110), a poem to the memory of Maria Falts,[9] is redolent of love and bereavement:

> Three small windows, three steps,
> Dark Virginia creeper.

Actual houses tend to be threatened or are already victims of war ('In the unpeopled steppe an eagle rests', p.97). Home is located in the past: 'The White Day' (p.156) is filled with nostalgia for a lost childhood paradise:

> Never again have I been
> As happy as then.

However, a house is also a metaphor standing for poetry itself. In 1963 the poet wrote to Anna Akhmatova about her latest volume of verse, declaring that now, whatever might happen to poetry in the future, readers would ensure that her 'poet's house would remain intact'.[10] In an interview of 1979 he spoke of world culture as 'the home, the daily life' of a poet.[11]

In the films the protagonist is often seen indoors, against a window, through which the outside world is perceived and through which it enters the house.

The father's house in *Solaris* is a copy of the latter's grandfather's home; for the hero childhood memories of it have been overlaid by adult responsibility and guilt, but the house is still an object of yearning, and in the ambiguous final episode the echo of Rembrandt's *Return of the Prodigal* suggests an archetypal, biblical father's house. In *Mirror* the painstakingly reconstructed replica of the director's childhood home is the locus of innocent oblivion and

The Father's house *Solaris*

growing awareness of the world. In *Sacrifice* the theme of home is central: Alexander has built his ideal dwelling in an ideal landscape, and it is this deeply personal material creation, where family life is enacted, that the hero is driven to sacrifice. This house too has its copy: the little son, helped by Otto the postman, has made a miniature model of his father's creation as a birthday present for Alexander. In all three films the 'doubled' house seems to represent at once an image of – or perhaps the search for – a setting for perfect familial harmony, and at the same time it is a reminder of the deep bonds that link succeeding generations.

The question of the place of *Mirror* in the rich tradition of the looking-glass in world art and literature has yet to be explored. As an essentially invisible surface that both repeats and reverses perception, the mirror is a significant motif in Arsenii's poems. In 'The Actor' (p.19) and in 'Testament' (p.180) a mirror shows someone other than the person facing it, which is reminiscent of *Nostalghia*, in which Gorchakov sees Domenico's image instead of his own. In *Trees* Arsenii wrote of looking into the mirror of nature and recognising one's own face, and his son talked of his own films in identical terms.[12] In 'First Meetings' (p.115) what lies beyond the mirror is the intimacy of love. In 'And I have dreamed of this, and this is what I dream' (p.164) the poet, outside time and personifying poetry itself, is surrounded by mirrors: poetry is open endlessly to reproduced, shifting reflections of reality and of human experience.

'You were such bitter stuff, so blind' (p.197) is based on the play of multiple reflections between an hourglass, cut glass and a mirror. While Marina Tarkovskaia is sure her brother Andrei did not know this poem,[13] his diploma film, *The Steamroller and the Violin*, includes a scene of mirrored clocks in a sunlit shop window. The parallel between the hourglass and clocks may be an indication of how father and son were fascinated by similar things, whether or not Andrei was indeed ignorant of the poem.[14] The screen-play elaborates: 'The mirror surfaces slice up the sparkling space and heap on to each other the reflected objects, which are cast from one dimension into another, engendering a new, wonderful and fantastic world of colour.'[15] The poem finishes with a single, endlessly repeated, miniature portrait; the film sequence opens up the viewer's vision to street scenes, sky and puzzles of space and time.

In Arsenii's poem 'At Right Angles' (p.137) the couple's lives are compared to a sheet of glass, and the elusive quality of the imagery seems to reflect their estrangement: it is not possible for the two of them to be holding their window pane as they emerge from different sides of a crowd, yet that brittle, transparent sheet is what they share. In *Mirror*, a man is seen running through a panicking Spanish crowd during an air raid,[16] carrying a pane of glass; perhaps Andrei chose that scene because it is incongruous and poignant, and perhaps because it recalls his father's poem.

Sometimes the reader is shown the poet (or protagonist) looking into the frame of the mirror, seeing himself and the person addressed, and both are reflected back into the reader's line of vision. Both father and son are concerned with questions of percep-tion, representation, mirroring reality; perhaps with the Bergso-nian notion that 'our actual existence, while it is unrolled in time, duplicates itself along with a virtual existence, a mirror-image. Every moment of our life presents the two aspects, it is actual and virtual, perception on the one side and recollection on the other'.[17] In cinema such an mirror-image becomes 'the reality of a reflection', as the young painter says in Jean-Luc Godard's *La Chinoise*.[18]

Angels occur in Arsenii's poems and Andrei's films. In the poems they are often associated with artistic creation. In 'Photog-raphy' (p.121), the picture is more than a visual record because 'the angel of the lens' has preserved an experienced moment: 'being dead, you are alive', and you relive what was 'dear'. The intensity of the emotion evoked seems close to Roland Barthes's notion of the 'punctum', the 'lacerating emphasis of the *noeme* ("that-has-been")', which Barthes sees as the 'pure representation of time'.[19] The beginning of a work of art is 'angel and infant' (Arsenii's 'Inscription in a Book [1]', p.137). Arsenii devotes a poem to the ikon-painter Theophanes (known in Russian as Feofan the Greek), in whose work he saw:

> ... a distant roar take flesh
> And chalky wings that stirred and came alive

Arsenii's angels have something in common with those in Rainer Maria Rilke's *Duino Elegies*: 'transcendent beings of perfect consciousness, beyond time and the limitations of physicality ... [who] guarantee the recognition of a higher reality'.[20] But mortals too can possess shining wings: the poet sees them on his child ('After the War'); they are destroyed in the Gulag ('Air heavy with iron and rotting potatoes', p.192); they grow dim as the poet ages ('Sight is fading – my power', p.175); a young poet finds his voice only when his 'wings have grown'.[21] The poet's angels are never visually precise, at most we 'see' the glow of their wings; they point towards the heightened reality of poetic vision or love. They rarely suggest the protective figure evoked by Mikhail Lermontov, whose work was part of Arsenii's poetic universe, though there is perhaps an echo of Lermontov's 'Angel of Death' (Arsenii's favourite poem in his childhood)[22] in the vengeful angel of the cycle of ten war poems, 'Chistopol' Notebook'.

Andrei intended to make a short film based on 'As a child I once fell ill' (p.155), where the mother flies and the nurse has wings, which was to end with a shot of an angel.[23] An element of this idea was incorporated into *Nostalghia*; an angel appears by the Russian house in the hero's dream as a distant white silhouette, but because it is visible this image has none of the power of the angels in the poems. More ambiguously, the white feathers floating down from the sky in this film could be from angels or birds – although clearly not from the sparrows in the church. Generally in the films angels appear in ikons or other paintings, or as statues – remnants of earlier moments of civilisation and elements of the director's and viewer's aesthetic world. In the poems they are metaphors; in the films (apart from the one instance in *Nostalghia*), recorded works of art.[24]

Also winged, and also often metaphorical, are the poet's butterflies; the poet gazed at things that attracted him with the same rapt concentration as his son. Sometimes they are quintessential images of fragility, sometimes symbols of departed souls ('Invitation to a Journey', p.190) as in the Greek myth of Psyche; in one poem the flickering greenish light of a cinema is likened to a butterfly. In 'Butterfly in a Hospital Garden' (p.99), the creature conjures up the poet's earliest awareness of nature's beauty, and here the light tone only makes his plea for her not to fly away the more wistful. The one filmed butterfly is in the opening episode of *Ivan's Childhood*, and is typical of that innocent, idyllic evocation. However, in *Solaris* a display case of butterflies hangs decoratively on the wall: an ambiguous collection of beautiful insects to remind the scientists of native earth, but also, perhaps, transfixed emblems of departed souls. Traditionally the emergence of the butterfly from the coffin-like chrysalis served as a symbol of new life or resurrection. Hari's simulacrum is as beautiful as the true Hari, but in fact she may be as lifeless as the open-winged butterflies.[25]

Intertextuality in the work of both Tarkovskys is a complex topic that invites rewarding study. Arsenii echoes Ovid and refers to Greek myth; the *Iliad* and the *Odyssey* are 'sacred texts'; the language of poetry is that of the psalms; and the poet is possessed of Adam's gift – he names things;[26] Dante and Goethe have a place in his universe. Father and son look back to earlier Russian writers, above all to Fëdor Dostoievsky, for Arsenii the 'highest point' in the Russian literary tradition which has from its earliest beginnings been 'spiritual' in its 'punctilious demarcation of good and evil … its feverish, awed, yet audacious thinking that seeks out the very truth, the deepest roots, the innermost core'.[27] Preparing to direct *Hamlet* in 1976, Andrei wrote in his notes that Hamlet's revenge stemmed from an urge 'to embody the idea of self-sacrifice', from 'what Dostoievsky calls the desire to suffer.'[28] Dostoievsky's two central ideas – the human propensity for self-sacrifice and the ultimate unity of humankind – seem to run through the director's veins. He thought of making a film about the writer, entitling it *Golgotha*.[29]

Some of Arsenii's poems hark back to the earliest Russian literature ('There was nothing you would not do') or to oral and folk tradition.

Pushkin is alive in the world of both Tarkovskys; his impeccably harmonious, succinct verse, 'overwhelmingly' truthful, sounded unceasingly in Arsenii's memory and his heart,[30] and often in his work. Andrei quotes Pushkin's 'To a Poet':

> You are a king. Live alone …
> You are your own supreme judge.

He twice quotes 'The Prophet'(the full text of the poem is given here in 'Appendix I: Pushkin Poems'), first in the screenplay of *Mirror*[31] (though it was not used in the film) and then in *Sculpting in Time*, in the chapter on *Sacrifice*, which ends with the poet hearing the voice of God:

> 'Rise up, prophet, see and hear,
> Be thou charged with my will,

And going out over seas and lands –
Fire men's hearts with the word.'

'The Poet' (p.127), Arsenii's poem about Osip Mandelshtam, has as its epigraph the first line of Pushkin's poem 'The Poor Knight'. The effect is to have, as it were, at the entrance to the poem: Pushkin himself; Prince Myshkin who recited it; Dostoievsky, Myshkin's creator, whose favourite poem it was; Don Quixote, the original prototype; and Cervantes. Beyond them lies the world of the nineteenth-century Russian drawing-room, and beyond that the chivalric tradition of medieval Spain. Myshkin's ancestor, as Viacheslav Ivanov wrote, was Don Quixote, 'the most complete ... of all figures in Christian literature' but 'beautiful only because he is at the same time absurd'; and his description of this character reads like a portrait of Stalker. Andrei wrote of Cervantes that he was 'if possible even more faithful to his hero than the latter to Dulcinea';[32] and he hoped to make a film of Dostoievsky's *The Idiot*.[33]

Arsenii's 'Pushkin Epigraphs' (p.166), in each of which a line of Pushkin becomes the starting-point of a new poem, are both homage and dialogue, but there are many echoes elsewhere – of Pushkin, Lermontov and Fëdor Tiuchev – in a phrase or the rhythm of a line. His poems also contain more recent literary 'reminders'. For instance, in 'Joan of Arc's Tree' he writes that his 'soul is listening/To itself' and compares the voices it hears to those heard by Joan of Arc. This is one of many poems about poetry, and is remarkable not only for its ideas and elaborate imagery, but also for the way it places the here and now of poetic creativity against a wider historical and literary background. The soul's demand for 'silence' reminds the Russian reader of Tiuchev's poem 'Silentium' and the much-quoted line 'a thought once spoken is a lie'. The tree of the title is also 'the magic oak', which takes the reader to Pushkin's lines about how the poet, once seized by inspiration, has to hurry from the frivolous world to desolate shores and 'broad-soughing oak groves'. For a Russian of Tarkovsky's generation these two allusions point towards Aleksandr Blok's speech on Pushkin of 1921,[34] in which both these poems are quoted, and where Blok spoke of how the poet must commune with elemental chaos, drawing away outer veils and catching the hidden sound waves where the raw sources of poetry lie hidden. His task is to 'free' the sounds, giving them form through the power of harmony, and bring them into the world. He quotes Pushkin's play *Mozart and Salieri*, about the dichotomy between art defined in terms of genius and inspiration on the one hand, and painstaking labour and analysis – in Salieri's metaphor, 'dissecting' – on the other. Blok also spoke of the lethal role of the bureaucratic 'rabble' and its hold on culture. His conclusion was that Pushkin's death was the result of 'lack of air' – of which Blok himself was to die some months later. Blok's speech, to which Andrei refers both in *Sculpting in Time* and in interview,[35] lies unmistakeably just below the surface of the poem.

The film-maker's literary allusions open up new horizons and depths in much the same way, and some examples will be looked at later. Often the director's quotations are from earlier films. He declared that the scene in *Mirror* where his old mother approaches her younger self in the looking-glass was a tribute to Ingmar Bergman; however, it is also reminiscent of those moments in Jean Cocteau's *Orphée* where Death comes to watch Orphée sleeping;[36] and the Zone in *Stalker* recalls the Zone in *Orphée*, another place of ruins and mysterious winds. To a Soviet ear 'zone' had strong connotations of the Gulag.[37] No doubt some cinematic echoes are unconscious. Robert Bird has an excellent summary of the echoes in *Andrei Rublëv* of films by Sergei Eisenstein (of whom Tarkovsky tended to be so damning), Vsevelod Pudovkin, Akira Kurosawa, Carl Th. Dreyer, Federico Fellini and others.[38]

Quotations and allusions throw open vistas of association. At the same time they draw on the reader's own memory, making him a participant. Mikhail Iampolski gives a fascinating analysis of this process in film in his work on intertextuality, *The Memory of Tiresias*. He compares the viewer's position, at once 'pivotal and peripheral', to that of the blind seer Tiresias, who remembered all that had ever been and also knew all that was to come; by contrast, Odysseus's mother, having no memory, could not recognise her son, for seeing without remembering means not understanding.[39] References to works of earlier poets or film directors, echoes of literature or of the Bible, whether recognised (or half recognised) or not by reader or viewer, provide other levels of memory, 'placing a number of texts and significations one on top of the other'.[40]

Personal memories are the very stuff of Arsenii's work; 'the poet writes only from memory. Memory is his muse, his pen.'[41] It is also, as it was for Henri Bergson,[42] a spiritual concept. Many of the more or less autobiographical poems raise questions of his own guilt or of setting the past right. One of his poems 'In Memory of Marina Tsvetaeva' ('As It Was Twenty-two Years Ago', p.131) ends with the question:

And how am I to blame? How am I to blame?

Andrei saw the Russian tradition of memoirs of childhood and youth as an attempt to settle accounts with the past, a kind of repentance.

In memory and memories we have direct experience of time. An example of Arsenii's treatment of time can be seen, for instance, in 'Just Before Leaf-fall' (p.78), the poem which he chose to put first in every edition of his verse. The word 'before' in the title has the precise sense of 'immediately before'; the first sentence is about immediate past and present absence, and the lyric hero has been given a short-lived parting gift. The third stanza is both present and conditional future, but the last two lines narrow the frame to the briefest of moments – the time it takes for gravel to settle after a footstep, which is at the heart of the poem, its *now*, expressed in crunching gravel – although even that split second can be divided into untold numbers of 'presents'. The final questions leave the poem unfinished and the drama open. The departing woman's (possible) wishes relate to a potential future, and he relates them, negatively, to her memory of him, his memory of her, and his recollections of his own past.

Arsenii wrote that although the poet's own epoch will inevitably put its stamp on his verse,[43] poetry contains elements of all the arts, 'even ballet and circus; representations, rhythm, colour, sound, temporality'.[44] The word he uses is *vremennost'*, emphasising 'timeness' rather than, or as well as, transience. Virtually all his poems deal with time, overtly or by implication, and time is often manipulated, different plates of time are juxtaposed, different strands interwoven. 'In the last month of autumn' (p.176) has a burst of sunlight shining from the lyric hero's future into his past. 'Psyche' (p.195) is based on the juxtaposition of Greek legend, nineteenth-century romanticism and, through the mention of the kolkhoz, Soviet political reality. In 'Komitas' (p.133) the poet either becomes or walks alongside the Armenian musicologist of that name at the moment of the 1915 massacre, and Lazarus appears, but from his final tomb rather than after his Gospel resurrection. The poet has a certain mastery over time:

> I measured time with my surveyor's chain,
> Walked through it as though walking through the
> Urals. ('Life, Life')

In his reminiscences, Arsenii recounts how he confronted the phenomenon of time in early childhood, when news came that his uncle had been killed at the front in the First World War; that evening he stood hidden from sight in the garden, rigid, concentrating on the death 'ordained' for his uncle, convinced that 'if you really want ... past and future can intersect, join together, merge'. Such meditative, purposeful concentration is typical of father and son. Next morning he woke hoping the miracle would have occurred.[45] Arsenii's seven-year old notion of time may have been based on childish intuition or been informed by grown-up talk about Henri Bergson, many of whose works were translated into Russian almost as soon as they were published.[46] Bergson's ideas were much in the air for the first decades of the twentieth century, and both Tarkovskys were close to his way of thinking. He held that all our memories remain with us, and that a remembered past in becoming a mental picture coincides with, or becomes part of, our present. Time is not a linear sequence but a duration – *la durée* – a whole, past and future, which we know by intuition rather than analysis.[47] Intuiting our *durée* opens our awareness to the totality of durations; analysis limits it to elements that are already known. Mandelshtam, who was reputed to know at least one volume of Bergson by heart,[48] defines time in Bergson's system as the internal connection between phenomena, like a fan that can be opened out, or alternatively 'closed in a way intelligible to the human mind'.[49]

Andrei saw time and memory as 'two sides of a medal'.[50] He used as the epigraph of an earlier version of *Mirror, A White, White Day*, the first line and last stanza of Pushkin's 'What can my name be for you',[51] where the poem's 'you' is brought back from oblivion by the memory of the poet's name.[52] The director saw his task as 'the creation of my own, personal stream of time, the realisation on screen of my own perception of the movement or flight of time'. Time is the supremely important mystery, where 'extraordinary discoveries' await us. He could feel 'tormented' by how little we understand of it,[53] but his article entitled 'Imprinted Time' (which appeared in the journal *Iskusstvo kino* in 1967 and with very few changes became Chapter III of *Sculpting in Time*) shows how clearly he grasped the implications for film of 'Bergsonian' – as opposed to 'Newtonian' – time. With the invention of cinema 'man found the means to take an impression of time' and to reproduce 'that time on screen as often as he wanted ... He acquired a matrix for *actual time*.' Film as an art he defines as 'time printed in its factual forms and manifestations'.[54] Whether consciously or not, his reflections contain strong echoes of Book III of St Augustine's *Confessions* and Book XV of Ovid's *Metamorphoses*, as familiar of course to St Augustine as to Arsenii, who took from it the epigraph to his poem 'Inscription in a Book (1)' (p.137).

Bergson's thought became the basis of Gilles Deleuze's seminal works on film, *Cinema 1* and *Cinema 2*, and Deleuze saw Tarkovsky's theory of the pressure of time in a shot and the 'fixing of time in its indices perceptible by the senses'[55] as a new awareness in the evolution of cinema. From a Russian perspective Mikhail Bakhtin's concept of the chronotope, the inseparability of time and space, has been applied to Tarkovsky's theory and treatment of time, and the idea of 'spatial and temporal indicators ... fused into one carefully thought-out, concrete whole'[56] is relevant and enlightening. In relation to the work of both Tarkovskys what matters here is that past time, and indeed the time of dreams, is as real as 'real time'; time may be reversible, 'in any case it does not go in a straight line', as Andrei remarked in his diary.[57] Terence McSweeney defines Tarkovsky's technique as 'observing rhythm and cadence in a film, matching shots together based on their inherent capacity for recording time's flow',[58] thus achieving, in the director's words, 'the possibility of printing on celluloid the actuality of time'.[59] Pavel Florensky, whom Tarkovsky quotes in *Sculpting in Time*, writes of the 'fact' that 'time flows backwards as well as forwards'.[60] (Florensky's English contemporary, R.G. Collingwood, wrote of 'man as standing with one foot in time, the other in eternity').[61] Alexander's apparent reversal of time in *Sacrifice*, however, seems to be based also on the Nietzschean concept of escape from the thrall of 'what has been' by its sublimation into 'what I will'.[62]

Gilles Deleuze writes of cinema's capacity to move imperceptibly from one level of reality to another so naturally that 'we no longer know which is imaginary or real, physical or mental ... not because they are confused, but because we do not have to know, and there is no longer a place from which to ask'.[63] All Tarkovsky's films demonstrate this specifically cinematic phenomenon, but his father's verse could be said to foreshadow it. Scenes, images and levels of consciousness, as well as times, emerge or merge, drawing the reader into unfamiliar, shifting areas of awareness. Arsenii's 'Azov' (p.158) is full of such transitions. The matter-of-fact opening sentence is followed by the 'resting' engine; steam is evoked by texture and smell and given mystery by being made into spheres, before becoming an ancient Assyrian. The poet's soul is drawn into the opened steppe; 'towers' of moonlight solidify, the edge of earth can be sensed far in the distance, the space between it and the poet filled by night as a vast, unwinding bolt of cloth; the poet's personified youth walks away from him. His knapsack is heavy, his food is both physical and sacramental; he shares the meagre bread and salt of hospitality with the earth, keeping a magical seventh part, then sleeps alongside ancient kings and slaves; the abundant Azov waters are associated with mourning; he dreams a prophetic dream and wakes, Adam-like, to a new dawn, naming the earth to which he is now bonded. The last line, which is translated here as 'And turned my tender chest to face the heat', reads more literally: 'towards the intense heat I turned my not-yet-strengthened chest': there is an overwhelming disparity between the slight lad and the scale both of his imaginings and of the steppe itself.

Borders between reality and dream or imagination, if they exist at all, are tenuous. In 'Dreams' (p.144) the poet has Night reading a dream-book, her staircase endlessly leading upwards, with no railing, over what seems to be a vast cave full of shades engaged in debate. The image suggests dizzying space, containing the wisdom of human experience, which 'we' must strive to see and to utter for the sake of our 'sons'. Dreams are limitless but have meaning for our day-to-day lives. In 'And I have dreamed of this, and this is what I dream' the suggestion of shared dreams indicates an element of objective reality in their content; and it is clear that they relate, in however 'miasmic' and ill-defined a way, both to individual experience and to that of humanity as a whole. The poet seems to strive to see the stuff of dreams or of imagining more clearly, but never to doubt its reality.

The dream sequences in Tarkovsky's films have been much discussed. In *Ivan's Childhood* they recall happy pre-war years and the boy's mother and sister. In *Mirror* the dream about the wood around the country house, with the wind blowing through the trees and bushes and over the table, is virtually the same yet each time subtly different; the narrator talks about repeatedly dreaming that he cannot enter the house. In *Nostalghia* the hero dreams more than once of the home for which he yearns, while his dream of seeing Domenico in the mirror makes him take on the latter's mission. Igor Evlampiev suggests that in Alexander's dream of a small child in *Sacrifice* the hero has gone back to his own infancy, for the whole of his life has been a preparation for the moment when he will save the world from nuclear disaster.[64] Like Bergson, both Arsenii and Andrei are aware that 'our faculty of sensory perception, far from shrinking when we are asleep, broadens its field of operations',[65] and dreams often open on to other times and places which are nonetheless part of life as it is lived here and now.

Arsenii's childhood heroes included the eighteenth-century poet and religious philosopher Grigorii Skovoroda, to whose work he was introduced at the age of seven and to whom he wrote two poems some sixty years later, his affection and respect undimmed ('Where burial mounds, face down in grass' (p.170) and 'Grigorii Skovoroda'); and the astronomer genius Angelo Secchi, tirelessly devoted to his work, suffering debilitating illness and political tribulation ('Angelo Secchi', p.88). In 'The Poet' he draws a portrait of Osip Mandelshtam, whom he revered, as an inept figure in worldly terms. (Arguably the greatest Russian poet of the century, Mandelshtam died of starvation in a transit camp near Vladivostok in 1938 and was buried in a common grave.)

These selfless outsider heroes are germane to the concept of art shared by the two Tarkovskys, for whom the role of artist involved sacrifice and suffering. To Arsenii any poet is a Promethean figure ('Aeschylus'), his service a heroic feat; his very life is at stake and he has to be the 'double' of his work.[66] For Andrei, too, the artist is always 'a servant, perpetually trying to pay for the gift that has been given him as if by a miracle'.[67] Rublëv strives to realise his ideal of artistic beauty in the face of a brutal reality – 'his battleground is the human spirit'.[68] All Andrei's main protagonists are driven: Ivan is child-soldier and child-martyr; Kelvin battles for his own humanity on the outer edges of scientific endeavour; Stalker drives himself to extremes of physical and emotional exhaustion, obeying his vocation to bring people face-to-face with themselves, and to preserve hope – 'the last of the idealists, whom nobody believes'.[69] Gorchakov identifies with the eccentric Domenico because he sees truth in the latter's perceptions, and dies while carrying out his request; and Alexander sacrifices what is most dear to him in order to avert world catastrophe.[70]

In the late 1920s, when Russian culture was expected to play a vital role in the building of a new socialist society, Arsenii Tarkovsky and his young fellow poets 'raised a flag which hardly anyone noticed' and defined the central tenet of their art, the one point on which all could agree, as 'a system where the artist is honest alone with himself'.[71] Fifty years later he considered his favourite among his own poems (not necessarily the best) to be those which most closely correspond with his own view of the world. Andrei's poetic vision, too, is grounded in the artist's interior world, and demands 'total honesty and sincerity towards himself', for it is by transmuting 'what is most important and precious' to him that he will touch the viewer to the innermost depths of his soul – like Wordsworth who believed that 'What we have loved/Others will love; and we will teach them how' (*The Prelude*).

Through the artist's search for his own truth and his own language his work becomes a system of discovery, 'a means of knowing', essential to the quest for knowledge and for what Andrei termed 'the wholeness of existence'. Arsenii saw the poet as humanity's 'organ' for exploring reality, and poetry as a 'cognitive' process for exploring the world and the essence of being. He subscribed to the classical concept of the poet as 'prophet and madman': 'the poet's intuition runs ahead of his conscious awareness';[72] he himself sometimes foresaw events 'by a year, or a day' before they happened;[73] Akhmatova's later poems 'express the future'.[74] Andrei was convinced that 'every true artist – regardless of whether he wants to be or not – is a prophet'.[75] One may see this phenomenon in terms of the poet's being possessed of hypersensitive antennae; Osip Mandelshtam spoke of hearing the 'overtones of time'.

Poetry is the 'harmoniser' of life; and it 'creates life'. By reaching the deepest understanding of the world and the human soul, art can transform awareness. Arsenii's terminology and vision are remarkably close to those of his son, and also to allied areas of film theory: Terence McSweeney writes that Gilles Deleuze and Andrei Tarkovsky 'share the belief that cinema is a philosophical tool with the potential for revealing essential truths of consciousness and identity',[76] and Robert Bresson that 'cinematography becomes a method of discovery ... because a mechanism gives rise to the unknown, and not because one has found this unknown in advance'.[77] Andrei felt very close to Bresson.[78]

Like life itself, poetry is a 'miracle'. Its creation is ultimately 'imponderable',[79] and much of Pushkin's 'enigma' remains 'sealed with seven seals'.[80] However, Arsenii Tarkovsky has left us some of his thoughts on poetic technique. First, structure: he refers to Pushkin's perfect sense of balance and his gift (rare among Russian poets but shared by Evgenii Baratynsky) for the harmonious arrangement of the internal 'mass' of a poem; he admires Baratynsky's unerring 'architectonic intuition'. Precision is a word that recurs, and he praises both Baratynsky and Akhmatova for the 'precision' of their use of epithets, 'driven into the line like nails'. Words are wider than the meaning we put into them; almost every word is 'metaphor, trope, hyperbole'.[81]

It is the meticulous placing of words (and sounds) that create the quasi-electric 'contact' that makes words 'light up'.[82] The 'light' of words is a recurring trope, and may be based on Martin Heidegger's analysis of the Greek word *phaenomenon*, which is connected with *phaos*, 'light', and with *apophansis*, 'statement' or 'speech'; the sequence of ideas is thus: revelation-light-language.[83] But it could equally well be the poet's own analysis of what happens to words in poetry.

Arsenii praises Akhmatova for her 'perfect coincidence of syntax and rhythm.'[84] He looks back to his mentor, Georgii Shengeli, whose (unfinished and lost) study – filled with 'accordion-like' diagrams – of the connection between the rhythm of a poem and its recitation raised questions of how the deepest human intuitions can achieve 'plasticity of expression' in the rhythm, imagery and movement of verse.[85] Rhythm is as intrinsic to our make-up physiologically as breathing. Traditional patterns of rhythm and rhyme allow the meaning of a poem to be spread evenly over its surface.[86] Far from being mere decoration, rhyme has the function of signalling that one wave has passed and another is imminent. The material of poetry ranges from 'what is underfoot to the music of the spheres',[87] and the process of transmuting any material into verse will involve conflict, often painful, between the artist's original inspiration and the 'changing world'. Poetic creation has something in common with musical composition; the strictures of the sonnet are akin to those of the sonata. Pushkin has often been compared to Mozart, Arsenii points to Bach as an artistic prototype, and of course Bach was all-important for Andrei.

Arsenii's own verse illustrates his comments. Almost every line is a syntactic unit; enjambments and broken lines are quite rare and always deliberate. Rhymes are regular and never insistent. Images have a sharp clarity. The recurring image of a needle, as simile or metaphor, conveys the piercing effect of a new awareness; or that of mica – layered, mineral, flaking, translucent. He applies fractions to things heard or felt, not normally associated with accurate measurement. His images can be startlingly unexpected – the mountain ridge seen as a crucifix; the homeless woman cast as Psyche; wooden paving laying itself down at dawn at the approach of the first tram.

Andrei constantly writes of accurate factual recording, and every account of his work on set emphasises meticulous preparation for every scene. Poet and film-maker would subscribe to Bresson's note: 'Master precision. Be a precision instrument myself.'[88] Or to Paul Klee's succinct formula: 'Exactitude winged by intuition.'[89]

More than once in interviews Andrei declared that his father was the best living Russian poet, a view also expressed by Akhmatova. Though his diary suggests that his relations with his parents could at times seem 'tortured, complicated, unspoken',[90] one only has to read his 'I Live with Your Photo', written in 1962,[91] to see how devoted he was to both of them. The ubiquitous father image in the films has often been discussed, and it does seem that the director was trying to reconcile the trauma of childhood abandonment with filial love. In *Solaris* Andrei thought of basing the film which the hero was to take with him into space on one of Arsenii's poems,[92] and the film ends with an archetypical image of a father's forgiveness and a son's humility. Asked in Sweden whether his father had written the poems in *Mirror* specially for the film, Andrei said he had used published poems and would never ask his father to write anything just for him. Praise from his father was uniquely important. In the same interview he said that when his father had told him, 'What you make are not films, ... it immediately became easier for me to live'.[93] Most of us will know what his father meant: particularly after watching *Mirror* one can feel that it is a poem before it is a film. Andrei said he had always seen himself as a poet rather than a cinematographer.[94] He noted in the diary that his father 'categorises *Solaris* not as a film but as something akin to literature, because of the internal, authorial rhythm, the absence of banal devices, and the enormous number of details each with a specific function in the narrative'.[95]

The artistic and psychological kinship between father and son is sometimes patently illustrated in the poems. In 'Theophanes' (p.32), the poet declares:

> I must ...
> ... be apprenticed to Theophanes.

Andrei Rublëv, although not Theophanes' apprentice, certainly regarded the older painter as his teacher; and in the course of making his film, Andrei Tarkovsky in his turn undoubtedly learned a great deal from, as well as about, Andrei Rublëv. The painter had been the subject of official celebrations in 1960, and it is possible that these prompted both the poem and the 1966 film; the former is dated 1975–6, so it could in theory be a question of the son's influence on the father. In any case, they were inspired to produce work on the same subject.[96]

Leafing through a later edition of the poet's collected works, one comes across 'Testament', (sometimes wrongly called 'Dedication'), which includes the lines:

> I thought: My hands must be released,
> And as I woke I did set my hands free,
> In order once again to learn to speak.

It seems that we are reading what the poet wrote as a result of seeing the prologue of *Mirror* – until we see that the poem was written between 1934 and 1937, when his son was a small child. Later in the poem comes the stanza:

> I am the first of all your birthday guests,
> It has been granted me to live with you,
> To make my way into your nightly dreams,
> And to be reflected in your mirror.

In the course of the poem he passes on to his son, formally, trees and town, the radiance of lightning flashes flying like swans, the bitterness of experience – all of which in one way or another would find their place in Andrei's work. At the same time, he casts himself as 'guest': however dominant in his son's life, he was never domineering.

For all the affinities between poet and film-maker, there are also some notable differences. Arsenii Tarkovsky's poems written to or about the women he loved have no counterpart in his son's films, where only mothers are portrayed with devotion. Ivan's mother was killed; Kelvin's wife killed herself; even though the director calls the devotion of Stalker's wife 'the final miracle',[97] the relationship could not be called happy; both the wives in *Mirror* are divorced – the elder is loving and courageous but deserted, the younger rather brisk, while (from what we see of her) the Redhead seems cold and self-centred; Eugenia is frustrated by Gorchakov's lack of interest in her – his own wife has a passive role and has been given the mother's name of Maria; and the wife in *Sacrifice* is an hysteric. Only Maria in *Mirror* is a wholly sympathetic character, and of course she is modelled on Andrei's mother.

Arsenii was married three times and had a number of other lovers, but he retained a deep affection, almost reverence, for his earlier loves. He even wrote of unhappy love that although it is a torment to remember it, doing so makes a man kinder.[98] To his first wife, Andrei's mother, he wrote few poems but many letters both before and after they parted, and these are always full of affection and trust. To his first love, Maria Falts, he wrote many poems while she was still alive, and more over the decades after her death; they are among the most lyrical and poignant of his poems, and will be looked at in the next section and in the notes to the verse translations. Twice the poet writes of her carefree laugh, and he mentions her open, undemanding gaze. The only female character who laughs in the films is Ivan's mother, the moment before she is killed; and the children laugh joyfully only in Ivan's dreams of pre-war happiness. Both artists meld nature and art, personal and universal, past and present; only Arsenii's work can also be playful.

Anyone who falls under the spell of Arsenii's poems or Andrei's films finds that as reader or viewer they are engaged as participants and their way of looking at the world is changed by the experience. Perhaps the greatest difference between father and son is that the former often writes of his own joy – not only in love but more broadly in life itself.

> For my daily bread, for every drop of water
> I give thanks.
> For my repetition of labours done by Adam
> I give thanks ...
>
> That I'll go down into dense native earth,
> Flow into grass,
> That my path ascends from earth to highest stars
> I give thanks.
> ('For my daily bread, for every drop of water' p.179)

Both Arsenii and Andrei transfigure into poetry the pain of the human condition and the tribulations of the artist's calling, but nowhere in the films will one find such a confident expression of sheer happiness in being alive and being an artist.

II
The Poet's Voice

Arsenii Tarkovsky's poems are read in *Mirror*, *Stalker* and *Nostalghia*, but there is a fundamental difference between their function in *Mirror* and in the two subsequent works. In *Mirror* they are essential to the concept and structure of the film, and the poet himself is a central *persona dramatis*. In *Stalker* and *Nostalghia* the poems are quoted by protagonists, and although relevant and significant thematically, they remain quotations and without them the films would still stand, albeit in an impoverished form. Were the poet's role to be extracted from *Mirror*, it would not be the same film.

Mirror
The figure of the father-poet has to be considered in the complex scheme of the film's cast, actors and non-actors, who play single, dual or overlapping roles. The original proposal was 'for a film about a mother ... who will not be an actor'.[99] In fact, the film is about all family archetypes; out of the film's multiple mirrors different generations emerge, in their separate but shared identities.

The elderly Maria Tarkovskaia, Arsenii's first wife, appears as herself, but is largely silent, while the hero, her son Andrei (named Aleksei in the film), is constantly audible in the voice of an actor, but is not seen. We hear Maria's voice on the telephone in a relatively long exchange with the invisible hero but on screen she only speaks twice: first, when she and her grandson Ignat fail to recognise each other and she says, 'Oh, I think I've come to the wrong place'; and in a final episode when the small Aleksei (a fictional embodiment of Andrei as a child) tells her the oil-lamp is smoking, addressing her as 'Mum', as though she were young, and she asks, absently, 'What?' – her last disengaged word. Her younger self is played by Margarita Terekhova, who with deliberate blurring also has the role of her daughter-in-law, Natalia.

Andrei Tarkovsky himself, the hero, is invisible except for a brief shot of his shoulder and arm in the final episode, and his voice is heard only in its interpretation by the actor Innokentii Smoktunovsky. When we first hear the hero's voice it is clear that he is recalling his childhood in the setting at that moment on the screen; and once we have heard him answering his mother's telephone call we know that he is narrator and participant, and can locate him in the same room as his wife in the dialogue scenes. The childhood roles of Aleksei/Andrei are acted by two child actors of different ages – he is thus represented, visibly or audibly, in four different guises: (actor's) adult voice, little boy, twelve-year-old and once, fleetingly, the real Andrei Tarkovsky.

It is clear from the opening scene that the film is also about an absent father, whose part, at the age he was during the hero's early childhood, is played by Oleg Iankovsky. He appears in two dreams, the first – washing his wife's hair – apparently dreamt by the small Alexei/Andrei, during which he says nothing; the second – the levitation scene – seems to be Maria's dream and his words to her are full of tenderness. He comes to visit the family while on leave, greets his wife and asks where the children are; and at the very end the film loops back to when he talks to Maria about the imminent birth of their first child. In all, he utters scarcely more words than Maria Tarkovskaia. However, it is Arsenii Tarkovsky himself and not the actor who reads the poems offscreen, and these are the longest utterances in the film. Like the hero-narrator, he is invisible, but his voice is speaking his own texts; he is not interpreting the poems as an actor necessarily must, for he is in them.

This is direct communication from poet to audience, quite different from reading printed poems. Rhythm and rhyme make for musicality and, like music, the words are heard and gone; the poet's timbre and breathing are recorded as clearly as words and images, and his tone is restrained; the experience of hearing the poems is deeply personal. A voice, as Mladen Dolar has said, is unique, and 'the uniqueness of the voice brings out ... the most genuine part, the quintessential uniqueness, the pure exteriorisation of the most intimate';[100] Dolar sees the voice as 'the junction of presence and sense' and, as such, 'intimately involved with the very notion of time and hence with our hold on presence'.

Time and presence are at the very heart of *Mirror*, and the father's voice is a vital element in their realisation. Essentially it is acousmetric, to use the term coined by Michel Chion from the Greek *akousma*, something heard without the cause or source being seen. It is neither inside nor outside the image, seeming to come from everywhere because, unlike vision which is partial and unidirectional, hearing is omnidirectional and sound 'tends to spread out like a gas into whatever space there is'.[101] In some action movies the acousmetric voice is a means of creating suspense; it seems all-pervading because it is perceived as mysteriously powerful, and – again because it seems to be everywhere – it is readily internalised by the viewer and can thus become an 'I' voice as well as the voice of 'Another'. Having the diegetic space pervaded by an unseen voice speaking poetry is a particularly complex use of this phenomenon that belongs 'to cinema and to it alone'.[102] The acousmetric voice 'becomes invested with magical powers as soon as it is involved in the image'[103] – an appropriate designation for a poet who described the creation of a poem as 'wizardry'.

In Cocteau's *Orphée* there is a kind of precedent in so far as it is Cocteau himself who reads his poems broadcast on the car radio. However, not only are Cocteau's 'poems' surreal one-liners, like code messages, but they are listened to intently by the hero who is desperate to make sense of them, and the viewer's attention, like that of the actor, is concentrated on the one visual and aural image – nothing else is happening on screen. In Tarkovsky's films the poems are, formally speaking, complete in themselves, but at the same time they lead out far beyond themselves. The same can be said of the films and often, indeed, of particular images. The interaction between poems and visual images is subtle and complex.

It has to be said that for the viewer who does not know Russian, subtitles, particularly to a poem, are a problem: visually they intrude into the screen image; the viewer feels forced to read them and is distracted from listening to the music of the poem; and the translation appears in little bits. To a lesser degree the problem is there with any film in an unfamiliar language.

The narrator-hero's first words in the film seem to emerge from Bach's prelude 'The Old Year Has Passed'; Maria is seen from the back gazing over the fields, while her son's adult voice talks of the location of the scene and of his childhood belief that if a distant figure walking from the station were to turn at the bush, this would be his father coming home; if he did not, then his father would never return. It is in sharp contrast to the prologue in which the stammering adolescent is taught to speak. In order to release the boy from his tongue-tied state, the therapist has him concentrate all his will in his hands and then, using her own hands and voice, she frees his speech 'for the rest of [his] life'. He then says what she tells him to say; she is the expert, the session is being recorded, and the whole scene is viewed on television. Tarkovsky wrote of this episode as the epigraph to *Mirror*[104] in the sense that the film is his way of tempting 'into life the things that wanted to come out of' him; but the film is also about the technology of film-making and about voice. The adult hero's words are fluent, euphonic, and – unlike the definite, official, dictated facts spoken in the therapy session – they are about a conditional future, hope and uncertainty, and the child's psyche, open and delicate; also about time and identity. An unknown doctor intrudes on the scene, in the unwitting role of an impostor, asking Maria the way, needing a key or, failing that, 'an opener' (the Russian term for screwdriver) – practical requests that leave hints of deeper questioning; he wonders about man's alien-ation from nature and tries to flirt; Chekhov's bleak story about a doctor who finishes up as a patient in his own asylum is mentioned and dismissed. As he goes on his way there is a sudden gust of wind and he turns and looks back at Maria. We see her gazing out – but not towards him; then she turns away from the camera and walks slowly through the trees. Now we hear the opening words of the poem, which seem to come from the area into which she had stared; the acousmetric voice inhabits the image and thus blurs the bound-aries between onscreen and offscreen.[105]

First Meetings

Every moment that we were together
Was an epiphany, a celebration,
We two were alone in all the world.
You were bolder, lighter than a bird's wing,
Like vertigo you used to run downstairs,
Two steps at a time, and lead me
Through damp lilac into your domain
On the other side, beyond the mirror.

When night fell I was granted favour,
The altar gates were opened wide,
Our nakedness glowed in the dark
And gradually inclined. When I woke
I'd say: 'Blessings be upon you!'
And knew my benediction was too bold.
You slept, the lilac stretched out from the table
To touch your eyelids with a cosmic blue,
And you received the touch upon your eyelids,
They were peaceful, and your hand was warm.

Pulsating rivers flowed inside the crystal,
Mountains breathed with smoke, seas glinted,
And on your palm you held a crystal sphere,
As you slept there, high upon your throne,
And – God in heaven – you were mine.
Then you woke, and you transfigured
All the words that people use each day,
Speech was filled up to the brim
With ringing power, the word 'you'
Discovered its new meaning: it spelt 'king'.

Everything around us was made new
Even ordinary jugs and basins,
When between us two as though on guard
Stood water, many-layered and firm.

We could not tell where our delight might take us.
Cities that a miracle had built
Now moved aside like mirages before us,
Wild mint laid itself beneath our feet,
Birds were our companions on the way,
Fishes in the river swam upstream,
And the sky unrolled before our eyes ...

While Fate was following our footsteps,
Like a madman with a razor in his hand.

'Meetings' is an inadequate translation for *svidania* – namely 'seeing each other', being in each other's sight, and the first lines run literally: '[of our] coming/being together/seeing each other each moment/We celebrated like an epiphany/divine manifestation' ... the couple's embrace was radiant, every moment had an eternal dimension, the space around them was immeasurable. We see now Maria, back turned; often in Tarkovsky's films the back of a head is at once inscrutable and expressive. The poet's voice seems to be in the air and in her head, but she glances behind her (at the viewer?), and we see the small Aleksei, absorbed in his own world, and he too looks briefly out of frame; they seem not to see each other. In the poem the beloved was lighter than a bird's wing, now a leaf falls to the ground, then something is blown off the window-sill; all is earthbound. Then, ethereally, she had led the way beyond the mirror: they had reflected each other, merged together, outside time and space. In the second stanza the camera has moved indoors. The language is almost religious, the blue of the flowers spreads towards her eyelids from interstellar space, their world was a universe. Russian slips very easily into the historic present, but here all the verbs are past tense – happiness can only be remembered. The little girl is asleep, oblivious. At the word 'blessings' the camera is behind the two children seated at the table, deep in their own company; Aleksei lets sugar run from his hand on to the cat's neck as it laps milk; he's fooling around, but the falling grains of sugar remind us of passing time, of the passing sweetness of childhood; perhaps the incident was among the film-maker's memories.

With the line about her eyelids the camera moves from the children into darkness: for a moment the screen is black. We then see the curled wrought iron of the bedstead (perhaps the bed where the children were conceived) as Maria stands at its head, in half-darkness; she moves away at the lines about rivers and mountains, her shadow remaining on the bed for some moments, like a shadow of her memories. The screen again goes black and blank behind her, till a dim light spreads as the camera pans towards the window. The room appears empty for the first half of the third stanza; the 'ringing power' of speech coincides with the first sight of a notebook on the windowsill.

The repeated blackness is disorientating for the viewer; it may suggest a happiness so intense that Maria cannot bear to remember it, or the lacunae of memory, and it disrupts our attempts to interpret word/image coincidences. The jug on the table may be the one in the poem. Maria's face is unspeakably sad, the rain is like a curtain in front of her as she stares out, where the view moves upwards among the trees; the rain brings us down again and back to her in her grief. The poem evokes a walk, either actual or dreamed, where they wandered without knowing where they were going, at one with nature, which seemed to share in their happiness.

Chillingly, the last line brings the sounds *sbreetvoioo vrookie* ('with a razor in his hand'), sharp and discordant. As the poem ends, Maria picks up the notebook of her husband's work. The two have been severed by fate's blade but the material text remains. For us also, preserved by audio technology, the poet's recitation remains – that one recitation, made at one precise time, and delivered in just that way once and once only.

The poet himself was the only one who knew that 'First Meetings' was in fact addressed not to his first wife, mother of Andrei, but to another Maria: Maria Falts, an older woman of great charm with whom Arsenii fell in love as a very young man; he wrote his first poem to her in 1926.[106] He remained faithful to her memory long after they parted, and seems to have mourned her early death for the rest of his life. Marina Tarkovskaia only came to know about Maria Falts from her father's papers after his death, and well after the death of Andrei. Marina and Andrei had always hoped that 'First Meetings' was about their mother.

In the film the time remembered by the film-maker is the time to which Maria looks back, apparently that of the poem. The scene represents a crystalline concentration of different times. The poet's voice is heard reciting the poem in 1974 when the film was being made; the poem is dated 1962 and the time remembered by the poet is the 1920s; the film's scene takes place in the 1930s, after the death of Maria Falts and after the poet had left his family. Since the making of the film, audiences have related to this interweaving of narrative time, poetic time and historic time according to their own 'real' time, for the most part ignorant of these details. However, knowing them and their irony adds poignancy to the film. The poem can be read from the page either with all contexts in mind or 'restored', as it were, to its first addressee, who is never represented to us aurally or visibly in any explicit way. To a knowing viewer she is the final absent figure in the film – unseen, unheard and unnamed.

Arsenii wrote in his notes that the genesis of 'Yesterday from early on I waited' (p.81) was its opening sentence, heard from a patient in a mental hospital and 'translated as from a foreign language' into a poem.[107]

> Yesterday from early on I waited,
> They had all guessed you wouldn't come,
> D'you remember how lovely yesterday was?
> Holiday weather! I went out with no coat.
>
> Today you arrived, and we were given
> A somehow specially sombre day,
> It rained, and the hour was somehow late,
> And drops trickled down cold branches.
>
> This – no word can salve, no handkerchief wipe away.

The poem opens in the past with contradictory perceptions of an almost immediate future; in the next two lines that future has become the past to which the protagonist looks back, at the same time questioning whether his lost love also remembers. The second stanza is in the present, looking back to a more recent past, and then forward to a future which will be marked by what has ensued. The addressee, the world ('they' in the second line) and the protagonist all have different perceptions of what has or has not happened, or may have happened. The poem is recited as Maria is walking along the corridor in the newspaper printing works,[108] exactly halfway through that episode, which emerges from a telephone call to the hero in Maria's future, from her elderly self.

The mother's voice on the telephone is that of the real Maria Tarkovskaia, that of the unseen hero is spoken by Innokentii Smoktunovsky. His mother has rung to tell him of the death of her former colleague, Liza, whom he cannot immediately remember; he doesn't know the time, and when she tells him, he wants to know if she means six in the morning or the evening; and he wants to be reminded in what year his father left the family. He is too preoccupied and confused to respond to her grief for her friend; as in the opening scene she mourns alone. The conversation ends with his asking her forgiveness for their strained relations, perhaps rather more for his own comfort than for hers. Inability to communicate with the people most dear to him and concern with accurately recalling the past are recurring themes of both the poet's and the film-maker's reflections. The fact that the latter's mother is playing her own role at the other end of the line is disorientating: offscreen reality is the real world, borders between film and life are not delineated. The telephone line leads from the interior, but acted, world of the self-absorbed hero to the outside world of real people and real, though recalled, bereavement.

We see the young Maria running along the street and hear, asynchronously, the tram- or bus-stop announced on board the vehicle. She arrives at work in torrential rain, the doorman asks where she is rushing and she doesn't answer, she dashes to her office and asks for the previous day's proofs, then remembers the right cupboard and the young employee says, 'Of course, you put them there yourself.' Despite the disjointed communication, the girl, Liza and a male colleague are all drawn into the drama; as she starts anxiously checking the proofs for a mistake at the windowsill, other staff form a crowd, and their questions are deflected; then she walks back through the noisy printing works, past a poster of Stalin and a portrait of Felix Dzerzhinsky, founder of the Soviet secret police. We briefly see a banner slogan proclaiming 'The fiery word of Leninist-Stalinist Truth' (*Pravda* means 'truth'), grotesquely echoing the biblical phrase which occurs in more than one of Arsenii's poems and in Pushkin's 'The Prophet'.

The misprint she had feared – *sralin*, 'shitty', as opposed to *stalin*, 'of steel' – was not there.[109] The fatal word is not specified in the dialogue, and so there is a kind of negative echo of 'no word', heard in the final line of the poem.[110]

The poem then accompanies Maria's progress down a long corridor with windows on either side, which throw light on her as she walks towards us with purposeful tread, quite different from the previous frenzied rush, and the only time in the film when we see her as a young woman looking brisk and cheerful, at moments half smiling. The acousmetric voice is autonomous, happening somewhere else; but the forlorn waiting and the lasting sense of loss link the poem thematically to Maria, despite her air of detachment. She walks into shadow and disappears as the last line is heard.

In the office she tells Liza that she had 'seen that word' and the male colleague offers her a tail-end of vodka. (Is he an ambiguous character, could he want to loosen her tongue? Like the doctor and the doorman he disapproves of 'hurry'; there could be something sinister in his remark about fear – 'Some people can be frightened and others can get on with their work.') Then Liza compares Maria to Maria Lebiadkina, a character in Dostoievsky's *Demons*,[111] accusing her of being egocentric and demanding, of creating the situation 'with her own hands'. The character in question does indeed boast about ordering her brother about, telling him to fetch this and that; but the unlikely claim is not confirmed in the narrative. The introduction into the film of this novel, however, is relevant in a number of ways; the book is full of secrets, hidden guilt and skewed perceptions, and it includes a horrifying vision of a totalitarian state. Maria Lebiadkina is a more complex figure than Liza's words suggest: she is portrayed as a *iurodivy*,[112] or 'fool for Christ's sake', simple-minded but intuitive, perhaps with second sight, a representative of the folk tradition beloved of Dostoievsky that can equate Mother Earth with the Mother of God; she enjoins Shatov to 'water the earth' with his tears so that 'all will be filled with joy'. Her reverence for the earth is consonant with the love of nature that runs through Arsenii's poems and Andrei's films, and that provides the physical setting for Maria almost every time we see her in *Mirror*.[113] When Maria tells Liza impatiently to stop fooling, the word she uses is *iurodstvovat'* – 'play the holy fool' – turning the Lebiadkina simile back on to Liza, thus closing both the confrontation between them and the opening on to Maria Lebiad-kina and her context. But Maria, the mother figure of the film, has been fleetingly set alongside a peculiarly Russian archetype of feminine tenderness and strength. Generally speaking, educated Russians of Tarkovsky's generation knew Dostoievsky well enough for these associations to be picked up. Apart from Ivan, all the main protagonists of Tarkovsky's films are in the *iurodivy* mould.

After Maria slams the door of the shower in Liza's face, demanding to be left in peace, Liza gives a carefree sideways skip as she walks back along the corridor and quotes the first line of Dante's *Inferno*. She is halfway through life's journey, as was the director at that point in his career, and a window is opened on to *The Divine Comedy* which will lend another depth to the 'dark wood' of the final scene.

The shower episode provides a perfect epilogue to the inter-woven poem and narrative. When Maria was sitting by the window with the proofs we saw 'cold drops' and branches. Since then both women have been crying. The poem has evoked a longed for event that failed to happen, the film a catastrophe that did not take place. Now the comforting water of the shower peters out in a few derisory drops, leaving her wet, and she bursts out laughing because it is so unimportant; then in the final moments she covers her face with her hands and sobs, 'O, Lord!' Is she thinking of what Liza has just said, of her loneliness, of the political realities that remain unchanged? The next shot cuts to the burning barn, a reminder of the precar-iousness of well-being and an elemental contrast with the water images.

We cannot know the identity of the patient who inspired 'Yesterday from early on I waited' nor whom he had in mind. Yet by being incorporated into Arsenii's poem and Andrei's film, his words have become an element in a kind of time crystal that refracts the moment of their utterance and the memory to which they refer. The layers of time include the time when the poem was written; the time of the poet's recorded recitation; and the potentially infinite number of times when the poem is read or the film shown.

Like the printing-house episode and its accompanying poem, 'Life, Life' is indirectly introduced by a telephone call, leading this time to the Second World War in the father's memories (real and imagined) and in newsreel footage.

The repeated word of the title is equally apt for the indi-vidual life set in the context of a wider human family (kin, nation, humankind), of the continuity of cultural life from one age to the next, and here in the film for two lives echoing each other in interweaving memories. The poem is about inheritances and transitions between generations.

For an understanding of the poem's effect we need to look back to the events of the film that precede its recitation. The father's/grandfather's Leonardo album is being leafed through by either the teenage Aleksei or Ignat, it is hard to tell which, the significant point is their shared inheritance. The next scene emerges almost literally from its pages: Natalia is leaving Ignat alone in his father's flat; she drops her handbag on the floor and Ignat experiences 'like an electric shock' a sense of déjà vu as he helps to pick things up. Shortly after his mother leaves, a mysterious woman appears, with her maid, and has Ignat read aloud from Pushkin's letter to Piotr Chaadaev;[114] along the way he reads out Jean-Jacques Rousseau's view that art and science have failed to improve humanity. The doorbell rings, Ignat's grandmother (Maria Tarkovskaia in person) appears, she and Ignat fail to recognise each other and she leaves, thinking it's the wrong flat. Either Ignat and his grandmother have hardly ever met or they are separated because the boy now has a different consciousness of time as a result of communicating with the unexplained woman from an earlier era.

The Rousseau and Pushkin passages have been written down in a notebook (like the Tarkovsky poems earlier in the film) and thus also represent a family archive – possibly alluding to the poet's own. For Arsenii, as for Andrei, Pushkin was 'friend, brother, teacher, man of wisdom'.[115] The words of Rousseau, theorist and theoretician, are brushed aside.

Pushkin's point about Russia being a protective bulwark for Western Europe will shortly be illustrated by footage of a hostile Chinese mob. The woman chivvies Ignat – 'We haven't much time' – and her words run counter to the 'hurry' motif sounded by the doctor, the printing-works doorman, the male colleague and Natalia as she dropped her purse; they all say that people are in too great a rush, whereas she is declaring an urgent need to turn to what is timeless. Ignat's reading opens a vista on to centuries of Russian history, and the 'electric shock' seems to have flicked open a shutter on to another order of time to allow this meeting with the mysterious visitor, and an intimation for the young Ignat of his own living link with the generations that preceded him, the move from day-to-day bustle to 'duration'.

The telephone rings stridently as Ignat gazes at the slowly fading ring left on the polished table by the mysterious visitor's teacup.[116] He is clearly delighted to hear his father's voice, at a physical remove and reaching him along wires; the rarity of face-to-face communication in the family has just been shown in the non-recognition between grandmother and grandson. Aleksei's memories centre on the red-haired girl with whom he had been in love as a teenager; his words 'Are you listening?' suggest he is anxious for his son to share at least some sense of his past.

The scene changes to wartime and some boys, including the teenage Aleksei, are being given rifle instruction. Aleksei is played by Ignat Daniltsev, as is Ignat who (at the same age) is listening to his father's words about that scene. The camera cuts to the Redhead, the personification of self-conscious good health and good looks; as she glances aside the camera follows her gaze to show the back of a naked soldier carrying a heavy box to the water's edge. The sound is again of drum- or heart-beat. The nude figure with its load is at once an Atlas image and the very type of physical vulnerability. It opens the newsreel of the Lake Sivash crossing, which Tarkovsky, impressed by its intensity and authenticity, chose as 'the centre, the very essence, heart, nerve of this picture that had started off merely as ... intimate lyrical memories'.[117] The newsreel shots appear to be superbly composed, though the groups of men are simply as they were, in those actual moments of 1943. Scraps of paper floating on the surface of the water might seem like scraps of memory, but again are factual, as are the smiling soldiers looking back at the camera; this could be a series of cheerful snaps rather than a day which for many would prove to be their last. The cameraman himself was killed later that day.[118] Dmitri Salynsky sees Tarkovsky's focus on the last things seen by someone about to die as the quintessential film image that creates an immediate, total sense of time.[119]

In an earlier draft of *Sculpting in Time,* which Tarkovsky revised when the English translation was already in progress, he wrote:

There seemed to be something Dantean in these scenes ... because they were of real people, with lives offscreen ... And all this gave the moment imprinted on film extraordinary range and depths, awakening a complex mixture of emotions equivalent to a heightened state of moral awareness ... What was exciting was that the image had emerged from an utterly concrete situation, it had not been constructed on the sort of theoretical basis that I was anxious to avoid.

The first sounds are of footsteps in water, as the camera shows groups of soldiers, some pushing rafts loaded with guns and equipment. The faint sound of a choir is heard, the drumbeat grows now more intense, now fainter.

Life, Life

1

I don't believe forebodings, nor do omens
Frighten me. I do not run away
From calumny or poison. In this world there's no death.
All are immortal. All is immortal.
Death must not be feared at seventeen
Or seventy. In this world nothing but
Reality and light exist, no death, no dark.
Already each of us is by the sea,
And I am one who hauls the nets ashore
When shoals of immortality sweep in.

2

Live in the house – the house will not fall down.
Whatever century I summon up,
I shall enter it and build a house.
For that very reason now your children
And your wives are with me at one table,
One table for great-grandfather and grandson:
The future is accomplished here and now,
And if I just raise my hand before you,
All five beams of light will then remain.
Every day that went into the past
I shored up with collar-bones like pit-props,
I measured time with my surveyor's chain,
Walked through it as though walking through the
Urals.

3

I picked out an age of my own stature.
We headed south; made dust rise on the steppe;
Coarse weeds smelt rank; a grasshopper cavorted,
Brushed horseshoes with his whiskers, prophesied,
And told me like a monk that I would perish.
I took my fate and strapped it to my saddle;

And now, in future times, I still can stand
Upright in my stirrups like a boy.

My immortality is all I need
For my blood to flow from age to age.
For some corner, safe and always warm,
I would traffic my life willingly enough,
Were it not for life's flying needle
Drawing me like a thread around the world.

The first words of the poem are spoken as we see a small group carrying a long, weighty object, and because they are walking away from the camera the impression is that the scene – coinciding with the word 'forebodings' – is in the past. Calumny and poison conjure up the image of Socrates, to whom in his poem of that title (p.87) Arsenii gives the words 'we're in times to come'. 'All are immortal' is heard as we see legs and feet, fully shod, walking through the water, so that cameraman and viewer see what the men saw as they trudged. The words 'reality and light' coincide with the moment when two men catch up with a group clustered round a large object, behind which a soldier is pointing towards camera and viewer. The distant figure pointing towards the advancing soldiers, the viewer and 'reality'[120] appears only briefly, but because he has stopped and is facing the opposite way from the others, he disrupts the viewer's sense of a steady march forward; in this instant of hiatus we hear the words 'no death', as the screen is filled with an expanse of flat white water and sky, with no people or movement. As Deleuze wrote: 'A clairvoyant function is developed in water, in opposition to earthly vision ... the promises or implication of another state of perception'.[121] The still water becomes a background for the images ending the first stanza, filled with movement, weight and energy, hauled nets and immortality.

The first stanza is full of negatives, rejecting the linear time scheme where forebodings and predictions can suggest a predetermined future, even as we watch precisely recorded images of men whose fate was already sealed. The imperative, 'Live', at the start of the second stanza is addressed directly to the listener-viewer, evoking solid house, table and assembled family. Although the house here is that of world culture, 'the home, the daily life of the poet',[122] who is at home in any period or place, it also emphasises – in this film about ruptured family relationships – links of kin. In his *First Philosophical Letter* Chaadaev wrote of the need to 'tie up the severed links' between the generations; and well before Bergson he was writing of 'duration' ('*la durée*', he wrote in French) as the only 'true time'.[123] There seem to be echoes, too, of the thought of Nikolai Fedorov,[124] much discussed by the intelligentsia in the early part of the last century and certainly familiar to Arsenii; Andrei refers to him in his diaries.[125] Fedorov was a highly original, unworldly thinker, whose central thesis is that we are all responsible not only for each other but also for preceding generations, and he saw the prevailing 'disrelatedness' and 'non-kinship' as fatally destructive.[126] In all his films Andrei sought to 'establish links which connect people ... I need to have a sense that I myself am here as a successor'.[127]

At the word 'house' we again see a harmoniously composed group on the gun transporter; 'your children' comes with a sudden change of view: for the first time the camera is ahead of the men, who walk in a long, widely strung out line towards the viewer, striding and leaning forwards. The poet's 'collar-bones like pit-props' are relevant to the men marching with loads on their shoulders, and the poet bearing the weight of the past again suggests Atlas.

At 'prophesied' the camera cuts to a snowy hill with a river below, toboggans and a horse on the hillside; and the orphaned waif Asafev, whose fate seems to parallel that of the poet himself,[128] who now looks back to a prophecy heard in his childhood, and repudiates its warning. His words 'I took my fate' are heard as Asafev slips and falls, then rises wearily, in tears, to walk higher, glancing behind him down the slope at the picturesque groups below. His frailty and isolation, and the cold, contrast with the poem's dusty steppe and the boy standing up in his stirrups. Asafev walks steadily towards the camera, and only when he is seen in close-up does it become clear that he is whistling; beyond him the snowy landscape extends into the distance, 'creating a short circuit of the near and the far',[129] as the camera is panning and the poet anticipates immortality. As the poem ends with the flying needle image, the film extends it through the world in time and space. Asafev is suddenly central. Now his air of concentration, the intensity of the close-up and his whistling all assert individual strength. He will resist the temptation of a warm haven; and his whistling evinces artistic creativity.

With the poem still resonating, he glances aside and the camera cuts to scenes of the liberation of Prague and other newsreel footage of victory, including a shot of a man on crutches (like the poet himself) and of a cameraman photographing the corpse of

Hitler's double: a reminder of how modern history is recorded and, hidden inside the shot, of political deception. After footage of the atomic bomb, the camera returns to the hilltop, we hear electronic music rather like choral singing, and then again the beating drum is heard as Asafev turns towards the tree; the music grows louder and a bird flies on to his hat. A cut to newsreel footage shows a Chinese mob and countless identical busts of Mao, grotesquely meaningless by comparison with the frail child who is uniquely himself, for whom the poem has opened up the possibility of being master of his fate. The 'needle' that leads him on may recall Bergson's celebrated cone image, where the pointed end is the individual's present moment, continuously driven forward into the future; the thread creates an unbroken tie with the past.[130]

Here, as in the poem 'Joan of Arc's Tree', the bird may have its origins in the birds charmed by Orpheus; certainly at this moment Asafev personifies the organic link with nature that is fundamental in the work of Arsenii and Andrei. A link has also been made with *Solaris*, where the director singled out the detail of the bird perched in a tree in Breughel's winter landscape. The episode, unlike the newsreel footage, has been set up; Asafev takes the bird in his hand, prefiguring the end of the film when the hero, perhaps at the moment of death, will release a bird. It creates a poetic link between poet, hero and orphan, and is significant above all for that moment's singularity.

The newsreel was chosen well after initial planning.[131] The poem celebrates artistic vocation and the sacred bond and succession between generations. Its accompanying Sivash newsreel is an authentic record of an epic moment in the war which cost a huge number of lives, and its aesthetic impact is akin to that of classical tragedy; it is the high point in the series of pre-war, wartime and post-war newsreel extracts, which together fix the moment in history and in the nation's memory.[132] All these areas of human experience are relevant to Asafev's individual fate; his powerlessness and insignificance in worldly terms make him a typical hero in the work of both Tarkovskys.

With this poem the voice is classically acousmetric in that it could not possibly be taken as sounding in any character's head. At the same time it encapsulates some of the poet's fundamental convictions. He wrote for years with little hope of publication but always knew that his poems 'would not perish'; they were made from life itself and had nothing to do with official 'literary dictatorship' based on theories of 'how to organise the world'.[133] 'Life,

Life' is the most philosophical of the poems quoted and the only one to be combined with newsreel footage; thus the most abstract of the poems accompanies the most precisely recorded event. The newsreel is an actual imprint of time, here combined with the poet's reflections on time and immortality, which belong to those 'aspects of human life that can only be faithfully represented through poetry'. And despite disparaging remarks from official Soviet critics, the poem evidently spoke directly to the Soviet viewer: fan letters to Andrei Tarkovsky quoted in the first chapter of *Sculpting in Time* speak of communication through feeling and images; of removing obstacles between people; of there being no death; of time being one and undivided.

The final poem is heard just after the visit of Maria and twelve-year-old Aleksei to the doctor's wife, to whom she hoped to sell some earrings. Maria Tarkovskaia had in fact sold a pair of turquoise earrings during the war, an heirloom of which her husband was particularly fond, and was able to bring home a bag of potatoes.[134] The doctor's wife (played by Larissa Tarkovskaia, Andrei's second wife) tells them to wipe their feet because the maid, 'Masha' (a familiar form of 'Maria'), has washed the floor, somehow making it sound as if Maria is also of servant status; in the end Maria has to escape empty-handed from the stifling, pretentious fussiness of the house and its owner.

While the women are negotiating in another room, Aleksei is left on his own and literally reflects on himself in a looking-glass. As if we are reading his thoughts, a shot of the girl's hand in front of the fire (first seen just before the telephone call from Maria Tarkovskaia about Liza's death) is seen again, then the hand appears on the other side of the fire and on the edge of an opening door. As children Andrei Tarkovsky and his sister used to enjoy looking at the firelight glowing through their hands, held in front of the flames. A girl is seen sitting by the fire, namely the Redhead, played by Olga Kizilova, Andrei Tarkovsky's stepdaughter, who has already played the teenage Spanish girl in Ignat's childhood: perhaps his calf-love is a repetition of his father's, another 'mirroring' of one generation in the next, as the film-maker explained these doublings.[135]

After Maria has killed the cock, the snowstorm of feathers cuts to her dream, or daydream, of her husband at her bedside, stroking her hand, as she levitates above the bed. He tells her lovingly that all will be well, exactly the words he will utter on his deathbed at the end of the film. When he asks her, 'Are you ill?' she replies: 'It's so obvious, I love you.' This is the only time in *Mirror* that these words are spoken. Perhaps both Maria and Aleksei have experienced a moment of inner clarity in the alien setting of the doctor's house.

The two set off for home along the river bank. The first shot of the river is of a pool as calm as glass; the next, as the poem opens, of flowing water.

Eurydice

A person has one body,
Unique and all alone,
The soul has had enough
Of being cooped up inside
A bag with ears and eyes
No bigger than a tanner,
And skin, scar after scar,
On a bony frame.

Out through the cornea
It flies to the sky's pool,
Onto an icy spoke
Of a bird's chariot wheel,
And hears through the bars
Of its living prison cell
Rattling woods and cornfields,
Trump of seven seas.

Bodiless souls are sinful
As shirtless bodies are,
No intent – no action,
No design, not one line;
A riddle with no answer:
Who then will return
From dancing on the dance-floor
Where there's nobody to dance?

And I dream of another
Soul in other clothes:
Burning as it runs
From timidness to hope,
Spiritous and shadowless
Like fire across the earth,
Leaving on the table
Lilac in farewell.

On you run, child, do not grieve
For poor Eurydice,
Take your bronze hoop and your stick,
Go bowling through the world,
While earth's merry, dry reply
To every step you take
(If only as mere quarter-sound)
Still echoes in your ears.

Maria glances at the river three times and Aleksei walks out of frame as we hear the words 'icy spoke'. The soul can escape through the eye, and the water's 'clairvoyant function' is at work in a transition to 'other perceptions': as Maria looks again at the river, we hear the words about what the soul hears through the bars of its cell, and her gaze moves to the grove outside the dacha, shot in dark sepia, the scene of Aleksei's earlier dream. A strong wind is blowing through the bushes, as it does in previous dreams associated with the loss of husband and father. The camera moves left until we see the same table as we saw in 'First Meetings'; the wind wraps a napkin around the jug and a lamp is blown to the ground as we hear the 'riddle'.

At the start of the fourth stanza the camera cuts to the back of the small boy's head as he timidly pushes open the door and walks into the (still sepia) house. Just before the visit to the doctor's wife, the narrator spoke of his recurring childhood dream of not being able to enter the house. Now, at the start of the fifth stanza, 'do not grieve', the boy walks away from the camera into the darkened rooms, a very small, receding figure; the camera pans left to billowing curtains and, as the poem ends, the sound of the wind accompanies the play of light and shade made by dancing curtains, and this continues for several moments, the soundtrack quite loud – it 'Still echoes in your ears'. The camera moves to the right, towards a brightly reflecting mirror which gradually darkens, and the child appears in the mirror from the left, carrying a glass jug full of milk. He seems to sip the milk, or to smell it, perhaps even to kiss the jug. In the doctor's house in those hungry days, milk was allowed to spill and drip on to the floor, but this milk is precious, a source of life, symbol of motherhood, almost sacramental. In another poem, 'Thunder and clanging still fill our ears', fresh milk seems to summarise childhood happiness. For the Greeks it was also a libation for the dead, and this may not be irrelevant; death always seems to be an out-of-frame reference point. The camera dwells for some moments on the child – only his face and torso and the jug are brightly lit – against a dark background: he is at the centre of all that is happening, embodying an answer to the riddle in that as artist, as poet, he will hear the earth's response to his steps.

The final lines of 'Life, Life' are about following the trajectory of life's needle; here the circular image of the hoop still speaks of movement, but not of direction. Bowling a hoop is a playful pastime, sufficient to itself; the circle, essentially complete, is a also symbol of life or eternity. Where 'Life, Life' was followed by chronological scraps of newsreel, the end of 'Eurydice' points towards the end of the film and the completion of the circle.

After the poem there is little speech in the rest of the film. The small Aleksei's words to (the real) Maria Tarkovskaia are met by her absent 'What?' – enigmatic but full of weight. The deathbed scene is also enigmatic, made more so by the presence of the mysterious visitors from an earlier decade. We hear the doctor's brief diagnosis concerning the patient's conscience rather than his body; the hero releases the bird, and we do not know whether or not the hero, who 'only wanted to be happy', has died. The only other exchange is between the couple about the expected baby, when Maria is so full of emotion that she can barely restrain her tears.

The soundtrack, on the other hand, is eloquent. As Aleksei glances aside, holding the milk jug, there is a very faint sound of a train hooting, as in the opening scene of the film – his father presumably left by train and he may well do the same himself – then there is a cut to colour, and Aleksei dog-paddles across the stream towards his mother as she washes clothes on the far bank; a dog barks in the distance, at first faintly, then the sound grows louder. There is no sound of the boy's swimming, though he must have been breathing hard and splashing: the soundtrack is selective; the following scene inside the house with a Labrador puppy on the table is silent. The sound of the barking dog heightens the viewer's sense of offscreen space; the lack of natural sound in the other two shots makes them purely visual images. 'Factual' visual detail in combination with an incomplete aural record are one technical element in the dreamlike quality of the film which is partly created by natural and musical sounds; and we are reminded of the line, 'I dream of another soul'. A longish silence is twice broken by ringing birdsong. Gentle electronic music, or faint wind, sounds as little Aleksei approaches the old Mother. After the bird is released there is more birdsong and a long silence as the camera 'takes flight' over the meadow and wood, literally creating a bird's-eye view. Bach's *St John Passion* starts softly behind the young couple's conversation and grows louder as Maria Tarkovskaia walks with the basket of washing (just done by her young self in the stream?) and we see a complete cycle of nature at every stage from young shoots to rotting vegetation; there is a shot of the foundations of the original dacha and of debris in the well from which Maria once drank. Natasha Synessios calls this sequence 'the most poignant illustration of the fullness of time ... the life of nature is merged with human life, observing a common rhythm and language'.[136] Bach sounds triumphantly throughout this scene: 'Lord, ... whose name is glorious, show us by thy passion that thou, true son of God forever, even in the darkest hour will rise victorious.' Immediately after the final chorus comes Aleksei's full-throated whoop. Like the child evoked by the acousmetric voice, he will be in dialogue with the earth. Silence follows, broken at intervals of several moments by an owl hooting. At the third hoot the camera draws the trees closer together and the screen darkens into night.

Arsenii's poem is about poetry. Reflections on the physical limitations of the human condition, and the power of the imagination to escape them, lead on to the riddle, which can be read as both 'where there's nobody to dance' and 'where nobody can dance'. Poetry emerges from non-being into being; the mortal, physically limited poet has the power to make this happen. One cannot be sure whether the dance-floor exists; the question of returning from it carries a note of returning from the Underworld, from which nobody can be expected to come back – only the poet Orpheus did so.

Like 'First Meetings', the poem was secretly addressed to Maria Falts, and the other 'soul' of the fourth stanza is thus Maria-Eurydice. After Maria's death from tuberculosis in 1932, Tarkovsky wrote a total of twelve poems[137] to her memory, though her name never appeared. Maurice Blanchot writes that for Orpheus, 'Eurydice is the limit of what art can attain ... she is the profoundly dark point towards which art, desire, death and the night all seem to lead. His work is to bring it back into daylight, and give it form, figure and reality.'[138] This is indeed what Arsenii-Orpheus does. Only in two of the poems does he write the name 'Maria', and in one of them it is in order to say that it 'pains his heart'. In the other poems he refers to her name but does not specify it, almost as if, like his prototype, he were resolutely avoiding looking at her. In three of the poems she seems to be with him and yet not there.

If we follow Blanchot, 'Orpheus's impulse ... does not demand Eurydice in her diurnal truth and her everyday charm, but in her nocturnal darkness ... it does not want to make her live, but to have the fullness of her death living in her.'[139] Surely this is the sense of the last line of 'Rooms were low-ceilinged', also in memory of Maria Falts: 'And so – death is alive.' Arsenii believed that every poet loves life, however he may rail against it, for life is his mother and she feeds him; but he may 'also partake of the bread of death' for death too is his mother and nourishment.[140]

Maria-Eurydice is disembodied 'fire', his inspiration. Knowing the darkest reaches of grief, Orpheus can still sing of his beloved. The child of the last stanza of 'Eurydice' is the poet of the next generation; perhaps he may also be equated with the 'angel and young child' of the poem 'Inscription in a Book (i)': the opening of a new poetic work. The film-maker, ignorant of the identity of Eurydice for his father, used the poem for its significance as a statement about art and for the perfect way in which it harmonises with the image of the small Aleksei. The dark screen with which the film ends, reminiscent of Dante's dark wood, can seem like the dark of the Underworld visited by the poet: 'When Orpheus descends to Eurydice, art is the power that causes the night to open.'[141]

The four poems, woven into the film by the poet's voice, form a meta-narrative. The first tells of a supremely happy love; it happened sometime in the past and is irrevocably lost. The second also tells of a personal drama, where the protagonist's hope was dashed in the course of one day – namely today. In the third poem love may be understood to be an underlying reality, but the story is of the succession of generations, bound together by the power of art, which is stronger than death, and by the instinctive human sense of continuity. The timescale is past, present and future, the unity of time in duration. And the fourth poem celebrates triumph over death, and love as eternal reality. Transfigured by the poet, loss can become inspiration. The child, enjoined by the poet to play and to learn the language of the earth, will be his heir.

It is typical of the sensitivity of both Arsenii and Andrei that the physical link between the first and last poems is the bunch of lilac: that most joyful, promising and short-lived of early summer blooms. (Incidentally the Swedish translation of Arsenii's poems is entitled *En Klaser Syrener* – a bunch of lilac).

In cinema a poem works simultaneously with visual images; film also has the capacity to give offscreen reality as much immediacy as the moving images on screen. The poet's voice and poems in *Mirror* are a unique exploitation of this phenomenon.

Stalker

Now summer is gone
It might never have been.
It's warm in the sun.
And yet surely there's more.

All that could happen
Fell into my hands
Like a five-fingered leaf;
And yet surely there's more.

No evil was squandered,
No good done in vain,
Light never faded;
And yet surely there's more.

Life guarded and cared for me
Under her wing,
I've had such good fortune;
And yet surely there's more.

Not one leaf was burned,
Not a single twig broken ...
Today is clear as washed glass;
And yet surely there's more.

In *Stalker* the eponymous hero recites this one poem. He tells his companions that the poet perished in the 'Mincer' through the fault of his own brother, who was once Stalker's teacher; 'something broke' in this man, he betrayed his mission and became known as 'Porcupine'. He went to the Room to ask for his brother to be brought back to life; the response he received was fabulous wealth and days later he hanged himself. Andrei Tarkovsky thus casts his father, the 'subtle, talented poet', as victim of a brother's treachery, a sacrificial figure. The poem expresses a central theme of the film: the human need for something beyond the material and the worldly, which the director sums up as selfless love – 'the supreme value ... by which man lives and his soul does not want'.[142]

In the published screenplay,[143] the poem recited is 'Still from above on to time and space' (p.159), where the relevance to *Stalker* is clear enough: *need*, *want* and *futility* are precious elements in the search for self, and humans are bound umbilically to the earth. By changing to 'Now summer is gone' the director has Stalker make not only a more personal statement, but also a more open-ended one: although the poem's refrain hints at the existence of some higher spiritual reality, it also chimes with the vague possibility that the Zone may be fantasy, a psychological game or evidence of collective hysteria.

Stalker recites the poem in a state of physical and mental exhaustion, leaning his elbow against a window-frame, at one point rubbing his knuckles over his eyes; light from the window falls on to his face; halfway through the poem he turns round and rests his back on the wall. Light alternates with shadow and fades at the line about good fortune, then the screen brightens for the last stanza. Deleuze writes of alternating black and white – 'the white which captures the light, the black at the point where the light stops, and sometimes the half-tone, the grey, as indiscernibility', which can convey an 'alternation of terms instead of an opposition, an alternative, a spiritual choice instead of an opposition ... The spiritual alternative seems to correspond to the alternation of terms, good, evil and uncertainty or indifference, but in a very mysterious way.'[144] The idea is apposite in the context of this film's moral questioning. When he finishes, Stalker turns to his companions to say, 'It's good, isn't it?' and, despite the Writer's hostility, to tell them that their progress through the Zone proves that they are 'good, kind people'. He seems to be projecting on to them the ultimately optimistic sense of divine discontent expressed in the poem.

The quiet intensity with which Stalker recites the poem is partly due to the fact that speech is an effort for him – most of his utterances are instructions or warnings; like the speechless child in *Sacrifice* he has a bandage round his throat; the recitation is a significant act, an element of his life's task.[145] Very unusually the camera is on his face throughout; as a general rule in Tarkovsky's films the speaker is unseen or sometimes he or she is seen in a mirror. When speech is heard without the mouth being visible, the viewer is made aware of offscreen space, which adds weight and presence to the words. Exceptions are deliberate: for example, in the first exchange in *Mirror*, between Maria and the doctor, we see Maria's face only when she corrects the doctor – 'It's an alder' – and when she tries to tell him he has blood behind his ear and he doesn't listen. The coincidence of visible moving lips with heard words can make the words seem trite, less substantial; here it relates to the characters' lack of communication. Of course, there are many variations to the pattern – this is an area that invites exploration. As Stalker recites, the speech act coincides completely with the visual image of the speaker; and so – perhaps because we have grown used to the visual image not showing what the sound image utters, and more so if we come to *Stalker* already familiar with *Mirror* – we have a strong impression of the poet's voice being heard through that of Stalker. The poem is one of the longer 'visible' speeches in Tarkovsky's work.

Stalker could be said to be standing in for both the fictional poet and, by extension, for Arsenii, faithful to the latter's vision and seeing it as his duty to be the medium for the poet's thought; he is also clearly a projection of Andrei. The poem is not his only quotation: he prays in words from *Tao Te Ching*, repeats to himself the Gospel passage about the meeting on the road to Emmaus and dreams of his wife reading aloud from the Book of Revelation; his companions speak largely in clichés, whereas Stalker uses timeless words of human wisdom. He thus contrasts starkly with the Writer, whom Andrei calls 'simply a popular author';[146] what for Stalker, or Andrei or Arsenii, are precious elements of culture, are for the Writer the stuff of parody. He makes a crown of thorns, and as he puts it on his head contradicts its meaning by telling Stalker that he'll never forgive him.[147] The musicologist Natalia Kononenko suggests that he parodies Bach's 'Erbarme Dich' by whistling it in bits.[148] 'There is music, and there is Bach', as Andrei Tarkovsky said in conversation, and reducing his music to the level of a catchy tune is a kind of sacrilege.

Stalker could be quoting the poet when he talks of music as the purest of the arts because it only expresses itself,[149] or when he says that remembering past unhappiness makes you kinder.[150] In his closeness to nature he reminds us of many of Arsenii's poems, and in his innocence and dedication he is akin to Mandelshtam in Arsenii's image of him in 'The Poet', and indeed of Pushkin's 'Poor Knight' who figures in the epigraph to that poem; and he is of the same – more or less *iurodivy* – race as Grigorii Skovoroda.

Tiuchev's 'How I love your eyes', read in voiceover by Stalker's wife at the end of the film, was one of Arsenii's favourite poems.

It is as if the poet's work has grown symbiotically into the consciousness of the hero. The poet in his fictitious persona has perished, as has his brother; Stalker is bearer of the poet's vision and of the brother's betrayed mission. His life is lived as it were in the implied question of the poem's refrain: he knows that ultimately people need more than all the good things the world can give, none of which, in any case, have ever come Stalker's way, though his air of despair suggests that he *has* to go on being Stalker, against reason and against all the odds. Despair and hope seem to be at war within him, as perhaps they were for the film-maker.

Nostalghia

I have used the original Italian spelling of the title to prevent the reader from immediately associating it with the English notion of 'nostalgia'. For the film-maker the Russian word meant 'an illness, a life-threatening disease', stemming from a longing not only for the past or for home, but also for something distant and unattainable; and for an inner home. He connected it with the impossibility of living in a divided world.[151]

The first conversations relate to earlier films: the hero declares that he wants nothing for himself; a sacristan says that men are created for self-sacrifice and that there are more important things than wanting to be happy: this sounds like a direct comment on the dying words of the hero in *Mirror*.

The hero of *Nostalghia*, Andrei Gorchakov, is a Russian poet visiting Italy to do research into the life a of an eighteenth-century Russian musician, 'Pavel Sosnovsky', modelled on the historical figure of Maxim Berezovsky (1745–77), a serf whose master sent him to Italy to study. A letter from Sosnovsky to a friend, in which he recounts a dream, is heard in Italian voiceover as Eugenia, Gorchakov's Italian interpreter, reads it to herself: in the dream Sosnovsky was back in Russia and his master the Count was staging an opera in his park; Sosnovsky and his fellow serfs had to play the part of nude statues, painted white and standing motionless;[152] as the cold overwhelmed him, he woke up. He realised that this was 'no dream, but reality'; although he could stay on in Italy, the thought of not returning to Russia 'is like death'. The letter coincides with Gorchakov's suffering a severe nosebleed; the 'disease' of nostalgia/*nostalghia* is manifesting itself physically. He lies down, drifting into a dream about his wife and their Russian home, and his voice calls her name, 'Maria'; she looks around, trying to see him. The camera moves outside to a moonlit night by a misty river and members of Gorchakov's family appear. As the moon rises a woman's voice calls 'Andrei!' and the camera cuts to the hero, apparently turning in response, in the half-darkness of the hotel lobby. The soundtrack is of running water, and the camera cuts to the white statue of an angel lying partly buried on a riverbed, the pattern of its wing feathers repeating that of the surface ripples.

Not all the lines of 'As a child I once fell ill' are narrated in the film (the omitted lines are in square brackets here).

As a child I once fell ill
From fear and hunger. I'd pick
Hard skin from my lips, and lick them;
I still remember the cool, salty taste.
And all the time I'd walk and walk and walk,
Sit on the stairs in the hall to warm up,
Walk light-headed [as if led by the rat-catcher's pipe
Towards the river, sit down
On the stairs to warm up; and shiver every which way.
And mother stands and beckons, she seems
So close – but I can't reach her:
I start towards her then she's seven steps away,
Beckons me to come, I start again – and she's seven
Steps away, and beckons me.]
        I felt too hot,
Undid my top button and lay down –
Then trumpets blared out, lights beat
On my eyelids, [horses were galloping,]
Mother flying above the roadway, she beckoned me to come –
And flew away ...
     And now I dream
Of a white hospital, and apple trees,
[A white sheet at my chin
A white doctor looking down at me,
A white nurse standing at my feet,
Her wings stirring. And there they stayed.
But mother came and beckoned me to come –
And flew away ...]

Splashing footsteps sound together with the running water and, as the camera pans to dense green moss or weed on the riverbed and light mist floats above the surface – the leitmotiv mist of the opening episode, the baths and the Russian dream scenes – Gorchakov's voice is heard reciting the opening lines. Still more markedly than 'Life, Life' and 'Eurydice', the poem is preceded by 'clairvoyant' water, and water continues to dominate aurally and visually even after the hero starts to recite, so that it seems like a medium for the verse. At the line about his lips he is seen from the back, knee-deep in the river, walking slowly towards a doorway in the ruined monastery, an open book held behind his back: his father's poems are literally behind him, he holds them physically. At 'I'd walk and walk and walk' he goes through the doorway, turns left and vanishes at 'lightheaded', and remains out of frame until the poem is finished. As he disappears, the small figure of Angela is glimpsed very briefly through a low opening in a wall.

There is a painted red Greek cross inside a red circle on a wall, above the water, which is centre screen for several moments: a symbol belonging to the building's past, still present in the late twentieth century, perhaps actually harking back to Byzantine Christianity, the layers of history enclosed in a circular symbol of infinity, eternity or God. We hear Gorchakov's voice echoing inside the ruins, declaiming the lines about being too hot. He is drunk, and has missed out several lines of the poem, so that the little girl's appearance coincides with the *missing* reference to the Pied Piper. The word 'mother' is shouted loudly, after a pause where he can be heard muttering, 'Can't remember.' The final line of the abridged poem is uttered very quietly; a moment later he repeats the first line, in a low voice and without expression, as Angela reappears briefly through a low door.

This poem was important enough to Andrei Tarkovsky for him to consider including it in *Mirror*,[153] and in *Sculpting in Time* he gives his plan for a short film based on it, to include father, son, grandson, a fire, an angel and feathers floating down to earth.[154] In his diary he recounts a dream in which 'the sky was like fibres of a sunlit fabric ... light-bearing, living threads ... moving and floating and becoming like birds ... Music seemed to sound like the chiming of little bells; or else the bird's chirping was like music.'[155] The dream seems to be the basis for the soundtrack when we first see Gorchakov as he picks up a feather after the birds have fluttered out of the Madonna statue; the white patch of his hair reflects the feather, at which he gazes, and he sees the Russian countryside, with the angel beside the house.

Here the mother's angel-like flight takes her out of the child's reach; it may explain another title considered for *Mirror*: 'Why Are You Standing So Far Away?'[156] The theme of motherhood was introduced in the Church of the Madonna of Childbirth: the calm portrait by Piero della Francesca gazes down on the noisily praying women and the birds bursting out of the statue; Domenico prays to his mother as he is about to burn himself to death; Gorchakov hears his mother praying for him in the ruined cathedral of his dream; and the film is dedicated to Andrei Tarkovsky's mother.

After the poem, the camera cuts to the riverbank, a fire, remnants of a picnic, a vodka bottle and a paper cup, which Gorchakov refills. His first words are, 'I must see Father' – a sentiment recorded more than once in Andrei's own diary, for instance on 12 September 1970. He walks back into the water and turns as he senses the child looking at him. The poem is about innocent childhood, when grown-ups could be seen as angels; he looks thoughtful as she tells him her name: Angela. His mother's angelic wings had carried her from him so the image has a certain ambiguity. As he rails against the consumerism of modern Italy, sounding very like the director himself in interviews and in the later sections of the diary – and further blurring the distinction between himself and Andrei, between hero and film-maker – the child sits perched on her ledge of rock. Gorchakov suddenly declares in Italian: 'It's like Russia here, I don't know why.' For some moments Angela is centre screen; she drops a stone into the water, either to attract his attention or because she is in her own world, and as she does so 'Sight is fading – my power' is heard.

> Sight is fading – my power,
> Two invisible diamond spears;
> Hearing fails, filled with long ago thunder
> And the breath of my father's house.
> Tough knots of muscle weaken,
> Like ancient oxen on plough-land;
> And no more behind my shoulders
> Do two wings shine in the night.
>
> I'm a candle, burnt out at the feast.
> Gather my wax in the morning
> And this page will give you a hint
> Of how to weep and where to take pride,
> How to distribute the final third
> Of jollity, to die easily,
> Then, sheltered by some chance roof,
> Flare up after death like a word.

The poem is read in Italian translation in voiceover, and for the first five lines the camera is on Angela, as if the ageing poet were addressing this foreign child two generations younger than himself. The voice is acousmetric and the child appears to be listening, without surprise; the camera pauses just long enough on her motionless figure, centre screen, head slightly raised, to suggest that she is engaged by the words. At the line about the oxen, the camera cuts to shallow water, stones on the riverbed, bubbles rising and the candle burning on the shore: all four elements; time evoked in the flowing water; the candle burning 'like a word'. Behind the image of gathered wax is the Russian New Year custom of holding up the cooled wax of a candle so that its shadow, thrown by a candle-flame on to a wall, will depict an event in the coming year. The poem insists that the residue of life's experience, solidified and dull after the feast, holds a message as clear as words on a page about how to die, even if this is under a chance roof far from the father's house – as it will be for both hero and film-maker.

As the poem ends the hero is lying on the stones, eyes closed, while the book burns behind his head. The image suggests the physical fragility of written words; however, once it has been written, poetry exists. As Gorchakov was expounding drunkenly he was still holding the volume of verse, the contents of which are limitless and indestructible. His slurred delivery of one poem, and the translated version of another, illustrate what may happen to poems once they are out in the world; but even so they come to have a place in the consciousness of those who receive them; they remain alive. Perhaps the significance of Gorchakov's sense of the place being 'like Russia' has to do with the reality of Arsenii's Russian poem for any place or time. Moreover, fire may be creative as well as destructive. The poet, Arsenii tells us, 'burns' (in 'You who lived in this world before me'); and poetry is alive with a

... searing sense of prescience ...
That burns with fiery light above the precious rhymes.
('To a Notebook of Poems')

And, as we have just been reminded, the word will 'flare up' after death.

The camera cuts to Gorchakov's dream, in sepia, of the cobbled street, where he confronts the young Domenico's image in the mirror and starts to speak like him, adopting something of his identity. As the film goes back to colour and to Gorchakov still lying by the river, a feather (from an angel?) floats down through the ruined tower to the water. Now the hero's face is peaceful and sober: he has taken on the task set him by Domenico.

Earlier in the film Gorchakov impatiently told Eugenia to throw away an Italian translation of Tarkovsky's poems: they were clearly not worth reading since foreign cultures can never be understood. In an interview in Sweden Andrei dismissed equally categorically all attempts at translating because 'the culture of another people contains a mystery which no foreigner can fathom',[157] and the impossibility of translating Pushkin is a sign of the poet's greatness. Arsenii Tarkovsky himself said that everything Pushkin wrote is elementally Russian and once it has been separated from Russian it loses so much that it seems to have no flesh. True poetry is 'the highest form of existence of the language in which it is written'.[158] However accurate a translation, it will lose the sounds, associations and metaphorical connotations of the original. Such was the view of this master of verse translation. As Svetlana Geier says at the end of the beautiful documentary, *Die Frau mit fünf Elefanten* (2009), 'Translation is the word that escapes you'; and most practitioners would agree. And yet, 'it is this mourning for the absolute that produces the happiness associated with translation'; even if one must give up the idea of a perfect translation, it is possible 'to bring the author to the reader and bring the reader to the author'.[159] Tarkovsky translated from languages he hardly knew but never without scholarly, annotated literal translations, whenever possible consulting with the poet himself and always making painstaking use of dictionaries.[160]

Beyond the question of verse translation lies the wider theme of the universality of art; and world literature is given us largely through translation. Arsenii talked of great books as 'bridges' between different cultures and epochs, citing *The Divine Comedy* and *The Brothers Karamazov* as examples of works which, like those of Homer and the Greek tragedians, are 'soldered forever into the ring' of the universe, the ring of world culture. A great book is a 'true blessing', a treasury of the spirit, 'of that free and heartfelt spirit which from time immemorial has been ... persecuted and tortured by tyrants'.[161] Perhaps the child's hoop at the end of 'Eurydice' is a miniature emblem of that ring. Andrei also thought of great art as a unified whole, categorising the great artistic figures of the world – Leonardo, Bach, Shakespeare, Tolstoy – as poets, since 'in a certain sense each art is poetic in its highest and finest forms'.[162]

Although Andrei Tarkovsky declared that he should not be identified with his hero,[163] the parallels are undeniable. He, a Russian artist, is making a film about a fictitious Russian poet who is researching the life of a fictitious Russian musician, whose story is based on the life of a historical figure (Maxim Berezovsky).[164] He is desperately homesick and already ill. One is reminded of Arsenii's lines in 'Stone on the Path' (p.126):

> A poet's vatic power is helpless
> Every time a plot's strange whim
> Makes fate drive us, still alive
> Into her own story.

The film-maker seemed almost to feel that the film was dictating his fate; although he had come to Italy with no intention of staying abroad, as he watched his own film he 'got very frightened. The film had been creating the situation, was almost making *me*.'[165]

Gorchakov carries out his mission, a pointless, absurd act in worldly terms, and it costs him his life. His quiet deed seems to complete Domenico's self-immolation. In so far as the heroes of *Mirror* and *Nostalghia* share something of the same identity, Gorchakov's death also redeems his earlier counterpart. But he is also a counterpart to the poet Arsenii, whose director-son in turn saw himself as a poet.

Gorchakov's final clarity of vision springs directly from the two poems: the childhood vision of angels experienced during a grave illness, and the elderly poet's recognition of the fact that along with his physical faculties his wings have faded and death

The poet and his granddaughter Katia, Moscow 1987

is approaching. The motifs of bonfire, feathers and flowing water, the burning poems and the poet's belief that his words will flare up after death are all brought to consummation in the candle flame carried sacramentally across the baths.

The poems become a vital element in the interplay of shifting identities and dislocated time, presence and absence, remembering and forgetting, that we associate with Tarkovsky's films. The central figure of the absent father in *Mirror* is given no name in the credits (he is just 'Aleksei's father') and he appears only in the person of an actor; yet in the sound waves made by his vocal chords at the unique moment of recording, the real father is physically present to every listener-viewer. In 'First Meetings' the poet's son ostensibly assimilates his father's memories into his own artistic vision, but – all personal memories are that person's alone – the film-maker cannot in fact remember the poet's past, and never knew that the poem addresses Maria Falts, long since absent from the world but continually brought to life in the poet's memory and verse and, in that sense, present in the film. In the episode which is the context for 'Life, Life' Aleksei (Andrei) leads his son into his own adolescent memories, only for these to merge into newsreel footage proper to the collective memory of his father's generation; neither set of memories will ever belong wholly and personally to Ignat. In *Nostalghia* the hero (and son) recites his fictitious (and real) father's childhood images so ineptly as to obfuscate them; then comes a clear picture of the poet at the present time in which, in a different language, he looks ahead to his death, and this now seems like a prophetic intuition of the film-maker's own death. That future has become our past, and the 'word' still 'flares'.

Notes to the Introduction

1. See Andrei Tarkovsky, *Time within Time: The Diaries*, trans. by Kitty Hunter Blair, Calcutta 1991, entries for 14 March 1979. I have opted for references to dates of entries rather than page numbers in view of the number of versions of the diaries that exist in different languages.

2. For an excellent analysis of this episode see Robert Bird, *Andrei Rublëv*, London 2004, pp.74–9. Milky white liquid on flowing water recurs after the blinding scene: white paint runs from the flask of a painter as he falls dead; also when Foma, transfixed by an arrow, falls into a stream. Both craftsmen are thus associated with Calvary; neither is portrayed as a major artist, but both serve art and die a martyr's death.

3. In Andrei Tarkovsky, *Time*, 1991, 7 September 1970, the film-maker praises 'people who burn themselves alive in front of an impassive, wordless crowd'; he may have been thinking of the Czech student Jan Palach, who had burnt himself to death the previous year. However, the theme of the artist's figurative self-immolation is already to be found in his father's poems.

4. Arsenii Tarkovsky, *Sobranie sochinenii v trëkh tomakh [Works in 3 Volumes]*, Moscow 1991–3, vol.2, p.223.

5. T.S. Eliot, 'The Metaphysical Poets', *Selected Prose*, ed. and introduction by Frank Kermode, London 1975, p.64. See also note to 'There was nothing you would not do', no.24.

6. Andrei Tarkovsky, *Andrei Tarkovsky: Interviews*, ed. by John Gianvito, Jackson 2006, p.48. Geoff Dyer writes of Tarkovsky's treatment of nature: 'The simple things he notices and imbues with breathing magic always remain just what they are. Do they have a moral life? If so it is not one *given* by the artist; it's more like he responds to a tree's tree-ness and a wind's wind-ness which is the only moral life we can expect from a landscape. It is when there is some human interaction with landscape, when the landscape, having been manufactured or altered, is in the process of being reclaimed by nature – a source of abiding fascination for Tarkovsky – that its "inward meaning" is most powerfully felt.' Geoff Dyer, *Zona*, Edinburgh and London 2012, p.116.

7. Andrei Tarkovsky, *Andrei Rublëv*, trans. by Kitty Hunter Blair, London 1991, pp.95–6.

8. Ibid, p.33.

9. The poet's first love, who died in 1932 and to whose memory he remained devoted.

10. Anna Akhmatova, *Sobrannye sochinenia v 6 tomakh [Works in 6 Volumes]*, Moscow 2007, vol.2, p.312.

11. Arsenii Tarkovsky, 'Hope for the Future of Russian Poetry', interview, *Voprosy literatury*, no.6, 1979.

12. Andrei Tarkovsky, *Sculpting in Time: Reflections on Cinema*, trans. by Kitty Hunter Blair, London 1986, p.184. Page numbers are the same in other UK and US editions.

13. Arsenii Tarkovsky and Marina Tarkovskaia, *Sud'ba moia sgorela mezhdu strok [Between the Lines My Fate Had Burnt Up]*, ed. by V.A. Amikhranian; poems by Tarkovksy with commentaries by Tarkovskaia, Moscow 2009, p.121.

14. Fëdor Ermoshin points out the clear parallel between this scene and the mirrors

in Albert Lamorisse's *The Red Balloon* of 1956, and also the similarity between
the destruction of the red balloon and the expiring balloon in the prologue to
Andrei Rublëv. Fëdor Ermoshin, 'Dialogue through Denial: Lamorisse, Eisenstein
and Romm in the Artistic Consciousness of Andrei Tarkovsky', paper given at the
2nd International Andrei Tarkovsky Conference, Moscow 2013.

15. Quoted in Robert Bird, *Andrei Tarkovsky, Elements of Cinema*, London 2008, p.34.

16. Taken either from Roman Karmen's newsreels or Esfir Shub's *Spain* of 1939.
Ibid., p.137.

17. Gilles Deleuze, *Cinema 2: The Time Image*, trans. by Hugh Tomlinson and Robert
Galeta, London and New York 1989, p.76.

18. In an interview of 1968 Godard spoke of his own discovery of how 'you can't
separate the mirror from the reality'. Jean-Luc Godard, *Interviews*, Jackson 1998,
p.29.

19. Roland Barthes, *Camera Lucida*, London 2000, p.96.

20. Rainer Maria Rilke, *Selected Poems*, ed. by Robert Vilain, Oxford 2011, p.304.

21. Arsenii Tarkovsky 1991–3, vol.2, p.346.

22. Arkadii Khvoroshchan, 'Derzhava knigi' ('The Realm of the Book', interview with
Arsenii Tarkovsky), *Almanakh bibliofila*, Moscow 1979, vol.7, pp.72.

23. Andrei Tarkovsky, *Sculpting*, 1986, pp.92–3.

24. At the very end of Andrei Tarkovsky's production of the opera *Boris Godunov*
an angel child appears high above the back of the stage and stands motionless,
arms outstretched, gazing down on the pile of sleeping and dead bodies and the
lamenting *iurodivy* (Holy Fool).

25. Henri Bergson wrote of the need to free the 'fluttering, changing, living butterfly'
of metaphysics from 'the immutability of the cocoon' in order 'to restore to
movement its mobility, to change its fluidity, to time its duration'. Henri Bergson,
The Creative Mind, New York 2007, p.7. A word must be said about the director's
insistence that his films contain no symbols: in *Mirror* 'the images themselves
are like symbols, but unlike accepted symbols they cannot be deciphered. The
image is like a clot of life, and even the author may not be able to work out what
it means, let alone the audience … Symbolism is a sign of decadence' (answer
to a question after a talk on *Mirror*, April 1975, Andrei Tarkovsky, *Time*, 1991,
p.369). In *Sculpting in Time* he makes a distinction between symbols that work
on the level of allegory – generally didactic and explicable – and 'true' symbols,
quoting Viacheslav Ivanov's definition of the latter: 'inexhaustible and unlimited
in its meaning … it utters in its … language of hint and intimation something that
cannot be set forth, that does not correspond to words … It is formed by organic
process, like a crystal' (Andrei Tarkovsky, *Sculpting*, 1986, p.47). In other words,
all the things that clearly have symbolic significance, such as butterflies, houses,
the bird that flies on to Asafev's hat, the Anubis-like dog in *Stalker*, the Zone itself
and so on, are all physically and wholly exactly what and as they are, organic
elements of the reality of the film. Their introduction was sometimes quite
fortuitous: Tarkovsky originally wanted to use a trained fox in *Stalker*, according
to his sister Marina, because he was intrigued by Japanese legends of women
turning, werewolf-like, into foxes – or foxes into women (Arkady Strugatsky had
studied this topic). Because no trained fox could be found, the director opted for
a dog, which happened to be black. I am indebted for this detail to film director
Evgenii Tsymbal, who worked closely with Tarkovsky on *Stalker*.

26. N. Reznichenko discusses Tarkovsky's biblical references in N. Reznichenko,
'Slovar' tsaria Davida', *Voprosy literatury*, no.4, 2012.

27. Khvoroshchan 2009.

28. Andrei Tarkovsky, *Time*, 1991, p.378.

29. Ibid., p.71.

30. Arsenii Tarkovsky, 'Nobility of Spirit', *Literaturnaia gazeta*, no.7, 11 February
1987.

31. Andrei Tarkovsky, *Collected Screenplays*, trans. by Natasha Synessios and William Powell, introduction by Natasha Synessios, London 1990, pp.265–6. The poem was to sound in two sections, starting only with 'And he pressed against my mouth', interspersed with footage of an open coffin being carried; the lid put on; the coffin lowered into the grave, and then rising up again and opening, and the mourners 'walking away, their tears dried'.

32. Andrei Tarkovsky, *Sculpting*, 1986, p.52.

33. For his proposal for this film see Andrei Tarkovsky, *Time*, 1991, pp.371–7.

34. 'The Task of the Poet', given in St Petersburg in 1921 (the year of Blok's death) on the eightieth anniversary of Pushkin's death. Unfortunately no English version is readily available. 'O naznachenie poeta' is to be found in all complete editions of Blok's works. Arsenii quoted the speech in Arsenii Tarkovsky 1979.

35. Andrei Tarkovsky, *Sculpting*, 1986, p.36; Andrei Tarkovsky, *Interviews*, 2006, p.132.

36. Tarkovsky studied *Orphée* at film school. Mark Lefanu, *The Cinema of Andrey Tarkovsky*, London 1987, p.105.

37. See Dyer 2012, pp.17–18, for interesting comments on 'zone' and also 'mincer' or 'meat grinder' – slang for the Soviet repressive system; also, Anne Applebaum, *Gulag*, New York 2003, pp.xxix, xvi. After the Chernobyl disaster, the word 'zone' came to be used for the exclusion zone around the stricken power station, and this was one of the factors contributing to the film-maker's reputation for second sight.

38. Bird 2004, p.67.

39. Mikhail Iampolski, *The Memory of Tiresias: Intertextuality in Film*, Berkeley 1998, pp.2–3.

40. Ibid., p.35.

41. Arsenii Tarkovsky 1991–3, vol.2, p.300.

42. Henri Bergson, *Matter and Memory*, trans. by N.M. Paul and W. Scott Palmer, New York 2004, p.320.

43. Arsenii Tarkovsky 1991–3, vol.2, p.218.

44. Ibid., p.205.

45. Ibid., p.155–6.

46. Hilary Fink, *Bergson and Russian Modernism, 1900–30*, Evanston 1999.

47. The term 'intuition' is not to be equated with 'hunch': it is Bergson's term for a rigorous philosophical method based on the differentiation between phenomena that are different 'in nature' but often seen as different merely in degree, such as duration-space, memory-matter, recollection-perception, instinct-intelligence, etc. See Gilles Deleuze, *Le Bergsonisme*, Paris 1966, p.11. In *The Creative Mind* Bergson writes of intuition as intrinsic to 'the sympathy by which one is transported into the interior of an object in order to coincide with what there is unique and consequently inexpressible in it' (Bergson 2007, p.135) – a definition appropriate to the work of both Tarkovskys.

48. Georgii Ivanov, *Peterburgskie zimy*, New York 1952, p.113.

49. Osip Mandelshtam, *Complete Critical Prose and Letters*, ed. by Jane Garry Harris, trans. and by Jane Garry Harris and Constance Link, Ann Arbor 1979, p.117.

50. Andrei Tarkovsky, *Sculpting*, 1986, p.57.

51. For a translation of the poem see 'Appendix I: Pushkin Poems'.

52. Andrei Tarkovsky 1990, p.163.

53. Andrei Tarkovsky, *Time*, 1991, 15 February 1972.

54. Andrei Tarkovsky, *Sculpting*, 1986, pp.62–3.

55. Deleuze, *Cinema 2*, 1989, pp.40–1.

56. Maya Turovskaya, *Tarkovsky: Cinema as Poetry*, trans. by Natasha Ward, London 1989. See also Natasha Synessios, *Mirror*, London 2001, pp.70–9.

57. Andrei Tarkovsky, *Time*, 1991, 8 February 1976.

58. Terence McSweeney, 'Sculpting the Time Image: An Exploration of Tarkovsky's

Film Theory from a Deleuzian Perspective', in G.A. Jonsson and T.A. Ottarsson (eds.), *Through the Mirror, Reflections on the Films of Andrei Tarkovsky*, Newcastle upon Tyne 2006, p.90.

59. Andrei Tarkovsky, *Sculpting*, 1986, p.63.

60. Pavel Florensky, *Iconostasis*, trans. by Donald Sheehan and Olga Andrejev, New York 1996, p.35.

61. 'History, and the same is true of memory ... is the mind's triumph over time. It is a common-place of philosophy that whereas sensation is temporal, thought is eternal or extra-temporal. Sensation apprehends the here and now, thought apprehends the everywhere and the always. Hence the abstract psychology which splits the mind up into a sensitive and an intellectual faculty paradoxically presents us with a picture of man standing with one foot in time, the other in eternity. This is mythology, but it is true mythology.' R.G. Collingwood, *Speculum Mentis*, Oxford 1924, p.301.

62. Igor Evlampiev has produced a detailed study of this topic in Igor Evlampiev, *Khudozhestvennaia filosofia Andreia Tarkovskogo [The Artistic Philosophy of Andrei Tarkovsky]*, Ufa 2012. It is clear from the diaries (Andrei Tarkovsky, *Time*, 1991) that Tarkovsky was reading *Zarathustra* at the time he was working on *Sacrifice* and considered calling the film *The Eternal Return*; his entry for 3 September 1981 shows that he was reading Seneca with Nietzsche in mind. *Zarathustra* is cast as a kind of second Christ, and Evlampiev argues cogently that Alexander has a parallel role; Otto, Maria and even Victor and Martha are unwitting players in the drama of which Alexander's sacrifice is the culminating, world-changing act, achieved by liberating the forces of his own and all other existence. Certainly Alexander's omission from the Lord's Prayer of the words 'forgive us our trespasses' and 'for thine is the kingdom, the power and the glory forever' is consistent with Zarathustra's thesis that sin is unreal and God's kingdom is to be superseded by that of the Overman. In *Nostalghia*, Domenico gives a Zarathustran twist to the words spoken by God to St Catherine. The words recorded were: 'You are she who is not, I am he who is.' (Raymond of Capua, *The Life of St Catherine of Siena*, trans. by G. Lamb, London 1960, p.79); in the film they become: 'you are not who you are'. The original words state that God alone exists absolutely and that all other existence is contingent on him; Domenico's version seems to be informed by the Zarathustran motif of the creative individual's actualization of his potential, leading ultimately to the emergence of the Overman. This does not have to be taken as Andrei's own position: as an 'agnostic', he noted, he did not 'believe know-alls' (Andrei Tarkovsky, *Time*, 1991, 9 April 1982); and he seems directly to refute Zarathustra when he answers his own question, 'How can one live without God?' with: 'Only by becoming God, which is not possible'. On the other hand, in his speech on *The Apocalypse* in London in 1983, he declared that 'striving to become oneself, in one's deepest essence, is the wish to realise in oneself all those potentialities that make a person equal to God' (quoted in Evlampiev 2012, p.428). Andrei Tarkovsky's statements about his own world view could be contradictory; he was a passionate, impatient seeker, rather after the manner of Leo Tolstoy.

63. Deleuze, *Cinema 2*, 1989, p.7.

64. Evlampiev 2012, p.435.

65. Henri Bergson, *The World of Dreams*, New York 1958, p.34. Florensky speaks of dreams as 'the images that separate the visible world from the invisible – and at the same time join them ... A dream is pure meaning wrapped in the thinnest membrane of materiality'. Florensky 1996, pp.42–3.

66. Arsenii Tarkovsky 1991–3, vol.2, p.224.

67. Andrei Tarkovsky, *Sculpting*, 1986, p.38.

68. Andrei Tarkovsky, *Interviews*, 2006, p.40.

69. Ibid., p.51. In other interviews (Ibid., pp.55, 169) Tarkovsky said that the Zone

and the Room were (or may have been) invented by Stalker in order to give hope to unhappy people, but this was still 'an act of faith' on the latter's part. Stalker's genealogy is curious. In Arkady and Boris Strugatsky's novel *Roadside Picnic* he was a tough sci-fi bandit-hero; he was then slightly modified in the brothers' screenplay. It was only when the film had been in the making for a considerable time that he was transmuted by Tarkovsky into a self-sacrificing visionary. The name 'Stalker', first used by the Strugatsky brothers in the screenplay, was derived from Rudyard Kipling's 'Stalky' (Rudyard Kipling, *Stalky & Co.*, London 1899) whom the Strugatskys had admired since they were boys for his bad behaviour, inventiveness and generosity of spirit (Arkady and Boris Strugatsky, *Roadside Picnic*, London 2012, Postscript). Among the distant descendants of the Victorian public-schoolboy hero are the protagonists of three video games, all with the title *S.T.A.L.K.E.R.* The title of the novel is based on the suggestion – put forward by a character – that all the objects in the Zone are scraps and rubbish left behind by aliens who visited earth and had a picnic.

70. For an excellent discussion of the traditional Russian 'righteous', self-sacrificing hero in late Soviet literature, see Kathleen F. Parthé, *Russia's Dangerous Texts*, New Haven and London 2004, pp.132–59.

71. Arsenii Tarkovsky 1991–3, vol.2, p.199. Years later, Akhmatova praised him precisely for the fact that having started as a gifted young poet under the 'tyranny' of Mandelshtam and Pasternak, he had the strength to free himself and become 'the only poet who is totally himself, independent, autonomous ... I would say, the first of a line'. Quoted in notes to Arsenii Tarkovsky 1991–3, vol.1, p.444.

72. Arsenii Tarkovsky 1979.

73. Arsenii Tarkovsky 1991–3, vol.2, p.200.

74. Arsenii Tarkovsky 1991–3, vol.2, p.222.

75. Andrei Tarkovsky, *Sculpting*, 1986, p.221.

76. McSweeney 2006, p.81.

77. Robert Bresson, *Notes on the Cinematographer*, London 1986, p.58.

78. 'He looks for the possibility of talking about life, of showing its unique aspect, the singularity of every gesture on screen. But the contradiction is that each gesture is banal. He expresses what is typical through what is unique, and this ability to link the infinitely large to the infinitely small has always moved me. It seems to me that I have always understood what he means.' Andrei Tarkovsky, *Interviews*, 2006, p.25.

79. Arsenii Tarkovsky 1979.

80. Arsenii Tarkovsky 1991–3, vol.2, p.230.

81. 'A single word gives shelter to a whole range of thoughts born of couplings about which we know very little and which do not necessarily resemble each other very much.' Marc Augé, *Oblivion*, trans. by Margolin de Jager, Minneapolis 2004, p.9.

82. Arsenii Tarkovsky 1991–3, vol.2, p.196.

83. William Barrett, *Irrational Man*, London 1962, p.215. See also the poem 'World and Language', poem note 64, p.136.

84. Arsenii Tarkovsky 1991–3, vol.2, p.221.

85. Khvoroshchan 1979, p.8.

86. Arsenii Tarkovsky 1979.

87. Arsenii Tarkovsky 1991–3, vol.2, p.205.

88. Bresson 1986, p.3.

89. Sybil Moholy-Nagy, 'Introduction', in Paul Klee, *Pedagogical Sketchbook*, London 1953, p.8.

90. Andrei Tarkovsky, *Time*, 1991, 12 September 1970.

91. Andrei Tarkovsky, *Bright, Bright Day*, London and Florence 2007.

92. Andrei Tarkovsky, *Time*, 1991, 12 March 1971.

93. Layla Alexander-Garrett, *Andrei Tarkovsky: The Collector of Dreams*, London

2012, p.95.

94. Andrei Tarkovsky, *Sculpting*, 1986, p.198, p.221.

95. Andrei Tarkovsky, *Time*, 1991, 14 June 1972.

96. Both had read Florensky's description of Rublëv's ikon of the Trinity as 'a joyous message from the depths of existence'. Florensky traced the 'archaeology' of the work to St Sergius Radonezhsky, founder of the Monastery of the Holy Trinity outside Moscow, who preached on the visit of three angels to Abraham on the plains of Mamre, which in the Byzantine tradition became the model for depictions of the Trinity. Florensky 1996, p.84. Florensky also states, 'The most persuasive philosophic proof of God's existence is the one the textbooks never mention ... There exists the icon of the Holy Trinity by St Andrei Rublëv, therefore, God exists.' Ibid., p.68. In the *kinoroman* of *Andrei Rublëv*, the idea for the ikon comes to the painter because he comes across a trio of craftsmen (including the young Boriska) sitting together and forming 'a complete, assimilated, harmonious design', an everyday scene which reveals to him 'its most precious, deep-laid meaning.' Andrei Tarkovsky, *Andrei Rublëv*, 1991, p.149.

97. Andrei Tarkovsky, *Sculpting*, 1986, p.198.

98. Arsenii Tarkovsky 1991–3, vol.2, p.242.

99. Andrei Tarkovsky 1990, p.257.

100. Mladen Dolar, 'Which Voice?' in *In the First Circle*, exh. cat., Fundacio Tapies, Barcelona 2011, p.10.

101. Michel Chion, *Audio-Vision*, New York 1994, p.144.

102. Michel Chion, *Voice in Cinema*, New York 1998, p.4.

103. Ibid., p.23.

104. Andrei Tarkovsky, *Time*, 1991, p.300. In the documentary *Marina's House* by the Latvian director Dali Rust, 2012, Marina Tarkovskaia quotes her brother's words: 'I made *Mirror* in order to free myself from those painful memories. But when I'd finished it was even worse – a vacuum, there was nothing to take the place of the memories.'

105. Chion 1994, p.129.

106. Marina Tarkovskaia, *Oskol'ki zerkala [Fragments of a Mirror]*, Moscow 2006, p.68.

107. Arsenii Tarkovsky 1991–3, vol.2, p.201.

108. Maria Tarkovskaia was only qualified to work as a proofreader. As a girl she wrote both prose and verse, but she failed to complete her studies at Moscow University because in 1929 Arsenii asked her to join him in Zavrazhe and, impetuously and against her better judgement, she agreed (Tarkovskaia 2006, p.171). Work in the printing-house was relentless and mind-numbing, and she was never able to develop her literary talent. Her daughter suggests that in her severe expression in the final scene in *Mirror* her son caught something of her fundamental disappointment; in some of her photographs, too, he saw her as a 'tragic' figure (Andrei Tarkovsky 2007, p.23).

109. Synessios 2001, p.113.

110. In Grossman's *Life and Fate* a character has just been released after seven years in a camp for 'allowing a misprint in the surname of Comrade Stalin' (Vasily Grossman, *Life and Fate*, trans. by Robert Chandler, London 1985, p.364). I am grateful to Robert Bird for bringing to my attention an account of a similar case, this time reported as historical fact, in *Povsednevnaia zhizn' Moskvy v stalinskuiu epokhu, 1920-30-e*, Moscow 2003, p.319: on 26 February 1936 a typesetter in a local newspaper wrote 'r' instead of 't' in Stalin's name and was given a three-year sentence; then the prosecutor intervened, and the man's sentence was increased to ten years, not for the error but for 'political hooliganism'.

111. F.M. Dostoyevsky, *Demons*, trans. and annotated by Richard Pevear and Larissa Volokhonsky, London 2006, p.145.

112. The ascetic tradition of the Holy Fool, or fool for Christ's sake, had its origins in fifth-century Byzantium and developed widely in Russia from the sixteenth century onwards. Practitioners adopted the way of life of a beggar, often feigning feeble-mindedness; miracles and the gift of second sight were attributed to them. Their utterances were in the style of Old Testament prophets, and they boldly rebuked those in authority, even the Tsar. Literary *iurodivy* portraits include Grisha in Tolstoy's *Childhood* and the *iurodivy* in Pushkin's play (and Mussorgsky's opera) *Boris Godunov*.

113. 'Nature is always present in my films, and it's not a question of style. It's the truth … My mother took us to the country every spring … I associate nature with my mother.' Andrei Tarkovsky, *Interviews*, 2006, p.45.

114. Andrei Tarkovsky, *Sculpting*, 1986, p.195. Piotr Chaadaev (1793–1856) was a man of towering intellect and a lifelong friend of Pushkin. For an excellent annotated English translation of his *Philosophical Letters*, 1836, see Piotr Chaadaev, *Philosophical Letters and An Apology of a Madman*, trans. and introduction by Mary Barbara Zeldin, Knoxville 1969.

115. Arsenii Tarkovsky 1987.

116. It has been suggested that her resemblance to the young Anna Akhmatova is deliberate. Evlampiev sees her as 'the family's guardian angel' and a kind of embodiment of eternal Russian femininity. Evlampiev 2012, p.160.

117. Andrei Tarkovsky, *Sculpting*, 1986, pp.130–1.

118. Ibid.

119. Dmitri Salynsky, 'The Film Image: Tarkovsky's Conception', paper given at the 2nd International Andrei Tarkovsky Conference, Moscow 2013. The film-maker wrote of such scenes from real life in the first chapter of *Sculpting in Time*.

120. The word for 'reality' – *iav* – is most commonly used in opposition to dream. Here 'reality' feels too abstract for the Russian monosyllable which relates to what is in front of your eyes; in Slavic mythology it is the Second Kingdom, that which is 'seen'. Florensky wrote of the Platonic use of 'appearance' as 'the spiritual essence of a thing, its immutable, genuine nature' (Florensky 1996, p.153). Arsenii Tarkovsky uses *iav* in two other poems; in 'World and Language' I have translated it as 'world', and in 'Dreams' as 'all that is'. 'Light' may have been informed by Florensky's exegesis that 'everything that appears, the full content of every experience, everything existing, is light … Every darkness is unfruitful … the works of darkness are "unfruitful" … In Greek the word *Hades* means "without view, viewless". Reality is appearance, idea … unreality is appearancelessness, Hell, darkness'. Ibid., p.155.

121. Gilles Deleuze, *Cinema 1: The Movement Image*, trans. by Hugh Tomlinson and Robert Galeta, London and New York 1989, pp.80–2.

122. Arsenii Tarkovsky 1991–3, vol.2, p.240.

123. Chaadaev 1969, pp.37, 75.

124. For an excellent summary see Donald Nicholl, *Triumphs of the Spirit in Russia*, London 1997.

125. Andrei Tarkovsky, *Time*, 1991, 16 April 1982.

126. Following quite another path, Mary Warnock writes that 'our sense of continuity with the past, and with the future, carries with it an obscure sense of timelessness, past, present and future amalgamated into one … We will not survive, but we feel ourselves a part of something that has survived and will survive, and which we value as we value our lives.' Mary Warnock, *Time and Imagination*, Oxford 1994, p.128. 'Recollection reflected on … contains a significance which goes far beyond the individual whose recollection it is. Its significance demands to be expressed, and the purpose of its expression is to reveal a truth, and to make it available to whoever cares to hear it.' Ibid., p.136.

127. Andrei Tarkovsky, *Sculpting*, 1986, p.192.

128. Arsenii Tarkovsky suffered similar physical hardship at about the same age,

wearing outgrown clothes, with no shoes on his feet.

129. Deleuze, *Cinema 1*, 1989, p.107.
130. As Arsenii jotted down in the margin of a volume of Byron: poetry itself is 'fortified' by the 'living threads' that exist between poets, and between them and their readers from different eras. Arsenii Tarkovsky 1991–3, vol.2, p.216.
131. The decision to include the poem came still later, which illustrates how radically a film could change in the course of shooting: the idea came from the editor, Liudmila Feiginova, who felt that the newsreel needed more than accompanying music, and initially Tarkovsky dismissed the suggestion. He only started to integrate it into the work after she had deliberately misaligned poem and film in order to get him involved. Synessios 2001, p.53.
132. Dziga Vertov's writing about newsreel is very close to Tarkovsky's pronouncements; and Vertov was keen to make a documentary about the Spanish Civil War. Dziga Vertov, *Kino-eye*, trans. by Kevin O'Brien, ed. and introduction by Annette Michelson, Los Angeles 1984, p.144.
133. Arsenii Tarkovsky 1991–3, vol.2, p.198. Boris Strugatsky's postscript to *Roadside Picnic* (Strugatsky 2012), on which *Stalker* is based, gives a vivid account of the authors' fruitless attempts to get a realistic picture of perverse human behaviour past the censors.
134. Synessios 2001, p.75.
135. 'Wives resemble mothers, and errors repeat themselves – a strange reflection. Repetition is a law'. Andrei Tarkovsky, *Interviews*, 2006, p.44.
136. Synessios 2001, pp.78–9.
137. 'Let us quietly make ready', 'I said "Hullo!" and my heart contracted', 'Rooms were low-ceilinged', 'Some black day I'll dream', 'The Wind', 'Song', 'Eurydice', 'First Meetings', 'Just like forty years ago' (1), 'Just like forty years ago' (2), 'Praise – for their light and tears', 'The table has been set for six', Tarkovskaia 2006, pp.268–70.
138. Maurice Blanchot, *The Gaze of Orpheus and Other Literary Essays*, New York 1981, p.99.
139. Ibid., p.100.
140. Arsenii Tarkovsky 1991–3, vol.2, pp.205.
141. Blanchot 1981, p.99.
142. Andrei Tarkovsky, *Sculpting*, 1986, p.198 (in the Faber paperback edition the last six words are missing).
143. Andrei Tarkovsky 1990, p.407.
144. Deleuze, *Cinema 1*, 1989, p.116.
145. According to Evgenii Tsymbal, a close friend of the actor Alexander Kaidanovsky, Tarkovsky instructed the latter to speak in a high, thin voice rather than in his natural bass; speaking therefore really was a physical effort which the actor found tiring and frustrating. Conversation with Evgenii Tsymbal.
146. Andrei Tarkovsky, *Interviews*, 2006, p.51.
147. Andrei may also have been thinking of the poet Vladimir Maiakovsky, who in 'A Cloud in Trousers' pictured himself similarly crowned, in which case this is a double parody.
148. Natalia Kononenko, in a lecture at Cambridge, 2011. The copyright Russian text of her study of Bach's music as metafilm in Tarkovsky's work can be found at: http://tarkovsky.su/texty/analitika/Kononenko.html.
149. Arsenii Tarkovsky 1991–3, vol.2, p.245. He also wrote of music as the most mathematical of the arts, 'but it speaks of the most mysterious movements of the human spirit. It is the most enigmatic of the human arts.' Arsenii Tarkovsky 1979.
150. What Arsenii actually wrote was that it was torment to remember an unhappy love, but that it made a person kinder. Arsenii Tarkovsky 1991–3, vol.2, p.242.
151. Andrei Tarkovsky, *Interviews*, 2006, p.91.

152. In Act III, sc.2 of Andrei Tarkovsky's production of the opera *Boris Godunov* actors stand like marble statues in Marina Mnishek's garden.

153. Andrei Tarkovsky, *Time*, 1991, 23 October 1971.

154. Andrei Tarkovsky, *Sculpting*, 1986, pp.92–3.

155. Andrei Tarkovsky, *Time*, 1991, 6 April 1972.

156. Other titles were: 'Confession', 'The Bright Day', 'Raging Stream', 'Martyrology' and 'Redemption'. Andrei Tarkovsky, *Time*, 1991, 4 February 1973.

157. Alexander-Garrett 2012, p.93.

158. Arsenii Tarkovsky 1991–3, vol.2, p.231.

159. Paul Ricoeur, *On Translation*, introduced and translated by Richard Kearney, London and New York 2006, p.8. Arsenii Tarkovsky is very likely to have known Walter Benjamin's 1923 essay on translation, for Ricoeur a 'magnificent' and seminal text. In Benjamin's analysis, 'in translation the original rises into a higher and purer linguistic air ... The transfer can never be total, but what reaches this region is the element in a translation which goes beyond the transmission of subject matter. This nucleus is best defined as the element that does not lend itself to translation.' Walter Benjamin, 'The Task of the Translator', in *Illuminations*, London 1999, pp.75–6.

160. Khvoroshchan 1979.

161. Ibid.

162. Andrei Tarkovsky, *Interviews*, 2006, p.133.

163. Andrei Tarkovsky, *Sculpting*, 1986, p.206. Tarkovsky's statements are contradictory. J. Hoberman quotes his words to an Italian journalist: '[The film] is about the state of the soul ... of a Soviet intellectual in a foreign land; that is to say, my own condition at this moment.' Andrei Tarkovsky, *Interviews*, 2006, p.91. According to Tony Mitchell, in 'Andrei Tarkovsky and Nostalghia', *Film Criticism*, vol.8, no.3, 1984, p.5, the director said that the hero was a 'mirror' of himself. Cited in Thomas Redwood, *Andrei Tarkovsky's Poetics of Cinema*, Newcastle upon Tyne 2010, p.190.

164. Andrei Tarkovsky, *Time*, 1991, 27 May 1980.

165. Andrei Tarkovsky, *Interviews*, 2006, p.159.

Selected Poems

Poems have been selected either for their relevance to the films or simply by personal choice. In general the poems appear in the order chosen by the poet for the last collection published in his lifetime (1982). Even during the years when there was little or no hope of publication he liked to arrange his work in 'books'. His published books had the titles: *Star* (1929–49); *On the Eve of Snowfall* (1941–62); *Earth to Earth* (1941–66); *Herald* (1966–71); and *Winter's Day* (1971–9). The poems addressed to Maria Falts have been grouped together, as have the ones written about the poet's last, unknown love. Poems that remained unpublished in his lifetime are included at the end of the selection, as they were in the 1991 collected works.

Dates in brackets refer to the year in which the poem first appeared in print.

Information on the poems is provided in 'Notes to the Poems' at the end of the 'Selected Poems' section.

Just Before Leaf-fall [1]

Everyone's left. But as a memento
Yellow leaves flutter in panic outside,
At least a last vestige of autumn's rustle
Still stays with me here in my house.

Summer was dropped like a cold needle
From silence's stiff, numb hand,
To vanish in darkness behind the shelf
And the mouse-holey plaster wall.

I have no right – if we start to add up –
To even that blaze outside.
The gravel must still be scattering
From the cautious tread of her heel.

In troubled peace there, beyond the window
Beyond my being and dwelling,
Amid yellow, blue red – why should she
Want my memory? What's my memory to her?

1929 (1966)

The Cradle [2]

TO ANDREI T.

She:
Why do you wake all night, passer-by,
Wandering and never arriving,
Saying one thing over and over again,
And keeping the baby awake?
Who else is going to hear you?
What will you share with me?
He breathes like a snow-white dove
In his lime-bast cradle.

He:
Evening is passing, fields turning blue, earth is abandoned.
Who will help me scoop water from deep in the well?
I have nothing, all I had was lost on the way.
I see off the day, and welcome the star. Give me to drink.

She:
Where the well is, there is water,
And the well is on your way.
'Tis not for me to give you drink
I cannot leave the babe.
His eyelids now are heavy,
And the milky evening hop
Winds and washes round the crib,
Rocking it to and fro.

He:
Open the door and come out, take from me what you will –
Evening light, or maple scoop, or rose plantain.

1933 (1966)

'Sugakleia river runs away into the reeds' [3]

Sugakleia river runs away into the reeds,
A little paper ship sails downstream,
On the golden sand stands a child,
In his hands an apple and a dragonfly.
Its wing, all rainbow gossamer,
Thrums, on the waves the paper ship
Pitches and tosses, wind sifts the sand.
It will all go on like this forever.
But where's the dragonfly? Flown. Where's
The ship? Sailed away. And the river? Run dry.

1933–69 (1969)

'Dew swells on the grass's heart'

Dew swells on the grass's heart,
A child walks barefoot on the path,
Wild strawberries fill his basket.
From my window I watch him go
As though he carried the dawn.
If the path were running my way
And the basket swung from my hand,
I'd not look at the house down the hill,
I'd not envy another his lot,
And I'd never go home again.

1933 (1966)

Ignat'evo Forest [4]

In dense self-immolation the last leaves' fiery glow
Flies up into the sky, and in your path
All the forest lives in that same irritation
As you and I have lived these twelve months past.

The road is mirrored in your tearful eyes
Like bushes in a flooded field at twilight.
You mustn't fuss and threaten, let it be,
Don't jar the stillness of the sodden woodland.

You just can catch the sound of old life breathing:
Slime-covered mushrooms are growing in the wet grass,
Slugs have bored through into their very core,
And yet a humid itch is niggling at the skin.

All of our past now seems to be a threat:
'See, I'm coming back, watch out – I'll kill you!'
The sky huddles up, holds a maple like a rose –
Let it glow still hotter! – close before its eyes.

1935 (1966)

Arsenii,
Maria and
Andrei at the
farmstead,
1935

'When the bathing woman with heavy braided hair'

When the bathing woman with heavy braided hair
Walks out of the water alone in midday heat
To be concealed by shade, then the forest brook,
Decked out in green mirrors, sings a different song.

Above the cold, bright, brittle surface scales
The hundred-handed brook-god lowers his horns.
A dragonfly, like the first aeroplane,
Is the one reminder of new times.

1946 (1962)

The Portrait

There's nobody here with me at all,
Only a portrait on the wall.

Across the blind old lady's eyes
To and fro walk flies
                    flies
                            flies.

'Are you happy there,' I ask,
'In your paradise under glass?'

Down her cheek, slowly, crawls a fly.
Then comes her reply:

'How about you in your home?
Are you happy all alone?'

1937 (1966)

'Yesterday from early on I waited' [5]

Yesterday from early on I waited,
They had all guessed you wouldn't come,
D'you remember how lovely yesterday was?
Holiday weather! I went out with no coat.

Today you arrived, and we were given
A somehow specially sombre day,
It rained, and the hour was somehow late,
And drops trickled down cold branches.

This – no word can salve, no handkerchief wipe away.

1941 (1966)

The Skiff [6]

Why be so fanciful, crystalline lens?
You surely should take more care.
There's no rocking cockle-shell boat,
No pochard is taking wing.

The rushes on the shoreline
Are only there for a while.
Why do you wander rashly
Far from well-trodden roads?

All that is sacred, all that is winged,
All that sang me 'Godspeed',
Fades in the yellowing sunset flame.
How could you dare to look?

A sun-tanned child once sang there,
He did not want to go home.
And your white skiff lay rocking,
A blue flag at her stern.

1940 (1966)

'Opening my notebook I studied the grass' [7]

Opening my notebook I studied the grass,
And it started to sing like a flute.
I caught the connection between sound and colour,
And when the dragonfly set up a hymn
– Comet-like streaking her way through green times –
I realised that each drop of dew is a tear.

That in the vast compound eye's every facet,
In every rainbow of bright, chirring wings,
The fiery word of a prophet is dwelling.
And by a wonder I found Adam's secret.

I loved my painful toil, that laying of words
Joined fast by their own light, the enigma
Of vague awareness, the mind's straightforward answer;
In the word truth I could see truth itself,
My language was truthful as spectrum analysis,
And words would be lying there under my feet.

And what is more, my companion is right:
I heard only quarter and saw in half light,
And yet I wronged neither my kin nor the grass,
Was never unmindful of my fathers' earth,
And as I was working on earth and receiving
The gift of cool water and sweet-smelling bread,
Above me the fathomless sky always lay,
And stars fell down on to my sleeve.

1956 (1962)

Kelvin by
the river
Solaris

The Steppe [8]

The earth is swallowing herself,
Her head thrust into the sky,
She patches up memory's holes
Now with a human, now with grass.

Horseshoes have trampled the grass,
The soul's in a box of bone,
The word alone, the word alone
Still shines below the moon.

The steppe lies deep in deathlike sleep,
And boulders rest on burial mounds
Slumped like sentinel-kings
Sodden with moonlight's tin.

Last of all the word dies too,
But sky is moving on, until
The water's drill again bores through
The tough shield of dry land.

A burr's eyelash will stir and sigh,
A grasshopper's saddle gleam,
The steppe bird will stretch and preen
Her sleepy rainbow wing.

In mist-blue milk up to his shoulders,
Adam will come here from Eden,
And give back to birds and stones
The gift of straight, reasonable speech,

Breathe into grass roots like a soul
Wild love-words of self-knowing,
For he has made new in his dreams
All of their tremulous names.

1961 (1962)

Become Yourself [9]

werde der du bist
        Goethe

When you're really up against it
You'll find both cash and friend,
To find yourself is harder
Than either friend or cash.

You'll turn yourself the wrong side out,
Hunt through yourself from early dawn,
And muddle dreams with what is real,
You'll see the world – but from outside,

And find all well with folk and things.
But as if in Yuletide fancy dress,
You'll be playing hide and seek
With yourself, with art, with fate.

Hamlet wears another's garb,
Mutters some words about something –
He wants to play the part of Moses,
Not trounce his father's foes.

From a million probabilities
Just one is right for you,
But your mystery number seems to be
Wilfully withheld.

A genius has blocked half the sky,
Not for you to walk his way,
But even underneath his heel –
Be your own, become yourself.

A prophet too gives you a word,
But a word from a mute is better,
A blind man's colours brighter,
Once you've hit upon your viewpoint
And in a burst of light have seen
Outright – your very self.

1957 (1962)

Joan of Arc's Tree [10]

People talk to me but I no longer hear
What they say. My soul is listening
To itself, just the way it was
With Joan of Arc. Then – what voices sing!

And I have learned how to conduct them.
Now I call up flutes and now bassoons,

Now harps. From time to time I find myself awake,
And the music has been playing a long, long while,
And seems to be approaching the finale.

Greetings to you, lofty trunk and springy
Branches, with your green-rusty leaves,
Mysterious tree, whence every time
The bird of the first note flies out to me.

But I need only grab a pencil
In order to record in words the thunder
Of kettledrums, woodwinds' hunting-call,
Spring torrents flowing from bows and strings,
To understand exactly what is happening:
My soul has her finger pressed against her lips –
Silence! Silence! What makes death alive
And makes life complex, all of a sudden
Has a new, transparent, obvious sense, as clear as glass.
And I do keep silent. But I am all,
In my entirety, just as I am,
In the mouth of a funnel filled
With morning noise. That's why when we die
It turns out none of us has written
Even half a word about ourselves,
And what had seemed to be our very selves
Is moving round in circles,
Alienated, calm, outside comparison,
And we're no longer to be found within.

Asafev and
the bird
Mirror

Joan, Joan, ah, little Joan!
Yes, your king is crowned, but what of that?
The magic oak has never ceased its soughing,
And the voice is saying things, but you
Are blazing at the stake in your great, rough shirt.

1959 (1962)

'You who lived in this world before me' [11]

You who lived in this world before me,
My panoply, my blood-kindred,
From Alighieri to Schiaparelli –
Thank you for burning so well!

And do I not also burn well?
And do I charge you with indifference,
You, for whose sake I have lived
So much – grass, stars, butterflies, children?

My town, to you too I pay tribute,
For you're a blank manuscript pad
To be filled with inspired notation –
Once July rolls like kettledrums
Down the stone steps to the river,
And my red-hot pen cleaves to my hand.

1959 (1962)

Socrates [12]

I do not want power over people,
Or honours, or glorious wars.
So be it if I stiffen like resin on bark,
I am not a king – I am of other stock.

And you who drink my hemlock, to you also
It's given to taste aphony and deafness.
My back was not made to wear slaves' garments,
I am not alone, but we're in times to come.

I am flesh of your flesh, the height
Of all earth's mountains, oceans' depths.
As it fills the world up like a shell,
The void is ringing with Olympian sound.

1959 (1962)

Karlovy Vary [13]

Even songs are not given for nothing,
And if our work has been a hard slog,
By the power of what leaven, what heat,
Were these hills flung up long ago?

On to the hills' broad backs
Men set castles as if on to saddles,
And carried one tenth of the barley
From the fields to good Pilzen to brew.

May you flourish like the best rose
In the best three-dimensional space,
Dearest day to day prose
That has nurtured and made this land.

Sing away, honest Czech birds,
Sing, birds, while over the hills
Rosy-faced, stolid old Goethe,
Your devoted admirer, still roams.

1959 (1962)

Angelo Secchi [14]

'Farewell, dear Merz equatorial'
      Words of Angelo Secchi

From long exile returned once more to Rome,
Grey-haired, half blind, already close to death,
All alone amid the glowing heavens,
Bareheaded, he is standing here at last.

The very air of Rome is like dried herbs.
Greetings to you, final step of all!

Destiny is cunning, and the kings are wrong,
But even this day in the end has dawned.

From Merz's equatorial refractor
He cannot tear away his aged hands;
Urania will no more, as was her wont,
Make merry in this solitary tower.

And Secchi gulps the bitter air and strokes
The brass, so many years unpolished.
'Noble friend, we have to part forever,
Allow me now to go and die in peace.'

He climbs down the dilapidated ladder
Towards non-being, dust and the Last Judgement,
While swallows, high above the equatorial,
Dart about like heralds of oblivion.

I was still a child when I first mourned
This noble shade, as close as my own kin,
That, following in his footsteps through the world
I too might bless that final step of all.

1957 (1962)

'May Vincent van Gogh forgive me'[15]

May Vincent van Gogh forgive me
For not being able to help.

For not spreading grass underfoot
As he walked on the scorching road,

For not undoing the laces
Of his dusty peasant shoes,

Not giving him drink in the heatwave,
Not stopping him firing his gun.

I stand here and over me towers
A cypress, twisting like flame.

Chrome yellow and Prussian blue –
Without them I would not be me.

I should debase my own speech
If I cast that load from my shoulders.

And the angel's roughness, with which
He allies his strokes with my lines,

Leads you too, through his eyes' pupils,
To where van Gogh breathes the stars.

1958 (1962)

The Translator [16]

A sheep-faced shah sits on the throne,
On his hand sits Samarkand,
At his feet a turbaned fox,
A thousand couplets in her head.
Roses – species: saccharine;
Nightingale *paklava*.
Oh, you oriental translations,
How you hurt my head.

Torture-chamber: a half-naked thug,
Goggle-eyed, gulps down water.
Never mind. While it's still dark
They'll have the corpse sewn up in sackcloth.
Sleep like a log, king of nature,
Where are your sword and your rights?
Oh, you oriental translations,
How you hurt my head.

So let the refrain be a rose,
And the nightingale, moonlight's fledgling,
Soar high over hunger and typhus
And the salty mange of the steppe.
Why have I sold my best years
For words that were not my own?
Oh, you oriental translations,
How you hurt my head.

Well, translator, have you mugged up
The arithmetic of paired lines?
How d'you like dragging yourself over sand
With that old hag, your chagrin?
A pinch of soda, and desert rust hisses;
But – it's neither alive nor dead.
Oh, you oriental translations
How you hurt my head.

1960 (1962)

'Sometimes as you walk through town'[17]

Sometimes as you walk through town,
There'll come on you from nowhere,
Drumming a tremor down your spine,
A wild urge for a miracle.

Not for some centaur to be there,
Beside a shop, below a clock,
Nor for Serpukhov Street
To fill with sea and sails,

You won't hanker to zoom up
Over Moscow like a comet,
Or to float along the street
A bit above the ground.

If the comet hasn't zoomed,
You'll count that, too, success.
Pity that it's not the way
Spaces link, or times behave.

No miracles occur on earth
Except in expectation.
What keeps a poet going
Is that craving out of nowhere.

It waited for you wearily
By a lamp a hundred years ...
And, poet, you must cherish it –
It is your Serpukhov Street,

Your own town, your own earth,
And the grounded comet,
And even the ship's sail that sank
A hundred years ago.

We only live on earth and work
And recognise in others
Symptoms of that craving,
In order to turn it into verse –
That's if you're born a poet.

1946 (1962)

This Earth [18]

Had it been my fore-ordained destiny
  To be laid in a cradle by gods,
A heavenly nurse would have suckled me
  With the sacred milk of the clouds.

Then I'd have been god of a garden or stream,
  Standing guard over wheat-fields and graves,
But, being a man, I don't want to be deathless,
  Unearthly fate fills me with fear.

I am grateful my lips were not sealed with a smile
  In the face of earth's salt and earth's gall,
And so, fare thee well, Olympian viol,
  Don't mock me, stop singing up there.

1960 (1962)

'Around the threshold of the Lord' [19]

Around the threshold of the Lord
Snow-white wings press close
Each time an air-raid warning
Howls out here on earth.

While souls are moaning in distress
And human flesh trembles,

Then the Lord sends out his spy
To watch the town of death.

Through accursed darkness
And searching bluish beams,
The spy whom God sent through the night
Flies on unseen.

God's wondrous being is not afraid
Of either siege or guns,
He's not afraid of human fate –
Crazy and red-maned.

The angel sees us wretches
Down in hell till dawn,
And in our subterranean holes
His eyes gleam with greed.

No prayer will rise as high as God,
The angel's heart is diamond-hard.
The raid alarm does not let up,
The Lord pays us no heed.

God's angel cleaves the stifling air
And finds no mountain rose:
This angel is indifferent
To all our tears.

We've not stolen the Lord's raiment,
Nor trained our AA guns
On heaven's portals.
We are nothing – paupers,

Guilty only of going down
To hell below the ground –
But maybe the winged spy himself
Is doing us wrong?

25 October 1941 (1987)

'Put my St Nicholas into my hand'

Put my St Nicholas into my hand,
Bear me hence, lay me on seashore sand,
Show me a southern sail speeding from land.

How bitter my plight, and ever more bitter.
Sweeter than honey your salty seawater.
Bring me away from this place forever.

Under the ice a dull sturgeon still lurks.
My fingers are wracked by the shame of death.
Hurt done by Kama is the most cruel on earth.

I'd go back to the hut, but the cricket is gone,
I'd lie on the bench, but my hands hold no ikon,
Throw myself in the Kama, but waters are frozen.

11 November 1941 (1987)

'I call – there is no answer, Marina's sleep is sound'[20]

I call – there is no answer, Marina's sleep is sound.
Ielabuga, Ielabuga, yours is graveyard clay.

Your name should be given to a noxious marsh,
Its sound might lock a gate as with a bolt,

It could be used, Ielabuga, to frighten unloved children.
None but merchants or robbers should be buried in your graves.

But who was it you breathed on with your cruel breath?
For whom did you become a last retreat on earth?

Whose swansong did you hear just before dawn broke?
What you heard then was Marina's final word.

In your deathly wind I too grow icy-cold.
Diabolic, piny clod – give back Marina!

28 November 1941 (1987)

'There was nothing you would not do'[21]

There was nothing you would not do
　For the sake of a secret meeting.
You obviously couldn't sit still
　In that low-built house by the Kama.
You would spread yourself underfoot
　As spring grass, rustling so much
That I scarcely dared tread
　For fear I might hurt you.

As a cuckoo you'd hide in the woods
　And cuckoo so clearly that folk
Would grow envious: 'Hark at that –
　Your Iaroslavna is here!'
And if I caught sight of a butterfly –
　At a time when to think of a miracle
Could only be madness – I knew
　You were longing to glimpse me.

Or the peacock-eyed hawk-moth,
　With one drop of blue
Full of light on each wing ...
　I may well be swept off the earth,
But you will not desert me;
　Your wonderful power
Will array in grass, endow
　With flowers, both stone and clay.

As I gaze at the ground I can see
　Scales all shining with rainbows.
One would have to be blind not to read,
　Inscribed in the arches and stairs
Of these tender-green mansions – your name.
　The ambush of woman's devotion:
You've built a town overnight,
　Made a place where I may find rest.

And what of that willow you planted
　In a land where you never set foot?
Did those patient branches appear

In your dreams before you were born?
As it grew taller it swayed,
  Drinking in juice from the earth.
And it chanced that behind your willow
  I was shielded from death, by your tree.

Since then I have not been surprised
  When the worst has passed me by:
I must find a ship and set sail,
  On and on, worn and weary,
Till I moor where I see you truly –
  You as you'll always be with me –
And may I not burden with sadness
  Your wings, or your eyes, or your hands.

Appear to me, come to me, come
  Even one more time in my dreams.
War gives me nothing but salt –
  Salt that you may not touch –
Most bitter my anguish, my throat
  Is dried out and burning with thirst,
Give me to drink, give me water,
  Even one sip, one drop.

1942 (1962)

Song Under Fire [22]

We're firmly bound by discord,
Conjoined in every age,
I – wizard, and you – wolf, nearby
In earth's current dictionary.

Closely side by side like blind men
Wherever fate may lead,
In Russia's deathless dictionary
We both are bound for death.

Russian song habitually
Takes blood drop by drop on loan,
And becomes your nightly spoils.
That's what wizard and wolf are for.

The
destruction
of the zither
Andrei Rublëv

As in carnage snow smells sweet,
Above the steppe there's not one star.
And your backbone too, old man,
May be smashed by a lump of lead.

                                        1960 (1962)

'In the unpeopled steppe an eagle rests'[23]

In the unpeopled steppe an eagle rests
On the blackened chimney of a burnt-out house.
Since childhood I have known this very pain:
This vision, as it were, of Caesar's Rome –
A hunchback eagle, and no smoke, no home ...
And you, my heart, you have to bear this too.

                                        1958 (1962)

'The gun emplacement was just here behind the hill'[24]

The gun emplacement was just here behind the hill;
We can't hear any sound, yet thunder lingers on,
Corpses are still lying underneath this snow,
The sweep of arms flung up still here in the frosty air.
Signs of death obstruct, whichever way we turn.
Today again, again, the fallen are arising,
At any moment now they'll hear the bullfinch sing.

                                        1942 (1962)

Field Hospital

The table was turned to the light. I lay
Head down, like meat hung from butcher's scales,
Soul quivering on a thread,
And I watched myself from outside:
I was one lump, and I was balanced
By a greasy iron market weight,
In the middle of a snowy shield
Roughly broken on its western edge.
Around were marshes untouched by the frost,
And trees with shattered legs,
Substations on the railway line
With skulls split open, their caps of snow
Black, some of them were double and some treble.
That was the day when time came to a stop,
Clocks were motionless, and the souls of trains
No longer flew between embankments,
With lamps switched off and steam-grey flippers spread.
There were no crows' weddings, and no blizzards,
Nor any thaws there, in that limbo
Where I lay in shame and nakedness
In my blood, beyond tomorrow's
Field of gravity.

But a shift took place, and on its axis
The blinding shield of snow began to turn,
And low down above my head
A flight of seven planes deployed,
The gauze on my body grew stiff
As bark, someone else's blood
Was poured from a retort into my veins,
And like a landed fish I gasped,
Swallowing down firm, mica air,
Earthy, cold and blessed.

There were sores on my lips, and then
They fed me from a spoon, and then
I couldn't remember my name,
But on my tongue King David's lexicon
Came suddenly to life.

<pre>
                    Then later
The snow had gone, and early spring
Stood up on tiptoes, reaching to the trees,
And wrapping them about in her green shawl.
</pre>

1964 (1964)

Butterfly in a Hospital Garden [25]

From shade to light she makes her flight,
She herself is shade and light,
Wherever can she have been born,
With no identifying sign?
As she flies she bobs a curtsey.
Is she from China, could that be?
There is no other like her here.
She comes from these forgotten years
When the tiniest drop of azure
Was blue ocean in the eyes.

She swears that it will be forever!
She won't keep her word – never!
She can only count as far as two,
She's ignorant, she has no clue,
Not one letter does she know
Except the vowels A

<pre>
                              and
                                 O.
</pre>

And her name is like a drawing
Which there is no way of saying.
Why should she ever be at rest?
She's like a tiny looking-glass.
I beg you not to fly away
To China – please, my lady, stay!
Not China, no, you mustn't try,
As from shade to light you fly.
Dear heart, what's China to you? Why?
O my bright-hued lady, stay,
I beg you not to fly away!

1945 (1966)

Ivan's Willow [26]

Before the war Ivan walked by the stream.
A willow-tree grew there,
whose – no one knew.

No one knew why it lay over the stream;
Be that as it may –
the tree was Ivan's.

In his tarpaulin, fallen in battle,

Back came Ivan,
below his own willow.

Ivan's willow tree,
Ivan's willow tree,
Like a white boat
sails down the stream.

1958 (1962)

After the War [27]

I
Just as a tree above the woodland grass
Extends its leaves in a wide open hand,
And resting on bushes reaches with its branches
Obliquely, upwards, outwards –
Little by little I began to stretch,
My muscles swelled, my chest expanded,
My lungs were filled to the smallest alveoli
With stinging spirit poured from a blue beaker,
And my heart took blood from veins and gave it back
And took it once again: by transmutation
Simple happiness and simple grief became
An organ prelude and fugue.

II

I should have had enough for every living thing –
For plants and for the people
Dying at that moment close at hand
And somewhere at the far ends of the earth
In unthinkable torment, like Marsyas
Who was flayed. If I'd given them life
I should have been no poorer,
I'd have lost no life, or self, or blood,
But I myself was now like Marsyas. I had lived
A long time with the living, and become like Marsyas.

III

Sometimes as you lie in summer heat
And gaze into the sky, and torrid air
Swings above you like a cradle,
You come across an odd point of sensation:
The cradle has a crack, and through it
Comes a shaft of other worldly cold,
Sharp as an icy needle.

IV

Like a tree that topples off the edge
Of a scooped out bank, its roots in the air,
Flinging up great showers of earth,
Then rapids rearrange the branches,
So did my double, caught in other rapids,
Travel from the future to the past.
From high above I watch myself
Move away; I clutch at my heart.
Who was it gave me quivering branches, mighty trunk
And feeble, helpless roots?
Death brings decay, but in life decay abounds,
And life's despotism is unbridled.
Are you going, Lazarus? Well, off you go,
Half the sky is still ablaze behind you.
Now between us there is no connection.
Sleep, lover of life! Fold your arms
Across your chest, and sleep.

V

Come, help yourself, I don't need anything,
What I love I'll give away, and what I don't love too.
I want to take your place, but if I say
That I shall dwell within you –
Don't believe me, my poor child, for it's a lie ...
Oh, those hands and willowy fingers,
Moist, wide open eyes,
Tiny sea-shell ears,
Saucers filled with songs of love,
Wings arching in the wind ...
Don't believe me, my poor child, it is a lie,
I shall be stopped short, as if a torturer held me,
I cannot step across the disconnection,
Nor can I spread your wings, nor with your little finger
Touch your eyes, nor use your eyes
To see. You have a hundred times more strength
Than I, you are a song about yourself,
While I, substitute of trees and sky,
Am condemned by your judgement for my song.

1960–9 (1969)

Warning [28]

Still in the shell we hang from mare's tail,
    Nature's early experiment,
Our blood not yet red, in our cartilage
    Silurian waters' roar.

We haven't yet lit a fire in our cave,
    Nor have we drawn mammoths,
To neither white sky or black earth
    Have we given the name of god.

But we are here in the throat of the world,
    And with a hydrogen bomb
We revenge our own original sin
    On descendants still to be born.

So, all right, let's topple those gold-crowned towers,
   Galileo's science of motion,
Blow gusts of fire through Mozart's flute,
   Drunkenly breathing in fumes.

In our dreams we see a stone-dumb earth,
   A naked sky with no birds,
Seas without ships, without fish,
   Eye-sockets dried out and empty.

1960 (1974)

Arrival in
the Zone
Stalker

Titania [29]

Upright trunks bestow a blessing,
Milky mist hangs overhead,
I lie down on autumn leaves,
Breathing toadstool underwood.

My earth in sinful innocence
Now passes on to me
Her own ant-like patience,
Her iodine strength of soul.

My wanderings are at an end.
I'll enter the roots' labyrinth
And I'll find your throne, Titania,
And be lost in your domain.

What matter if my name has perished?
Your rusty leaf will be my shield.
Curse me, but don't banish me,
Kill me, only let me stay.

1958 (1962)

'Life has taught me gradually'[30]

Life has taught me gradually:
Now funerals are a habit.
We do – thank God – accept the order
That our years dictate.

But she was the same age as I
And my sometime companion,
Yet she left with no regard
For the wayward rules of being.

I've brought some pointless roses
To the funeral service,
And with the roses comes
A spurious memory.

We seem to be travelling
Somewhere in a tram,
And a watery rainbow
Falls on to the wires.

Seven-coloured feathers shine
Round yellow street-lamps.
Her eyes for one brief moment
Blaze with happy tears.

Dr Snaut
with
butterfly case
Solaris

And still her cheek is moist,
Her hand is cool,
She's still greedily in love
With happiness and life.

Silver brocade in the morgue
Catches milky light.
Conscience shudders and weeps,
Guilty for this death,

Strains to shift the wax mask –
If only by a fraction –
To let a flood of scalding salt
Swamp the fateful news.

1951 (1974)

The subject of the following fourteen poems, from 'Its yellow flame twinkling' to 'Praise – for their light and tears', is the poet's first love, Maria Falts. In total, he wrote about twenty poems about her, all except the first written after her death. Maria lived in Elisavetgrad, and from an adoring circle of young poets who were in love with her she chose Arsenii. She had been married to an officer who left for the front three days after the wedding, subsequently fought with the White Army, then vanished; Maria went on hoping he had emigrated rather than died. After the revolution she somehow managed to avoid repression as a 'hostile element' – her father had managed the estate of a relative, Baron Falts-Fein. Arsenii moved to Moscow in 1925, but the two met in Leningrad late in the following year, and she told her young lover that they must not see each other again. In 1928, when he was already married to Maria Vishniakova, he saw her in Zinovievsk (Elisavetgrad) when he visited his parents. She liked the photograph of Arsenii's wife. That year she remarried and moved to Odessa, but the marriage did not last. She went to live with her sister Elena in Slaviansk, where she died of tuberculosis in 1932. Her sister wrote and told Arsenii of her death, and also of the joy his last letter had given Maria; he kept Elena's letter on him, copying it out in ink in 1937, when the pencilled writing had started to deteriorate.

Arsenii Tarkovsky (left) with young poet friends, Elisavetgrad 1925

'Its yellow flame twinkling'

Its yellow flame twinkling
The candle is guttering.
You and I live like this –
Souls on fire, bodies melting.

1926 (2006)

'Let us quietly make ready'[31]

Let us quietly make ready,
Come, kiss the lifeless brow.
Let us set out on the road,
Bearing the pine coffin.

Custom has it that the coffin
Should be borne through streets,
Following fences, past locked doors;
No censer, prayer or choir.

I set up no cross for you
And sing no ancient hymns,
I shall heap no praise or blame
On your poor soul.

To what purpose burning candles
Or singing round your bier?
You cannot hear the things we say,
Nor can you remember

In the chill of native earth,
Deaf to all except –
Lighter than smoke, more mute than grass –
Your tender eyelids' weight.

1932 (1987)

'I said "Hullo!" and my heart contracted' 32

I said 'Hullo!' and my heart contracted –
'What's happening – but this is a miracle!'
She looked at me, laughing:
                                  'I've come straight from the station.'
'But how?' – I said, 'where from – where to,
Why no postcard to say you were coming?'
'Look, I've arrived, don't you hear,
Don't you see, I've come straight from the station
And called in to see you just for five minutes,
And how could I get it all on to a postcard?
Think what you want, do whatever you like –
I am just happy – because I am free ...'

                                         1935 (1987)

'The table has been set for six' 33

Your town of Slaviansk
Is all honey and salt.
I am too long alone –
Come, sit by me ...

The table has been set for six,
Crystal and roses –
But my guests are all beset
By grief and sadness.

Here with me is my father,
And my brother's here.
An hour goes by. And then at last –
A knock on the door.

And now, like twelve years ago,
The hand is cold.
And unfashionable blue silks
Softly swish.

From the gloom the wine sings out,
And glass intones:
'How we loved you then,
All those years ago.'

Father will give me a smile,
Brother will pour wine,
She'll give me her ringless hand
And will tell me this:

'My stylish heels are dusty,
My braid is faded.
And our singing voices come
From beneath the earth.'

30 July 1940 (1983)

'Fire like a golden bird'[34]

TO T.O.-T.

Fire like a golden bird
Trembles in the dark.
In a trice the match will die
In my hands.

A tiny pale blue heart,
Dear to me forever,
Must surely be alive
Within its flame.

And in the flickering light
(Though fallen from my hands)
I'll recognise one thing –
And know what is around me.

I'm sad we have no candle
Or matches anymore,
And that the yellow smoke
Will spin away in rings.

The final little corner
Is gloomy and ill-lit,
But for the briefest span
I'll take it as a gift.

Would that the transient heat
I've breathed into my verse
Might give you joy as long at least
As that short-lived match.

1944 (1983)

'Rooms were low-ceilinged'[35]

Rooms were low-ceilinged,
The air felt damp.
Saying her name – Maria –
Pains my heart.

Three small windows, three steps,
Dark Virginia creeper.
A poor life's poor genius
Looks out at the garden.

Chopin's B minor waltz
Will be cut short,
A wisp of fresh-mown hay
Run swiftly by.

You won't forget? You will be true?
You won't tell anyone?
Once the Rönisch has been sold
The only sound is silk –

The blue silk of a simple frock,
And the soul is still
Lighter than a bird's wing
From the last embrace.

Leaves blown down in the night
Carpet the low porch.
On thinning fingers
A little turquoise ring.

And a feverish flush,
Those blue-grey eyes.
Snow-flakes' early dance,
The blackened creeper.

Fur slipped on to shoulders, laughing,
Letting sleeves hang down;
Gusting wind, a swirl of snow ...
And so – death is alive.

1947 (1983)

'Some black day I'll dream'[36]

Some black day I'll dream
Of a star on high,
Deep down in a well,
Water icy-cold.
Dewy lilac crosses
Brush across my eyes,
But – the step has gone
And shade will hide us.

If there were two people
Walking out of prison,
They were you and I
With no one else on earth,
No longer are we children,
And I can't be wrong
When your sleeve is the brightest
Thing in all the world.

Whatever may befall us
On my blackest day,
On that black day I'll dream
Of a well, of lilac,
A delicate ring,

Your simple dress,
While rumbling wheels roll
Over the bridge.

On this earth all passes,
And this very night
Takes you as it passes,
Leads you from the garden,
And how could we ever
Bring back our own dawn?
I gaze at my happiness
Like a sightless man.

A knock. Who's there? – Maria.
You open – Who is there?
No answer. Living people
Don't visit us like that,
Their footsteps are more weighty,
And living people's hands
Are rougher and warmer
Than yours that can't be seen.

Where have you been? My question
Elicits no reply.
It may be that my dream
Is of distant wheels
On the bridge across the river,
To where a star shines,
Where the ring fell forever
Into the well.

1952 (1962)

The Wind [37]

My soul was filled with longing in the night.

I so loved the darkness when the wind
Whipped it up and tore it into shreds,
And stars that sparkle faintly as they fly
Above September gardens drenched with rain,
Like butterflies with unseeing eyes,

And the wobbling bridge that spans
The oil-smooth gypsy river,
A woman standing there, her loose shawl
Fallen from her shoulders over the slow stream,
Her hands held up as though against ill-luck.

And it seemed that she must be alive,
As alive as ever, yet her words
With liquid 'l's no longer signified
Happiness, or wishes, or dejection,
Nor were they any longer linked by thought
As is the worldly way with those who live.

Her words guttered in the wind
That snuffed them out, her shoulders seemed to bear
The sorrows of all ages. We walked
Side by side, but her feet never touched
This wormwood bitter earth, and then
She seemed alive no longer.

There was a time when she still had a name.
The September wind comes tearing
Into my house too, jangling locks,
Or touching my hair lightly with its hands.

1959 (1962)

Song [38]

Long ago my early years went by
Along the border,
Along the very border of my native land,
Over scythed mint, through a paradise of blue,
A paradise that I must lose forever.

On the far bank a willow is rustling,
It looks like white hands.
I cannot cross over this bridge to the end,
But when we last parted I kept as remembrance
The watery cadence of the dearest of names.

She stands by the meander,
Washing white hands in the water.
I owe her more than I could ever pay.
Would that I might tell who she is on the far bank,
On the river-meadow, a nymph behind a willow,
Leaning over the river,
Flicking her ring from finger to finger.

1960 (1965)

Eurydice [39]

A person has one body,
Unique and all alone,
The soul has had enough
Of being cooped up inside
A bag with ears and eyes
No bigger than a tanner,
And skin, scar after scar
On a bony frame.

Out through the cornea,
It flies to the sky's pool,
Onto the icy spoke
Of a bird's chariot wheel,
And hears through the bars
Of its living prison cell
Rattling woods and cornfields,
Trump of seven seas.

Bodiless souls are sinful
As shirtless bodies are,
No intent – no action,
No design, not one line;
A riddle with no answer:
Who then will return
From dancing on the dance-floor
Where there's nobody to dance?

And I dream of another
Soul in other clothes:
Burning as it runs

From timidness to hope,
Spiritous and shadowless
Like fire across the earth,
Leaving on the table
Lilac in farewell.

On you run, child, do not grieve
For poor Eurydice,
Take your bronze hoop and your stick,
Go bowling through the world,
While earth's merry, dry reply
To every step you take
(If only as mere quarter-sound)
Still echoes in your ears.

1961 (1966)

First Meetings [40]

Every moment that we were together
Was an epiphany, a celebration,
We two were alone in all the world.
You were bolder, lighter than a bird's wing,
Like vertigo you used to run downstairs,
Two steps at a time, and lead me
Through damp lilac into your domain
On the other side, beyond the mirror.

When night fell I was granted favour,
The altar gates were opened wide,
Our nakedness glowed in the dark,
And gradually inclined. When I woke
I'd say: 'Blessings be upon you!'
And knew my benediction was too bold.
You slept, the lilac stretched out from the table
To touch your eyelids with a cosmic blue,
And you received the touch upon your eyelids,
They were peaceful, and your hand was warm.

Pulsating rivers flowed inside the crystal,
Mountains breathed with smoke, seas glinted,
And on your palm you held a crystal sphere,

As you slept there, high upon your throne,
And – God in heaven – you were mine.
Then you woke, and you transfigured
All the words that people use each day,
Speech was filled up to the brim
With ringing power, the word 'you'
Discovered its new meaning: it spelt 'king'.

Everything around us was made new,
Even ordinary jugs and basins,
When between us two as though on guard
Stood water, many-layered and firm.

We could not tell where our delight might take us.
Cities that a miracle had built
Now moved aside like mirages before us,
Wild mint laid itself beneath our feet,
Birds were our companions on the way,
Fishes in the river swam upstream,
And the sky unrolled before our eyes ...

While Fate was following our footsteps,
Like a madman with a razor in his hand.

1963 (1966)

Arsenii
Tarkovsky,
Moscow
1928

'Just like forty years ago' (1) [41]

Just like forty years ago:
Footsteps sound, the heart beats faster,
The house, a window on the garden,
The candle, the short-sighted gaze
That asks for neither pledge
Nor oath. Bells ring in town.
Dawn is breaking in the rain.
Darkened, drenched Virginia creeper
Clings waif-like to the wall –
Just like forty years ago.

1969 (1974)

'Just like forty years ago (2)' [2]

Just like forty years ago:
I'm soaked with rain and I've forgotten
Something, someone's saying something,
I'm to blame, you'll be forgiven,
And the ten-fifty train
Approaches round the bend.
By eleven it's the end
Of all that forty years from now
Will be dragged out like a train,
With windows barely glimpsed through smoke,
Of all that you said wordlessly
As the train moved off.
Outside the station, lagging after
Those who've said goodbye, someone's youth
Goes blindly trudging home through puddles,
Biting the edge of his sleeve.

1969 (1974)

'Praise – for their light and tears'[42]

Praise – for their light and tears –
To eyes that measured heights
Of heaven's stars, earth's mountains.

Praise to work-weary hands,
For not being taken by your hands,
Not drawn away like wings.

Praise to larynx and to lips
That make it hard to sing
And make my voice turn thick and coarse
When from deep down in the well
A white dove comes bursting forth,
Its breast shattering on the rim.

No white dove, merely a name
That living ears find strange,
Filled with the sound of your wings,
Just like forty years ago.

                                        1969 (1974)

The Iurodivy in 1918 [43]

The iurodivy prays for his peely-wally soul
                     and for the dead tsar's body,
His hand is blue as he crosses himself,
His feet wriggle on crunchy sectarian snow:

Ah-ee mummy
daddy
granny
gooly-booly!
Give Fedia holy bread
give orphan Fedia a Kerensky-penny
give, sovereign-tsar
give, empelor Nikolai,
give for an ikon.
Tsaritsa-vixen
all fall down
smaller-smaller Alilei
give Fedia yum-yum,
make it better
don't shoot,
Pantelei.

What good ever came his way from golden Byzantine eagles,
What favours from the imperial standard fluttering over Russia,
Parades in front of the Winter Palace, Kshesinska, Lena slaughter?
What he heard he hearkened to, what he hearkened to – he never understood.
Ragged, dribbling, shivering in his lousy matting garb,
Nibbling like a squirrel at his crust,
He keeps butting the Red Guard's boot with his pate.
And the soldier says: 'Brother, don't shiver, there – eat your bread.'

                                             1957 (1962)

Lines from Childhood Notebook [44]

... O, mother Achaea, awake –
      – I am the last of your archers ...
           From a notebook of 1921

Why is it that once again now,
As in my far away childhood,
I long to compose solemn odes,
Not throw words away for a joke?

To storm the Olympian heights,
Go looking for nymphs in blue caverns,
And choose the rugged hexameter
Over verse forms in fashion today.

I know my ancient geography
As I did when it got me B-plus,
In fact Alcaeus's lyre
Could be my inheritance.

I was not mocked by the sailors
For reciting:
                    O, mother Achaea!
They would ply me with cigarettes
As they sighed for some girl called 'Achaea'.

Hexameters in that cold station,
Alive with freedom and youth,
Earned a reward from the troops:
The black bread of 1921.

So the road I walked was the right one –
The flint road the poet must follow,
It's not true that goat-leggéd Pan
Quit the world before I was born.

Barefoot in Budionny helmet,
Urchin boy in a sacred trance,
Ever true to the one Attic theme,
I had never a coin to my name.

Stale iambics and impotent rhymes
Are rubbish, obnoxious rubbish.
How much nobler:
                    ... O, mother Achaea, awake –
                    I am the last of your archers ...

                                        1958 (1962)

Photography [45]

TO O.M. GRUDTSOVA

A fine wind blows into the heart,
And you fly on and on,
While within the film love holds
The soul fast by her sleeve,

Bird-like stealing grain by grain
From oblivion – and now?
She does not let you fall to dust,
Being dead, you are alive –

Not wholly, but a hundredth part,
In muted tone or sunk in sleep,
As if wandering through some field
In a land beyond our ken.

All that's seen and dear and living
Flies on once again,
Once the angel of the lens
Takes your world beneath his wing.

1957 (1962)

In the Middle of the World [46]

I am human, in the middle of the world,
Infusoria lie in myriads behind me,
In front of me are myriads of stars.
Between them I lie stretched full length,
A sea that links two shores,
A bridge between one cosmos and the next.

I am Nestor, Mesozoic chronicler,
Jeremiah of ages still to come,
In my hands are clock and calendar,
Like Russia I am drawn into the future,
Like a beggared king I curse the past.

I know death better than the dead themselves,
Of all that lives, I am the most alive,
And to think – my God! – some wretched moth
Laughs at me like a little girl,
A scrap of silk – a shred of tinsel gold.

1958 (1962)

Riddle and Answer [47]

Who, as a still transparent schoolboy,
Teaches nonsense to the Muse,
Whose scalene triangle stands out
From a quivering burdock?

Who is Chiron's big-skulled grandson,
Half-rider and half-steed,
Who lifted from Anacreon's hands
Leaping, bounding fire?

Whose ceaseless song drove on Derzhavin,
For Khlebnikov a kindred soul,
Who from the shrine of ultrasound
Took a gold, serrated bow?

Who was it, angular and green,
King, acrobat or god,
Who preserved for me, red-hot,
A restive fiddle-bow?

Who chirrups, utters prophecies,
And whose antenna whiskers
Tickles the heels of time herself
As it were with clock-springs?

Grasshopper, my grasshopper,
Emblem of the Meadow Realm!
To me, too, he'll pass his pitcher
Filled with Ionian water.

1960 (1962)

On the Riverbank [48]

He was sitting by the river on some reeds
Mown by peasants for thatching,
And it was quiet there, and in his soul
It was still quieter and more peaceful.
So he took off his boots, and then

When he put his feet into the water
It began to talk to him, unaware
That he didn't know its language.
He thought the river deaf and dumb,
A wordless dwelling-place of fishes,
That dragonflies will hover over it,
Catching mosquitoes or horseflies,
That if you want you can wash, or drink,
And that's all there is to it, to water.

And the water's language, certainly,
Was strange: some tale going on about one thing,
It seemed to be like starlight, or the fleeting gleam
Of mica, or a warning of misfortune.
It had in it something of childhood,
Of not being used to counting life in years,
Of that which doesn't have a name
And comes at night before the start of dreams –
That menacing, vegetable
Self-awareness of our early years.

So that was how the water was that day,
And its language made no sense and had no point.

1954 (1962)

The Forester's Hut [49]

I lost my gun in the forest
As my shoulders pushed through the scrub.
Night creatures had me dazzled
With the flames that blazed in their eyes.

A forester gave me shelter
In his hut, and a mug of tea,
And I felt that my blind trudge
Through the wood had led me home.

My memory revealed to me
A mysterious world of pairs:
The mug and the table and bench
Were those I had known as a child.

We had just the same doors as these,
And the walls were just like ours.
And he went on with his story
Of what happened to him long ago.

He rolled up a smoke and glanced
Through the window as if with my eyes.
'Hark at that whistling. Don't mind them.
Nights here are often a riot.'

1960 (1962)

The Manuscript [50]

TO A.A. AKHMATOVA

I finished the book and put a full-stop,
And could not reread what was written.
Between the lines my fate had burnt up
While my soul had been changing its skin.

Thus the prodigal son tears his shirt from his back,
And the prophet blesses and curses
Sea-salt and earth's dusty roads, as he marches
To wage single combat with angels.

I am one who has lived in my times
But not been myself. Youngest scion
Of people and birds, I have sung with them all

And shall not forsake the feasts of the living,
Their honoured line's true armorial,
True lexicon of their deep-rooted bonds.

1960 (1962)

Poets [51]

We give away stars for birds' clarinets
And flutes, for as long as the poets are living,
The flutes we exchange for blue stamen brushes,
Dragonfly rattles, and herds' swishing whips.

How strange to reflect that our barter has given us
Rhymes, in which there can be so much sadness,
And voice, where there's bound to be whistling and tin-plate,
For our honour, deep-rooted under the earth.

And did you not love us, and did you not praise us,
So why do you lie row on row in your graves,
Sailing in silence, your coracles listing,
Reaper and psalmist and carpenter-prince?

1952 (1966)

Verses in Notebooks [52]

I have long been a stranger
To much in this world –
Music and word cannot
Answer for it all.

And as for a chance tune,
Or verses – what about them?
Life is lighter and more vagrant,
Without a stupid secret.

And how very little
Of it has been left,
Just a bit of pity
To make the heart contract,

And with that the habit
Of talking to myself,
Contention and exchange
Between memory and fate.

Sweet to the point of pain
Is this vertigo,

Stifling fall into the swirl
Of an alien will.

1947 (1966)

Aeschylus [53]

With my arm around my youth and always hurrying,
I gave paternal legacy short shrift,
And failed to see that Aeschylus's tragedy
Had already built its nest inside my verse.

With beak and claws so close I almost touched them,
Beguiled by a thousand-year-old tale,
I too was playing with fire like Prometheus,
Till I crashed on to the mountain top in Caucasus.

I implored that boy, winged minion of the gods,
That lackey to-ing and fro-ing above the stage,
'Look, here I am, here are my blood and bones,
Take what you want – why not the universe!'

From the chorus none will come to save me,
Nor cry: 'Forbear, or strike the fatal blow!'
And every line that sounds for longer than a day
Lives the very torment of Prometheus.

1959 (1966)

Stone on the Path [54]

A poet's vatic power is helpless
Every time a plot's strange whim
Makes fate drive us, still alive,
Into her own story.

To begin with we assume
We enjoy an overview
Of what clarity demands
Must be hell or heaven.

Then, when we're nearly at the end,
Inside the torture-chamber
Of our last four lines
We rush to flay ourselves.

Where do we get our power?
Whence that stone that blocks the path?
Is some new wonder-working god
Not able, then, to save himself?

1960 (1966)

The Poet [55]

Once there lived a pauper knight

This book was a present to me
From a poet – years ago
In a Statepress corridor.
It's scruffy now and dog-eared
And the poet is no more.

People said the poet's features
Had about them something bird-like,
An Egyptian sort of look.
He had a pauper's majesty;
And browbeaten honour.

How scared he was of spacious
Corridors, tenacious
Creditors! He received
Fees as though they were a gift,
In frenzied affectation;

As some old clown might squirm
On screen as if tipsy,
Bow and scrape, top-hatted,
Hiding his wound soberly
Inside a piqué shirt.

Feathered with a rhyming couplet
His calendric task is done.
Good journey to you and farewell!

Pay-day celebration – hail!
Black, white, round, crusty loaf.

A word askew had him amused,
He'd smile his bird-beak smile;
He'd greet you with a choking hug,
He was scared of being alone,
He'd reel off poems to strangers.

That's how a poet has to live.
I too scuttle through the world,
Afraid of being alone;
How often when I'm lonely
I turn back to this book.

He has hardly any landscapes,
It's all railway station mayhem
And theatre commotion,
Everybody there at random,
Markets – queues – prison.

It must be what life prated,
How fate spun the yarn.

1963 (1966)

From an Old Notebook [56]

Now all is linked, not in a dream but really:
The very air about you – to your stars,
Your little belt, each stubborn, springy step
You take, and your angular verse.

Your liberty is subject to no bail,
You are free to burn, to lavish as you will,
Only think: there was no separation,
Like the waters, times are closing in.

For joy, for sadness, for the years – a hand!
Do not open out your folded wings.
The fatal waters move at your command,
They must not be rolled apart again.

16 March 1941 (1966)

IN MEMORY OF MARINA TSVETAEVA

'Where is your thundering wave'[57]

Where is your thundering wave,
Black, surging, stifling surf –
You wingèd being, you falling star,
What have you done with yourself?

How radiant you were, munificent,
Perpetually gifting your all.
Why can't I stand, shout out, obstruct,
Catch you and bear you away –

Can't be held back – too late for regret,
You go breathless towards the sea-floor.
Just as a pearl might float down
Into the hallowed depths.

September 1941 (2009)

'I can hear, I'm not asleep, you're calling me, Marina'[58]

I can hear, I'm not asleep, you're calling me, Marina,
You sing to me, Marina, menace with your wing, Marina,
As angels' trumpets sing above the town,
And only by your bitterness that won't be healed
You'll take our poisoned bread to judgement's seat,
As from Jerusalem's walls those dear remains were taken
By exiled men, in days when David wrote the psalms,
And the enemy had ranged his tents in Zion.
But your call of death rings in my ears,
And behind black cloud your wing is burning
With prophetic fire on the wild horizon.

1946 (1978)

'Lovers of truth, friends, masters'[59]

Lovers of truth, friends, masters
Of times that are squandered in deaths,
What did Tsvetaeva quote to you
As she was leaving her burial?

There was clay sprinkled over the hair,
And the hand was more yellow than clay,
It grew so quiet that from far away
I could not catch the sound of her voice.

Maybe its only objective
Was standing on tiptoe not pausing
For breath, to bring out the stress
On the rise of an odd-numbered line.

There on the Kama, what were
The last words she remembered
In that bitter, still summer-time,
Fiery season on earth?

The earth which had said farewell
To soldiers leaving for war,
Widowed mother, yet with her way
Of giving strangers no warmth.

A wedge, in all your great power
There you are, beyond the last edge,
In all of your wrongful truth
In all your righteous error.

1962 (1978)

Washing [60]

Marina is doing the washing.
Her work-worn hands in their pride
Fling up swishing bursts of foam
That cling to the naked wall.

She wrings out her things. The window
Yawns on to the street, she hangs
Up her frock.
     Never mind,
Let them see even this crucifixion.

Outside an aeroplane drones,
The froth breaks apart in the bowl,
In the first daytime alarm
An air-raid siren howls.

From the grey frock in the window
Four cubits of shadow stretch
To the door.
     As on a riverbed
Marina stands in green gloom.

For two months she'll stubbornly toss
Her hair back from her brow,
After that Fate will be mistress,
And out-stubborn her by the Kama.

            1963 (1965)

As It Was Twenty-two Years Ago

And for everyone there's death, and for every
Blade of grass there's fire or crushing heel,
Yet even in that grinding pain I hear
Another death more loudly than all partings.

Why did I, an arrow, not burn up in the heart
Of the blaze? Why did I not travel my full
Semi-circle? Why do I hold in my palm
Life – like a swift? Where is my best friend,

Where is my godhead, my angel of rage
And righteousness? Blood to left and to right,
But yours, though bloodless, is a thousand times
More deathly.
                I've been flung to one side by the bowstring
Of war, and I shall not close your eyes.
And how am I to blame? How am I to blame?

1963 (1966)

Twenty-two Years On [61]

Not language –
                no, I do not want
Your treasures – vows, laments,
I will not retrain my pen
Or change my throat.

Not boldness in the face of death –
You bodied out all your designs
On paper, all the way
To where your ink ceased.

Not primacy –
              I'll waive my own
So that they will give you
There in the earth – your due:
A further day of earthly fame.

Not your passions' rashness,
Nor – that it doesn't matter,
No – from your grave, Marina,
Teach me only your memory.

How I fear I might forget you,
And in a moment substitute
For the straight, phosphoric thread
A doubling, a tripling
Of rhymes –
              and in your own poem
Bury you again.

1963 (1966)

Komitas [62]

My soul is without desire,
And with eyes closed fast,
It gazes into the sky,
Muttering like mad Komitas.

Heavenly bodies on high
Spiral in slow motion,
As if a spell was laid on them
By powers asleep in me.

My shirt is all over blood,
For around me too
The carnage of that distant time
Blows a squall of fear.

Once again Hagia Sophia
Stone is moving before me,
And my naked feet are burned
By earth red-hot with ash.

Lazarus has walked from his tomb
And he pays no heed
As white apple blossom flies
Through his empty eye-holes.

All night in my larynx
Air flakes off like mica,
And the untruth of Judgement Day
Glows with crimson stars.

1959 (1965)

The blinding
of the
craftsmen
Andrei Rublëv

THE STEPPE REED PIPE [63]

I 'They lived, they waged war, they went hungry'

They lived, they waged war, they went hungry,
Then they died alone, one by one.
I am not a painter, there's no point
In any details, I'll do better with the salt.

Of all the world's consumer goods
I was given nothing but a reed pipe:
I haven't taken much from earth for heaven,
I've taken a great deal from heaven for earth.

I shook sun and moon and stars from my cap,
I let birds go flying out of my sleeve.
A long while ago the earth forgot me,
Though it lives by my manual of rhymes.

1962 (1969)

II 'Every sound on earth has its own echo'

Every sound on earth has its own echo,
The shepherds' stew was bubbling in the pot,
Beside us sheep were scratching themselves idly,
Their dainty black shoes went clip-clop.
What is money to me, or fame or prestige
In the measureless evening steppe?
I want to share ewe's cheese with Ovid,
To be poor on the banks of the Danube,
Not listen for distant voices
Or wait for blessed sails to appear.

1962 (1965)

III 'Where Ovid translated'

Where Ovid translated
The snowstorm to Latin,
I drank the steppe's blueness
And brewed mussel soup.

And the fire of ill-fortune
Has blown through my pipe,
And therefore it sings
In tune with Mariula.

And so we too
Have our black sheep,
And this Danube freedom
Is my delight.

Where against winter cold
He warmed bread in his hands,
The south star still hangs
Above the horizon.

1964 (1966)

IV 'The bitter, parched earth of the steppe'

The bitter, parched earth of the steppe
Brings forth little, yet gives to the heart
The grasshopper's bony kit-fiddle,
And the honour trampled by Caesar.

Where might my future lie? God knows.
Remembering his Danube exile,
Like Ovid I too worked my way
Through paper – quire upon quire.

I so loved this land, its rancour, its bile –
I'd say: 'My grasshopper, play!'
And: 'Rome is seven years away!'

Now even the steppe is too far.
Live on, at least you – dry smoke,
Hut, fleece jerkin, sheep's milk.

1962 (1966)

'Oh, could I but move, come round, wake up'

Oh, could I but move, come round, wake up,
And in my darkest hour bless the labour
That waters meadows and gives gardens food,
Take one last sip of water's crystal core
From the curved saucer of a furry leaf.

Give me one drop, my earthly grass, and swear
To take as legacy my speech,
Sprout vocal chords, don't stop at blood,
Forgo all thought of me, shatter my lexicon,
And with my fire scorch your own parched mouth.

1965 (1966)

World and Language [64]

As sight to retina or voice to throat,
Number to reason, first tremor to the heart,
I swore I would return my art
To its life-creating source.

I bent it like a bow, and with the bowstring
Throttled it – and ignored my oath.

It was not I who word by word compiled
The lexicon – it made me from red clay;
Not I who placed, like Thomas's five fingers,
Five senses in the earth's wide open wound;
It was the wound that wrapped itself about me,
Life is alive, regardless of our will.
Why try to teach the plough straight lines,
The bow its curve, to birds – birdsong grove?
One pair of hands, you play a single string,
Oh, world and language – stretch my pupils wide,
Grant me commune with your royal might,
And let me be a bystander and witness
The soaring ship miraculously launched,
In unchecked flight.
Oh, pair of wings, you are vanes of a bastion
As constant as air and earth!

1965 (1966)

Inscription in a Book (1) ⁶⁵

... Even as a wave runs swiftly on a wave,
Driving that one onward while driven by the next,
So, too, do hours run ...

> Ovid, *Metamorphoses*, translated by S. Shervinsky

You are angel and young child, you are the opening page,
You bowl the surf before you like a wheel,
Wave follows after wave, and with the surf you drive,
Watchmaker-like, new hour upon new hour.

And all that wakes or sleeps or lives in dreams
Comes flying to the feast of green and blue.
I swear that fate is under my dominion
And therefore that you could not but come true.

I am beneath your hand, and here below my hand
Lie seven-coloured earth, the blue of seven seas,
Best hour of the day and best month of the year,

Best time of sleepless nights and anxious cares,
Whether or not the swallow's dizzying flight
Scares you off the moment you appear.

1964 (1966)

At Right Angles ⁶⁶

We're at right angles, you and I,
Against each other's grain,
Displaced in our own home,
We live on different planes.

We lost each other in the crush,
Then emerged on different sides,
Carefully holding, like a dream,
Our new-bought window-pane.

There's nothing that we don't reflect,
We're so quick to understand

Everyone except each other,
As we carry our lives like glass.

While we waste time bickering
In two conflicting tongues
Rainbow wheels are rolling
Along darkening passage walls.

1960 (1966)

Ruined
house with
cockerel
*Ivan's
Childhood*

Daghestan [67]

I lay on a mountain top,
The earth spread out around me.
The enchanted land below
Had lost every colour but two:
Light blue,
And pale brown where Azrael's pen
                              had written on blue stone.
Around me lay Daghestan.

How could I have guessed that day
That I never again
Would read Arabic script
                         on the stones of that proud land?
How dared I exchange for the odds and evens of love
That rarefied mountain air?

In order that here
I might smelt Daghestan silver
In a ladle, over yellow flame?
And sing:

> *'I dwelt there by a stream,*
> *And in its icy waters*
> *Washed my simple clothes.'*

1946 (1966)

Transformation

I was armed impeccably and knew
That I would have no need of any blade,
That Mars' warrior piping had bewitched me,
For all my martial gear I was unarmoured,
Weight floated from my shoulders to the ground,
Whichever way I might be turned by fate

I was weighty with the full weight of the earth
Like an anchor dragged along the sea-floor,
And behind my back the chain unwound –
I would not be pulled back to the sailors ...
I began to wish
              for airy lightness,
For my wondrous sister
                     a young, verdant shoot,

Longing filled me and I stole a peep:
Swallows darted to and fro like weaver's fingers,
While grass was thrusting up a tiny spear
Through every single ring of my chainmail,
There I lay, my muscles firmly grafted
With the gristle of a wayside elder-tree.

1959 (1966)

The Bull, Orion and the Great Dog [68]

Mighty architecture of the night!
A working angel overturned the dome
As it revolved about the crowns of trees,
And in between the trunks there opened up
Dark voids, like in an ancient church
Forgotten by God and man.

                                But here
My diamond Pleiades arose
Seven strings were tied to them by Sappho,
Who said:
        'My Pleiades are risen,
        And I'm alone in bed, I am alone,
        Alone in bed!'

        Below, and to the left
In a radiant peach glow are ascended
Like a sacrifice before the altar
The Bull's golden horns,
                        and his eye burns
Amid the Hyades
           like one more
Old Testament scroll.
                Time goes by,
But what is time to me?
I am patient,
           I can go on waiting
For Orion, unimaginable wonder,
To rise behind the sacrificial Bull,
Taking on the shape of a crazed butterfly,
With the font where Earth and Sun were christened
Held between its scraping, wiry feet.

I shall wait
                for the ascent
Of Sirius himself
                 with his sepulchral Egyptian
Dog's head.

I am destined one more time to see

This glittering embroidery,
Divine vault of happiness,
And whatever anyone might say –
I shall live to tick off every star,
To catalogue them one by one,
To read them over in the book of night.

1958 (1966)

Snowy Night in Vienna [69]

You are mad, Isora, you're evil and mad,
To whom have you given your ring with its poison! –
Biding your time behind the inn door:
'Mozart, drink, do not grieve, death is allied with fame.'

Ah, how splendid your eyes are, Isora,
Blacker still than your black, bitter soul.
Death is shameful as passion. Now wait –
There – he'll soon breathe his last, Isora.

Fly, never touching the snows with your foot:
So many ears to be flooded with deafness,
Eyes to be blinded, stomachs to starve,
Hospital lantern ... night-nurse crone ...

1960 (1966)

In Winter

Where is she leading me, my bride –
My destiny, my destiny?
We trudge, and lose the circle's edge,
And stumble against coffins.

No moon shows in the sky,
Crutches lodge in snowdrifts,
Souls' eyes gleam white above the ground
And watch as we pass by.

Tell me, old woman, do you recall
How we walked here, you and I,

Here beneath this same stone wall,
In bitter winter, late at night,
A long, long time ago; and half sounded,
Quarter heard, muted then as now,
At our backs an echo boomed?

1958 (1966)

Navigation Ended

Steamers cool in river harbours,
Inky waters turn to ice,
Leaden white is growing darker;
If it's true we've made earth suffer
She must surely be recovering:
Above the snows such stars are glowing,
Such deep silence has come down,
And from an icy prison now
The final hooter just, just sounds.

1957 (1966)

Life, Life [70]

1

I don't believe forebodings, nor do omens
Frighten me. I do not run away
From calumny or poison. In this world there's no death.
All are immortal. All is immortal.
Death must not be feared at seventeen
Or seventy. In this world nothing but
Reality and light exist, no death, no dark.
Already each of us is by the sea,
And I am one who hauls the nets ashore
When shoals of immortality sweep in.

2

Live in the house – the house will not fall down.
Whatever century I summon up,
I shall enter it and build a house.
For that very reason now your children
And your wives are with me at one table,

One table for great-grandfather and grandson:
The future is accomplished here and now,
And if I just raise my hand before you,
All five beams of light will then remain.
Every day that went into the past
I shored up with collar-bones like pit-props,
I measured time with my surveyor's chain,
Walked through it as though walking through the Urals.

3
I picked out an age of my own stature.
We headed south; made dust rise on the steppe;
Coarse weeds smelt rank; a grasshopper cavorted,
Brushed horseshoes with his whiskers, prophesied,
And told me like a monk that I would perish.
I took my fate and strapped it to my saddle;
And now, in future times, I still can stand
Upright in my stirrups like a boy.

My immortality is all I need
For my blood to flow from age to age.
For some corner, safe and always warm,
I would traffic my life willingly enough,
Were it not for life's flying needle
Drawing me like a thread around the world.

1965 (1966)

The Sivash
crossing
Mirror

Dreams [71]

Night settles on the window-ledge,
In her iron-rimmed spectacles,
And like a pagan priest intones
From a Babylonian dream-book.

Her staircase leads up ever higher,
No balustrade above the void
Where shades adjudge, as though on stage,
Your reason and its foreign tongue.

No sense, no figures, and no measure.
Who are these judges? Where's your sin?
We came out of the self-same cave,
There is one cuneiform for all.

We are doomed to view in detail
All that is – from Flood to Euclid.
Give what you took, say what you saw!
Your sons are calling you.

And some day, on someone's threshold,
You will find your journey's end,
While oxen wander on like gods,
Flank rubbing flank along the road,
As they chew the cud of time.

1962 (1966)

Insomnia

Furniture cracks at night.
Somewhere there's a dripping pipe.
At this time shoulders are freed
From their daily load,
At this time things are given
Wordless human souls,
And blind
              mute
                    deaf

They roam from floor to floor.
At this time city clocks
Despatch seconds
                hither
                          and thither,
And they drag themselves along,
                      lame
                          and halt.
Going up by lift,
                alive,
Not alive
            or half alive,
Waiting in the dark where water drips,
Taking glasses from their bags
And tripping a few gypsy dance steps,
Standing behind doors like disasters,
Slowly slipping drills into fittings,
At any moment now they'll snap the wires.
Actually they're more like creditors
Come here forever and ever,
Bringing bills.
                  It's impossible on no sleep
                          to pound water in a mortar.
                It's impossible to sleep –
                      so restless is this night
                          we were given just for rest.

                                  1958 (1966)

Bagrati
Cathedral,
Kutaisi,
Georgia
1960–70

According to his daughter, Marina, the following four poems are about Arsenii Tarkovsky's last love, whose identity is not known.

Kore [72]

When I must drink eternal parting,
Like mercury, ice-cold,
Don't turn away, but take my hand
And see me off on my last road.

Stand at the doorway of death
Like a shaft of daylight,
Stay by me until darkness falls,
Albeit six foot above me.

Queen Kore's horrifying mouth
Makes us welcome with a smile.
The hellish gaze of her blind eyes
Strips us to our naked souls.

1958 (1962)

Bust of Kore
in the poet's
room

'Dove-grey evening wings' [73]

TO T.O.-T.

Dove-grey evening wings,
Blessed light!
As though from my grave
I watch you leave.

Thank you for each mouthful
Of living water,
In thirst's final hours –
Your gracious gift.

For every movement
Of your cooling hands,
For there being no comfort
To be found.

For taking my hopes with you
As you walk away,
For your dress's weave
Of wind and rain.

1958 (1962)

Olive Trees [74]

TO MARINA T.

The road runs under the cliff,
Where grass is down on its knees,
Spectral wild olive trees,
Their antlers laid on stones,
Freeze like a herd of deer.
How strange that I'm still alive
Among so many visions and graves.

I am guardian of evening hours,
Of grey leaves over my head.
My roof is the autumn sky.
I do not remember my dreams –
I'm not worthy of your late tears.
A long time ago, far behind me,
Your call vanished into the stones.

And somewhere my Fate is hiding
Some keys by a fire in the steppe,
Her crimson-shirted companion
Seems to linger close by until dawn.
She's hiding the keys and weeping,

Because her own sister is Song
And it's time – she must be on her way.

And now, grey olive trees, lay
Your antlers on my shoulders,
Lay them down as if on to stones:
This land of burials, land of loss,
Has been my sacred cradle.

1958 (1965)

The Actor

It ends as if by the bell,
On the wretched stage my grief
Gets carried cardboard up –
Musty, rank mauve lilac.

I stand alone, hungover,
Like a beggar by his cap,
With a greasy rag my love
Wipes poppy paint from her cheeks.

I used to look down on your art.
To what else could I liken my life
If some ham was playing my part
In the fateful whirl of events?

Where are you now, happy double?
You must have taken me with you,
For here, in front of the mirror
Some old fogey is wrangling with fate.

1958 (1974)

The Blue Ray [75]

Then I locked up my house and left with the others.
H.G. Wells

I don't know what's happening to me:
Last in line and also prophet,
I can see as clear as daylight
What'll happen to the earth.

Who has never stolen milk
From Stepmother Europe?
Motorcycles, raucous Cyclops
Have devoured the crossing-point,

Rasping vehicles press forward
Heading hell-bent for the sea,
And the stench of heated rubber
Blows all over folk on foot.

Like ants teeming down the roadway
Joiners, tailors, laundry-women
Toil with overloaded barrows,
Drag great bundles of their things.

A mother looking for her baby,
Gaping fish-like gasps for air,
Clasping tight a nappy
And a bottle full of milk.

There a wheelchair paralytic
Topples over in the ditch,
Wall-eyes popping from his mask-face –
No one gives a damn.

A priest trips over as he runs,
Mutters grimly: 'God is dead',
Banknotes like so many pigeons
Flutter from beneath his feet.

All roads leading to the harbour
Are jam-packed as Europe gazes

Like a suicide, unblinking,
At the breakers straight ahead.

Knee-deep at the ocean's edge
White and bulky as a bull,
A listing transatlantic liner
Paws the foam beside the wharf.

And at any moment now,
Leaving Judgement Day behind,
Like a last hope of salvation
She'll cast off and won't return.

Every day a hundred times
You crucified me like a brother,
There's no way back now to your past,
And tube-lines won't protect you.

From the far edge of the Earth
The Martians howl – 'Ooh-la! Ooh-la!'
And through the fog each tripod
Shoots out a bluish beam.

1958 (1974)

Paul Klee [76]

Once upon a time an artist called Paul Klee
Lived beyond the fields, above the hills,
He sat alone there in his avenue
With different coloured pencils all to hand,

He would draw small squares and hooks and squiggles,
Africa, child on station platform,
Tiny demon dressed in pale blue shirt,
Stars, and on the distant skyline – animals.

He did not for one moment wish his drawings
To copy nature like a passport photo,
With people, horses, towns and waters
Ranged obediently in ordered ranks.

He wanted lines and patches to speak out
Like grasshoppers that swell the July air,
Harmoniously and making perfect sense.
Then suddenly one morning on his board

A wing appeared, and then a sinciput:
Death's angel was beginning to take form.
Klee realised that the time had now arrived
For him to say goodbye to Muse and friends.

So Klee made his farewells and breathed his last.
It was as melancholy as could be!
If Paul Klee had been the least bit evil,
Death's angel might have seemed more natural.

Then the lot of us would have been swept
Together with the artist from this world,
That angel would have shaken all our bones!
But tell me: what good would that have done?

Better far than graveyards are museums,
Where now and then you take a stroll, alive,
Past Klee's pictures hanging side by side,
Blue and yellow and fantastical.

1957 (1966)

Ward 4 [77]

Anna from the orphanage,
Small in her grey gown,
Knows all there is to know
About Women's Ward 4.

Medicine smells and douches,
Duty Nurse's orders,
And a never-never land
In cracking, grimy paint.

She peeps like a caged blue-tit
From underneath her blanket.
Has her neighbour woken up?
Is it morning yet?

Nose-tip sharp, fingers
Waxy, plait pale as flax.
Live people walk past her bed.
'What is it, Anka?' 'Can't sleep.'

The clinic angel's misty robe
Shines behind the blind.
'I've come for the patient.' – 'Which?'
'One from the orphanage – Anna.'

1958 (1966)

'And I come from nowhere' [78]

And I come from nowhere
To cleave asunder
The integral wonder
Of soul and flesh.

The kingdom of nature
I have to divide
Between song and water,
Dry land and speech.

And, having tasted
Of earthly bread,
Reach the starting-point
In word's light.

I am your son,
Your joy, Abraham,
And my times do not want
Any victim.

So much hurt and labour
Are mine in this cup –
And after the sweetest
Of cups ...
          nowhere further?

1967 (1969)

'When nature and lexis launch into dispute'[79]

When nature and lexis launch into dispute,
And word strains to tear from phenomenon,
Like mould from face, colour from chiaroscuro,
Am I beggar or king? Scythe or reaper?

But I never gave names to things in my world:
Adam scythed reeds whereas I weave a basket.
Scythe, reaper and king, I am still quasi-beggar,
Undivided as yet from myself.

1966 (1969)

'From a volume of stone I learn language that is beyond time'[80]

From a volume of stone I learn language that is beyond time.
Turning around like corn in a mill I float between querns,
I have thrust myself up to the throat into two-dimensional space,
And millstones of life and death have pulverised my spine.

What am I to do with your straightness, O staff of Isaiah?
The tympanum finer than hair has no time, no top, no floor.
Folk had assembled on stones in the wilderness, and my skin
Was cooled in the heat by the bast of my kingly regalia.

1966 (1966)

'War with Germany had not yet broken out'[81]

War with Germany had not yet broken out,
1913 was only halfway through,
Unawareness racked the household like a mania –
Three palm-trees parched with thirst in desert sands.

Mother's room smelled of oil-lamps and violets,
Of her stole on a hanger in the wardrobe;
The whole of my innocent, fond childhood
Was marked by burning lamps and *violets de Parme*.

Father, still, like an exile in Siberia,
Had Herzen beside him, and a Garibaldi rug.
From the dusty town came a scent of vanilla,
Odours from the outskirts were of horse-sweat and tar.

It was as if the people living in this house
Were set for all time in their own pre-war Europe,
As if there'd never been, could not be, Sarajevo,
And where on earth are the Mazurian marshes? ...

1966 (1969)

'A ghost, an empty sound' [82]

A ghost, an empty sound,
A legacy too late,
Childhood's simulacrum,
My own poor town.

My shoulders are burdened
By so many years.
This meeting is pointless
When all's said and done.

Beyond the window now
There's another sky –
Pallid, smoky-blue,
And a small white dove.

The poet
outside his
childhood
home
c.1955

A scarlet curtain
Hangs in the window,
Jarringly red
From afar.

The waxen mask
Of times long gone
Watches blank-eyed
As I pass.

1955 (1969)

'As a child I once fell ill'[83]

As a child I once fell ill
From fear and hunger. I'd pick
Hard skin from my lips, and lick them;
I still remember the cool, salty taste.
And all the time I'd walk and walk and walk,
Sit on the stairs in the hall to warm up,
Walk light-headed as if led by the rat-catcher's pipe
To the river, sit down
On the stairs to warm up; and shiver every which way.
And mother stands and beckons, she seems
So close – but I can't reach her:
I start towards her then she's seven steps away,
Beckons me to come, I start again – and she's seven
Steps away, and beckons me.
                                    I felt too hot,
Undid my top button and lay down –
Then trumpets blared out, lights beat
On my eyelids, horses were galloping,
Mother flying above the roadway, she beckoned me to come –
And flew away …
                          And now I dream
Of a white hospital, and apple trees,
A white sheet at my chin
A white doctor looking down at me,
A white nurse standing at my feet,
Her wings stirring. And there they stayed.
But mother came and beckoned me to come –
And flew away …

1966 (1969)

Swallows [84]

Swallows – go on flying, do not let your bills
Take up drill or saw, don't make discoveries,
Don't copy us, it's enough that you can speak
So fluently in your barbaric tongue,
That your stately retinue is blest with sharpest eyes
And the sacred joy of nascent green.

I have been in Georgia, I too made my way
By grass and shattered stones to Bagrat's church –
A broken wine-jar, above whose mouth you spread
A hanging net. And Simon Chikovani
(Whom I loved and who was like my brother)
Said he'd failed you in this world, for he'd forgotten
To write lines about your weightless convocation;
That he'd played here as a boy; that on Bagrat himself
Your clamorous speech may once have cast its spell.

In Simon's place I render you all praise.
Don't copy us, but here, in the land where Simon
Sleeps in earth, in your own language
As in a trance – sing one line of my verse.

1967 (1969)

The White Day [85]

By the jasmine lies a stone,
Beneath the stone a treasure.
Father's standing on the path,
It is a white, white day.

The silver poplar's flowering,
And the centifolia,
Beyond them – curling ramblers
And tender, milky grass.

Never again have I been
As happy as then.
Never again have I been
As happy as then.

There can be no returning,
Nor has it been given
To tell of the sheer joy
That filled my garden heaven.

1942 (1969)

'Now summer is gone'[86]

Now summer is gone
It might never have been.
It's warm in the sun.
And yet surely there's more.

All that could happen
Fell into my hands
Like a five-fingered leaf;
And yet surely there's more.

No evil was squandered,
No good done in vain,
Light never faded;
And yet surely there's more.

Life guarded and cared for me
Under her wing,
I've had such good fortune;
And yet surely there's more.

Not one leaf was burned,
Not a single twig broken ...
Today is clear as washed glass;
And yet surely there's more.

1967 (1969)

Azov [87]

I got out at the halt. The engine rested.
Round it hung great spheres of oily steam,
An Assyrian king with bunchy, curling hair.
The steppe was opened out, a whirlwind funnel
Sucked my soul into its expanse. Behind me
Were no more clay houses; moonlit towers
Wavered and grew firm to the far edge of earth.
Into space after space the night unrolled
A tightly wound bolt of stiff canvas.
My youth walked away from me, my knapsack
Bowed my shoulder. I loosed the straps, took out bread,
Sprinkled it with salt and fed the steppe. One seventh
Was enough to satisfy my patient flesh.
I slept, and by my pillow all the while
Ashes of kings and slaves grew cold, at my feet
A cup brimmed with a leaden Azov tear.
In my dreams I saw all that would befall me.
Morning came, I woke and called the earth – the earth,
And turned my tender chest to face the heat.

1968 (1969)

'A star dances before stars'

A star dances before stars,
Water dances like a tinkling bell,
Bumble bees dance and pipe a tune,
David dances in front of the Ark.

A one-winged bird weeps for her loss,
A wretch weeps in his burnt-out house,
A mother weeps by an empty crib,
Strong stone weeps under a heel.

1968 (1969)

'In the universe our happy reason'[88]

In the universe our happy reason
Cannot build a solid home,
People and stars and angels have life
By gravity's spherical pull.
Before ever a child is conceived,
Already from under his feet
A film arches out towards nowhere,
Describing his orbital path.

1968 (1969)

'Our blood does not yearn after home'[89]

Our blood does not yearn after home,
But ahead is a yawning void,
For the earthly sets limits on earth
For all that belongs to the earth.
In her dream the demented mother
Hears the neighing of four steeds,
She sees Phaethon and his chariot,
And incarnadined cubes of stone.

1968 (1969)

'Still from above on to time and space'[90]

Still from above on to time and space
We shall lay the palms of our hands,
But shall come to know that the star of need
Is most prized in the royal crown,
The star of want, of futility,
And fretting about our sad bread –
Accounts with alien galaxies
We shall clear on our motherly earth.

1968 (1969)

IN MEMORY OF ANNA AKHMATOVA

'I made up a bed of snow'[91]

I made up a bed of snow,
Culled heads from fields and groves,
And forced to nestle at your feet
Sweetest laurel, bitter hop.

But April never followed March
To safeguard rules and schedules,
And I set up your memorial
On earth that was drenched in tears.

I stand before the northern sky,
Before your white, poor, yet unbowed
Lofty mountain height,

And do not recognise myself,
In my black shirt, alone, alone,
In your future as in heaven.

1968 (1974)

'At St Nikola by Sea'[92]

At St Nikola by Sea
Poverty lay piled with flowers;
An outlandish, humble word
Shone severely, sombrely
On her regal, waxen mouth.

But its sense could not be fathomed,
And if grasped would not be held,
So dim it might have been unreal
But for the fitful play of light
Cast by guttering candles.

And the shade of homeless pride
Flew out across black Neva ice,
Out over snowy Baltic wastes,
And over Adriatic blue
Before our very eyes.

1966 (1974)

'Home, home, home'

Home, home, home,
To Komarovo's pines,
Oh – my angel of death
With wreaths at your pillow,
With lace round your head,
With wings poised for flight.

No more than snow for trees
Is your uncovered ark
A burden for the earth
As it floats before us
To your new century,
Out of time into time.

Winter carried the last ray
High above our heads,
Like the first sweep of a wing
From below Karelian pines,
And night set stars ablaze
Over bluish snows.

All night long we promised you
Immortality,
Begged you for your help
To leave the house of grief,
All night, all night, all night,
And now night starts again.

1966(1974)

'Over ice, over snow, over jasmine'

Over ice, over snow, over jasmine.
On her palm whiter than snow,
She took with her into her kist
Half a soul, half the greatest
Song ever sung about her.

Distrustful of earthly acclaim,
Her earthly arc at an end,
Only half avowed, like a heresy,
Through a pall of frost, through
Swirling light –
                 She stares south.

What is seen by the sightless gaze
Of the wary, luminous eyes?
The opening shutters of miles
And winters, or the bonfire
That holds us in its embrace?

                                   1967 (1974)

'White pine trees'

White pine trees
                 sing 'Amen!'
                 My dove – your hand.

Bitter my bread,
                 my voice – wormwood,
                 bitter my road.

In my throat lies
                 heavenly blue –
                 your icy As:

Your name
                 is Angel and Canaan,
                 you are set apart,

You are estranged,
                        desert of deserts
                        feast evoked in Lent,

Phosphorus of furthest stars
                        through seven centuries
                        come within sight.

1967 (1987)

'And this shade too I saw along the road'[93]

And this shade too I saw along the road,
The final road towards the final threshold,
And the two wings shining at her back,
Like rays of light, have gradually grown dim.

A year has gone by, circling wide.
From a forest cutting winter calls,
Its bugle answered by the ragged sound
Of Karelian pine trees' mica gloom.

What if memory outside earthly bounds
Is powerless to restore day in the night?
What if a shade, on leaving earth behind
Does not drink immortality in the word?
                        Be silent, heart,
Do not tell lies, gulp down some more blood,
Give blessing to the rays of dawning day.

1967 (1974)

'When like a bonded slave beneath the pines'[94]

When like a bonded slave beneath the pines
My soul was carrying my mutilated frame,
Earth was hurtling up towards me,
Horses neighing and scattering the birds.

Black pine needles and scaly bark,
Crimson whortleberries spurting underfoot.
I tear wildly at my eyelids with my fingers,
My body wants to live – and how can this be me?

How can it be me, this burnt-out mouth that seeks
For knotted root nodes? As in ancient times
Earth swallows blood, and Phaethon's sisters
Metamorphose and start shedding amber tears.

1969 (1974)

'And I have dreamed of this, and this is what I dream'[95]

And I have dreamed of this, and this is what I dream,
And some day I shall dream of this again.
And all will be repeated, all be made incarnate,
And you will dream all that I have seen in dreams.

There, at a distance from us, distanced from the world,
Wave follows wave to break upon the shore,
And on the wave are star, and human being and bird,
Waking, dreams and death, wave after wave.

I have no need of dates, I was, I am, I shall be,
Life is miracle of miracles, and on its lap
Like a lonely orphan, I lay myself down,
Alone amid mirrors, surrounded by reflections
Of seas and cities glowing in miasmic haze.

And a weeping mother lifts a child on to her knee.

1974 (1982)

Theophanes [96]

When I saw a distant roar take flesh
And chalky wings that stirred and came alive,
I realised I had passed my own life by,
My epic task was halted in mid-course.

The testament of graves that lie agape
Like so many knife-wounds, I must bring
To the Bible sharpness of white lead,
And be apprenticed to Theophanes.

I recognised him by his claws: a lion,
Bone of the bone of his own wilderness,
And dreaming dreams I thirst, consumed with heat,
On the fiery coals of beauteous works.

Throughout six centuries I've breathed his fire,
Six hundred years been torn by jealousy.
Are you coming, Good Samaritan,
To swathe my body in cool linen bands?

1975–6 (1982)

The River
Sugakleia

PUSHKIN EPIGRAPHS

I 'Will you tell me why, my sister'[97]

Sing to me about the blue tit
Who lived quietly overseas.
                                        'Winter Evening'

Will you tell me why, my sister,
You desired to drink your fill
Not from God's own ladle,
But instead from ours, my soul.

A human being's body
Is not a sure abode,
It was rash of you to fly
Inside my narrow heart.

Bodies can become exhausted,
Or, unwitting, swallow venom,
Then you'll fly off like a bird,
To return the way you came.

And yet when you obeyed the call
To come into existence,
The weight of my poor burden
Seemed too much for me to bear –

Maybe it could even happen
That you would make your flight
And then your wings would beat, beat, beat –
But the gates would be kept shut.

Sing of how you drank the pain,
The salt and gall of earth,
Of how living flesh was pierced
By a needle bearing death.

Sing, then, roamer, sing on, blue-tit,
For whom there is no food,
Sing of snow that like a shroud
Drapes itself on apple-blossom,

Sing of wheat growing ever taller,
Of the hail that beat it down ...
Sing though time itself should end,
Sing, for that's why you're a singer,
Sing, my soul, you'll be forgiven.

1976 (1982)

II 'Like that prisoner in his pit'[98]

... Like a fleeting vision,
*   Like a genius of pure beauty.*
'To ***'

Like that prisoner in his pit
In highland Caucasus – I too
With clumsy hands from pauper's clay
Made whistle-pipes for children.

Since they were not fired in ovens
They must have crumbled soon enough,
Little billy-goats and sheep,
Tiny cockerels and camels.

Children used to throw me scraps,
For they valued my poor art,
And from above they gazed at me
As if on some caged beast.

I lulled the disquiet in my heart
Forgetful of my mother's songs,
In time I started to make out
Some snatches of their babble.

My life was baned, and yet to save
My sluggish, pining soul,
Like a fleeting vision
The Muse appeared to me once more,

And, lowering a ladder, led me
Out into the light of day,
And forgave my heart its torpor –
Albeit only in my autumn years.

1976 (1982)

III 'I have worked out the conundrum'[99]

Why do you disturb me?
What do you signify? ...
                    'Lines written during a sleepless night'

I have worked out the conundrum
But I cannot recompose it.
Do at least tell your descendant
How to live life in this world.

Is it for heaven's sake, or just
For bread and earthly trifles,
Or words entered in a notebook
For someone who'll succeed me?

Outside are marshy vapours,
And the river of oblivion,
Elation from another age
Both troubles and attracts.

I cry out, he does not hear,
His candle burns till dawn,
As if to answer me he writes –
'Why do you disturb me?'

I am not worthy of one half
Of one word in his rough draft,
Each word is for someone else,
Through centuries and years.

Surely, righteous God, I do not
Have to follow in his steps
Into life from life, by-passing
The very aim and point of being?

                              1976 (1982)

IV 'I was given short change in the shop' [100]

Each time I want to open
My coffers ...
             The Covetous Knight

I was given short change in the shop
The girl's need was greater than mine.
But how many matchless sorrows
Have been granted me during my life:

In this snowy world full of laughter,
Where diamond heights radiate light,
My breast was a firing-range target,
My soul a sought-after prize.

My body was riddled with wounds,
Costing me never a groat,
While my precious jealousy, gratis,
Ate its way into my heart.

Slander laid snares to entrap me,
Their colour was turquoise blue,
The great and the good of this world
Graciously lied to my face.

As long as there's bread. Wealth and fame
Could never be stored in my chests.
But he did not guess, my sly donor,
That with his gifts came the right
To free, straightforward speech.

                                        1977 (1982)

Grigorii Skovoroda [101]

He sought no food, no place to lay his head,
Feuding against falsehood, at variance with the world,
The most tongue-tied, the most indigent
Of all masters of the psalms.

He lived his life in lowly pride,
In concord with the Book of Books,
The very tariff of love of truth,
Soul of this created world.

Nature sets a limit to self-will:
Velvet steppe glides beneath your feet,
Spreading Sivash salt to your stale bread
As you tread the waggoners' road.

Birds pray, ever faithful to faith,
Garrulous brooks glow softly.
Home-loving, neat little marmots
Stand, candle-straight, by their holes.

And yet through the world's seductions
From behind its alphabet letters,
The sky shines bluer than sapphire,
Wide open to reason's wings.

1976 (1982)

'Where burial mounds, face down in grass'

The world tried to entrap me and failed
Grigorii Skovoroda's own epitaph

Where burial mounds, face down in grass
Like hunchbacks, kissed the steppe,
And herds drummed a staccato beat
And swirled up clouds of dust,

Where oxen balanced on their horns
Steppe waggoners' own sun,

And fumes of bitter, treacly grief
Rose from campfire dung,

Where great stone figures slumbered
In a calendar long past,
And toads would gather in the night
To bow at their flat feet –

There I made my way to Azov:
Turned my chest to face the wind,
Walked south, barefoot, obeying the call
Of my vagabond fate.

On native soil I trod on thyme,
I don't remember where I slept,
Without meaning to I lived
Like Grigorii Skovoroda.

I would bite into his blessed
Sacred stony rusk,
But he had walked all through my world
Already – like a king.

Before his eyes alluring nets
Would vainly change their shade.
Their meshes had me spellbound,
Even now I hold them dear.

I can but marvel at the greatness
Of his happy thoughts.
But grant me birdsong and the steppe –
To what end – is it not, in time

To come by light of later stars,
Rejoicing in earth's wonder,
Back to the country churchyard
Of my village home?

1976 (1982)

'Thunder and clanging still fill our ears' [102]

Thunder and clanging still fill our ears:
What a din the driver made with his bell.

That's where the tram used to go, and there
Was a river, sluggish and shallow,
All rushes and weeds.
                              Valia and I
Sit astride cannons by the gates
Of the Treasury Gardens – oak-tree
Two hundred years old, ice-cream men,
Lemonade stall, musicians in a blue scallop.

June shines brightly over the Treasury Gardens.

A trumpet sounds, drums tattoo, a fife whistles,
But the sounds seem to come through a cushion:
Half-drum, half-bugle, half-fife,
Quarter-dream, an eighth of life.

We two
            (in summer hats with elastic,
Sandals, sailor-suits with anchors)
Do not know for the moment
Who will survive, who be killed,
Our fate is not yet in question.
Fresh milk, still warm, awaits us at home,
Butterflies settle on our shoulders,
And swallows fly high overhead.

                                        1958 (1978)

Arsenii (on
left) and
his brother
Valerii
2 June 1913

Once Upon a Time [103]

All of Russia suffered hunger,
Clung to life through biting cold.
Gramophones and rugs and blankets,
Chairs, warm hats, and this and that
Got exchanged for salt or millet
In that year, 1919.

Elder brother had been slaughtered,
Father was already blind,
We had bartered all our chattels,
Home was like an empty grave.
There we lived, drank only water,
All we baked was nettle bread.

Mother was grown stooped and haggard,
Old and grey at forty years
On her wasted little body
She would wrap a pauper's rags.
When she lay asleep I'd listen:
'Mum is still breathing, isn't she?'

There were hardly any visits
In that year, 1919.
All soft-hearted neighbours' wives
Also lived like birds in cages,
Hanging from a withered branch,
Each in her own private hell.

But one day our neighbour brought us
Some only slightly rotten spuds.
'Time was,' she said, 'when even beggars
Lived without knowing want.
God must be punishing Russia
For things that Grisha did.'

That evening mother said: 'Eat up!'
And she served potato cakes.
The muse, who'd never come before,
Now appeared, arrayed in pink,

In the hope that I would never
Have another peaceful night.

Then my first poem was composed
In something like delirium:
'On Sunday what did Mother bake?
Beautiful potato-cake.'
So – I first knew inspiration
In that year, 1919.

1975 (1982)

'Damp, earthy smells were borne through the window'

Damp, earthy smells were borne through the window,
Acidic decay more heady than wine;
Mother walked over and glanced through the window,
And earth-smells came hovering in.

Sleep in your mother's home, wearied with winter,
Sleep like a grain of rye in black earth,
And do not fret that the end may be death.

Lie dreamless as Lazarus lay in the tomb,
Sleep until spring in the mother's womb,
Till you walk from the tomb, crowned in green.

1977 (1979)

House
and well
Mirror

'Sight is fading – my power' [104]

Sight is fading – my power,
Two invisible diamond spears;
Hearing fails, filled with long ago thunder
And the breath of my father's house.
Tough knots of muscle weaken,
Like ancient oxen on plough-land;
And no more behind my shoulders
Do two wings shine in the night.

I'm a candle, burnt out at the feast.
Gather my wax in the morning
And this page will give you a hint
Of how to weep and where to take pride,
How to distribute the final third
Of jollity, to die easily,
Then, sheltered by some chance roof,
Flare up after death like a word.

1977 (1978)

Arsenii
Tarkovsky
1987

'The body is waking'[105]

The body is waking
And hearing grows tense.
Night is drawing to a close,
The third cock has crowed.

The old man sits up,
His bed makes a creak.
That was with Pilate.
Why think of it now?

And what is this thing
That's gnawing at my heart?
And why should Peter
Make me feel grief?

Who is dearest to me,
Most longed for of all?
Who was it last night
I denied in my dream?

The cock's cry goes out
In the first morning gloom
Over valleys and hills
And around the wide world.

1976 (1978)

'In the last month of autumn'

In the last month of autumn,
Towards the end
Of my most bitter life,
I walked
Heavy-hearted
Into a leafless, nameless wood.
It was filled to the brim
With a milky white
Glass of mist.
Over grey branches

Dripped such pure tears
As are shed only by trees
On the eve of winter
That drains everything
Of colour.
And now a miracle occurred:
In the sunset
A shimmering blue emerged out of the cloud,
And a ray broke through as if in June,
From my future days into my past.
And trees were weeping on the eve
Of happy labour and the festive bounty
Of joyous storms that swirl in a blue sky,
And blue tits led into a round-dance,
As if hands were running over keys
From earth up to the highest treble note.

Mid-1970s (1979)

'What a mass of leaves. They are our trees' lungs'

What a mass of leaves. They are our trees' lungs,
Devastated, flattened oxygen bubbles,
Roofs for birds' nesting-places, the summer sky's support,
Wings of weary butterflies, ochre and purple of hope.
For the sake of precious life, for quarrels and reunions,
Fall obliquely to earth, burn in bonfires, rot away
Under our feet – you tiny boats for foolish sylphs. The children
Of northern birds fly south, bidding no one farewell.
Leaves, my brothers, give me a sign that half a year hence
The naked trees will be dressed by your green successors.
Leaves, my brothers, grant me utter faith
In my powers, my happy sight, my sense of touch.
Leaves, my brothers, give me strength for this life.
Leaves, my brothers, hold fast to your branches till snow fall.

Mid-1970s (1979)

'Moths laugh as if they've lost their wits' [106]

Moths laugh as if they've lost their wits,
Dancing their sweet foolish way

Through blue conglomerations
Of stereometric figures,
Instructed in these mathematics
By a naked, rose-pink Cupid.

There's something of the ballet-school,
Of carnival-time young wine,
In the helter-skelter swirl
Of June moths playing with fire,
Throwing themselves like tiny beads,
With their swift-winged leader.

Till their unthinking childish band,
Weak-willed and frail, is blown away
When the wind comes tearing into life.

Late 1970s (1979)

'I was not killed in the war' [107]

I was not killed in the war,
Which means I was really lucky.
But my brothers knock on my door,
'Remember,' they tell me, 'Remember.

Remember that we also had
Our mothers, we had our children ...'
'I died in a doom-laden hour ...'
'I was killed as dawn was breaking ...'

'We too loved life and aspired
To one unique destination,
And the more ardent our love,
The happier were our songs.'

Forgive me for being still alive,
And heading nowhere from nowhere.
Now you see dreams in reality:
What miracle do you behold?

Early 1980s (1986)

To the Memory of Friends

They were so very few, those friends of mine,
And all are dead, all dead. I do not know
To what paradise I might entrust
Their final breath. I do not know
To what earth I might entrust
Those cold remains. Our cheeks were scorched
By the same wind. We shared
One fate. They were more worthy
And are dead, while I am still alive.
Not that I could thank them
For the wondrous gift allotted me,
I did not want to pay so high a price.
How could I dare admit to them
That I still breathe and that their widows
Gaze into my eyes – or rather, gaze
Past my eyes. Admit that without reproach?
No – I'll not speak ill of widows to the dead,
A widow will pass by me and she'll say ...
But what she says can't interest the departed.
How could I thank them for wanting to bring flowers
For their graves in my still living hands,
Breathing in fragrance, stepping through grass,
Over their grass, while they are lying
In moist earth, and cannot move at all –
How would they move, since they no longer are?
They don't need me or you or anyone.
But what of me, with whom shall I break bread,
With whom drink wine on my day of joy,
To whom shall I say: 'What a wind today,
How green the grass, how blue the sky.'

1945 (1984)

'For my daily bread, for every drop of water'

For my daily bread, for every drop of water
I give thanks.
For my repetition of labours done by Adam
I give thanks.

The poet's
grave,
Peredelkino

For this my gift, my senseless mantic gift,
For knowing that ill-luck
Will not be warded off by word or bird's spell,
I give thanks;

That I'll go down into dense native earth,
Flow into grass,
That my path ascends from earth to highest stars
I give thanks.

1945 (1983)

Testament [108]

I
Inside me lives the muffled agitation
Of treetops that remain awake all night,
Like poetry I can foretell the features
Distinguishing a person or a thing.

Because I've always breathed as a word breathes,
I have been an echo among pupils,
The reverberation of a different voice
Drowned in a chorus of others.

The world is as malleable as a child of seven:
When thunder swells, it falls silent like a babe,
But in those days inherited mistakes
Were lying in great masses on my hands.

My whole life came up and stood beside me,
As if long years had really come and gone,
And the looking-glass responded to my glance
With someone else's greenish gaze.

Any untrue note would make me shudder,
I thought: My hands must be released,
And as I woke I did set my hands free,
In order once again to learn to speak.
Scared, I ran my fingers over objects –
Medusas' bodies felt in flickering waters,
Woody root made warm by music,
Marble tilted up to face a star.

And so I learned to speak as in my childhood,
Tormented by my stumbling tongue.
If the children will recall their heritage,
I hereby leave them everything I have.

II
Each will remember the bright town of childhood,
Village and river, or mountain aul,
Where we received as our fathers' bequest
Love of land to be cherished forever.

Where our mothers watched by our cradles
All night long; where we went to school,
And our young minds first knew fire
As we sat over our books.

Where we first loved, too timid to declare it,
Where we grew up amid the heat of battle,
Where each swore upon his conscience
Forever to be faithful to you.

The trees on the avenue are rustling,
Blazing like torches with green fire.
I'll give them up, you need them more than I,
Come now, take away my trees.

Come, take my whole town, now it's yours,
You will fall asleep lying on my grass.

And be woken by the whistle of my swallows,
I give them up, you need them more than I.

All that I have lived by, many years from here,
Many miles away from your memory,
You will summon without miracle,
Without breaking the agreement of the shades.

I am the first of all your birthday guests,
It has been granted me to live with you,
To make my way into your nightly dreams,
And to be reflected in your mirror.

Arsenii and
Andrei on
the latter's
birthday, 4
April 1934

III
The lingering trace of all that I held precious
Is stretched out like a scrap of spider's web,
And I'm afraid that I might leave my heirs
A mere imagined, insubstantial imprint.

It may be that children as they play
Will remember me in passing,
But take incoherent interjections
As words that signify a lack of sight.

I was not blind. I could see everything,
All that made my generation's lives.
All that time fixed with its signature,
And carried past blind people's sleepy eyes.

I saw all that those with sight could see,
Like dawn light through branches' tracery.
The bitterness we try in vain to hide
From our sons and daughters – take this too.

IV
So I learned to speak from the beginning,
Receiving this grave gift in a dread year,
When love seared my cheeks with fire
And pressed the ice of death against my heart.

And jealousy would nestle on my pillow
To whisper in my ear: 'Look,
While you've been sleeping, hunted down by love,
The street-lamps in the town have all gone out.

I'm good and true, I'll open your eyes for you,
Set you free for evermore,
On the sheets, beneath a rosy dawn
Your last star is lying …'

And I left my house and ran away
To where light strikes the face a swingeing blow,
I was driven round the town by my alarm,
And saw lightning flashes intertwine.

In full flight, as a flock of swans –
More than a hundred strong, I did not count –
Over the empty square they flew away
And the height was swaying in their bills.

So slowly were they flying that it seemed –
And let the new day burn close to my eyes –
That like the bitterness that never leaves
Their reflected light would always stay.

So take them too, you need them more than I,
Let them feel the touch of your infant hand;
Touch jealousy with still more tenderness
So that you will be at ease with love.

V

Then the sky turned blue and came alive,
The heights began descending low,
The lofty bridge's wooden paving
Lay down before the wheels of the first tram,

And at the hour when your gigantic town
Rises to the dawn in splendid green,
You lie there, infant, in your mother's womb,
Inside your translucent, tender bubble.

It may be that you cannot see at all,
But still – above your head the sun drifts by ...

1934–7 (1987)

The Olive Grove [109]

Long ago in Asia Minor
Stood the town of Lydia.
No fortress, river, houses
Or fair ladies,
No wealth or luxury goods
Had brought it fame.

People never went there
To buy and sell,
Drink and be merry, or marry.
In Lydia by the bazaar
Grew a small olive grove,
Where leaves were covered
With grey dust.
Under the dull, joyless branches
Was very little shade,
No birds or butterflies
Found shelter there.

Anyone coming to town
Could go into the grove
And, without swearing an oath,
Could beg for a gift.
Not that you would get

Anything useful,
Not food or drink or clothes,
Not wealth or renown –
Only a senseless gift
Which no one on earth could want,
Merely a poor little flower,
The kind of which you'd get scores
In the market for tuppence.

You had to pay for whatever
It was you received –
Whether a memory,
A bright bird's feather,
Or a glass ball –
With a strange movement of the hands,
A bit like the letter A.
For a moment after the palms had drawn it
That movement would hang
In the dusty air
As a barely perceptible
Blue glow, in proof of payment:
The price you paid was a particle
Of your life.

Very few people minded
About that town and its wonders,
But I would have gone there,
Entered the olive grove,
And sketched a pale blue A.
I'd have been given the useless
Gift of a senseless song,
I'd have forgotten the muteness
Of words written on paper,
I should not have sung like a bird.

I don't want those trills
That torture the poor souls
Of busy people,
Nor silvery chirrups, or whistling,
Or sparrow songs, which are closer to tears
Than earth is to constellations;
I should have sung like the earth

When nobody treads it,
Like trees when nobody sees them,
Like grass when we've forgotten
That it's already green,
Like spring water in a desert.

I have seen that town in my dreams.
Somewhere it may exist:
It cannot be that restless, bitter verses
That have found no home on earth
Will vanish without trace,
I have seen that grove in my dreams,
And still the notebook
Has not burnt to ashes,
Nor the verses crumbled to dust …

Let them crumble to dust,
Let grasses grow through them,
Let them change into leaves of trees.
I have loved this earth,
I have lived on this earth.
When I wanted to drink
I would look for a spring,
I learned to sing from birds …
May my voice teach song
To the very stones.

1945 (1987)

Medem [110]

At one time I had piano lessons.
Note by painful note I picked out tunes,
Toiled at a childish sonata,
Never made it as far as Ganon.

Each Wednesday I'd come with my music,
Give the front door bell a turn,
And Medem was there to greet me,
Wearing his fustian coat.

A giant, ungainly and cunning,
He would bring down his bear-like hand,
One and a half octaves wide,
On the aged piano's dark dream.

Then hounds would swirl through the bass notes,
The hunt in full cry in deep woods,
A chorus of huntsmen's voices
Hovering on high by the brook.

It would end with a joke in German,
One blue eye half-closed in a wink.
His grey hair had a little-boy cut,
His speech tumbled head over heels.

Before I quite knew where I was,
Before I'd walked out of those woods,
I would timidly go through my pieces,
Medem's hand lying on my shoulder.

The sleepy-head grand piano
Was alive with black and white fire,
I felt the keys scorching my fingers,
And Medem used to get cross.

Then childhood grew bored and ran off.
Today if I went to my town
I'd be lost in the dark of the station
With no idea which way to turn.

Why follow after me, childhood?
Why won't you step out ahead?
Or might Medem's old hand be poised
Once again over the keys?

1933 (1983)

'From out in his yard the dog stares into the window' [111]

From out in his yard the dog
                              stares into the window.
Cold, terrible cold, the ground wind cuts you through!

At home stoves are stoked up,
                              the cat purrs and purrs,
It's ever so nice at home –
                    food to eat, plenty of clothes, shoes on our feet.

Furs and more furs, fluffy-fine shawls, stockings and scarves,
So much camel-down spun
                         and warm woollies knitted.
We sat by the stove with a nice cup of tea
                                   and agreed:
'That's the way housewives do things in December.'
Then we thought –
                  and called to the dog to come in:
                                         'You stop the night here.
It's hard at thirty below
                    if you haven't got clothes or shoes.
Don't pick a fight with the cat,
                         get warm by the stove, Tyke Mongrelich,
Out in your kennel the frost
                      will bite your tail off you in no time.'

                                            1940 (1991)

'A town stands on the river'[112]

A town stands on the river,
But the river has no fish.
A beggar dozes on the bridge,
Holding out a plate.

Whoever used to cross the bridge
Will have seen the plate,
And given one kopek, or five,
Or maybe none at all.

How merrily the plate sings out
And balances and rings.
It tells a tale about itself
And the beggarman.

Since it is not made of tin
It's no weight for the hand,

Nor is it clay, so if it falls
It's light enough to bounce.

Whoever used to cross the bridge
Remembers nothing now.
He forgot his town, the bridge
And the beggarman.

But I want to recall myself
And the river town.
I want to recall the man
With the outstretched hand.

If the wind would only talk
With that lively plate,
Then for me the town would still
Be really, truly there.

1930 (1987)

'Easter chimes floated down the Volga from Iurovets'[113]

Easter chimes floated down the Volga from Iurovets,
The town could be seen far away in airy cloud,
Riverside smoke lay round houses and jetties,
And above on a steep bank stood a white church.
But no matter how much water I drink from other rivers,
Adamantine ash still hangs before my gaze,
No matter if a haze descends upon my eyes,
My town's liberated bells
Are still silent.
          And there was breath in them,
And the gentle cooing of grey doves,
My foreboding; in them lived and whispered
Like slender, dried out reeds,
Those ringing needles, every word a tumult,
The clap of pigeons' wings, and the youthful stir
Of frightened blood ...
          Deep in the grass
Of my town's graveyard lies a peaceful grave,
Its cross bears no inscription. – Yet he breathes,
Even there he still can hear the rustling wind

And the lingering boom of bronze, there in his native soil.
His blind eyes, open to the depths
With no fleeting screens to veil them,
Gaze before them into gaps of blue.

1932 (1989)

Invitation to a Journey [114]

We are leaving, we are leaving, start packing right away:
I queued until fate dealt me thousand rouble tickets.
At last we're going to visit my own distant lands,
The towns of Childhood Bliss and Family Graves.

If you like we'll take a trip to the town of Lovers' Fear,
The town of Centifolia and the town of Open Piano.
A butterfly of cherished dust flies above each town,
But nonetheless there is a town of Wounds.

An armoured train, tarpaulined, stands outside the station,
And my brother's teaching me to fire a Lefaucheux.
In Music town the children play sonatas by Clementi,
And to a shaken soul the town is strange and empty.

You can tell from the damp salt or read in the grass
That far away, where earth comes to an end
Beyond the steppes, the sea roars in its freedom,
And ships ride at anchor in the bay.

And if a single jot of all I've promised
Can be realised, I'll make you a gift
Of the town of Sea, the town of Steamer Smoke,
And the town of Sea at Twilight.

You will say: 'Your towns depress me. Loving no one,
I don't know how I should live in Music Town,
And as for twilit sea, sea with its curving rim –
The blue sea was mine already without you.'

1937 (1983)

Inscription in a Book (2) [115]

I walked away from family, from warm home,
My hair was whitened by an early frost,
In my native land my voice became
A voice crying in the wilderness.

Like a bird, penniless – lame, like Israel,
I have never yet betrayed myself,
My language has become the voice of pride,
A language others cannot understand.

I hear my own lamenting or my laughter
Only as an evanescent echo,
And – gracious God – surely I'm not singing?
How would I give you all that's sacred to me,
Even as I've given you my life?
And yet there was a time
                    when I burned and lived and sang ...

                                        1946 (1987)

Doorbell in the Night [116]

Why do you chain up your door at night
As if your home were a prison?
Ivan Ivanich, while you're asleep
I'm standing outside your front door.

Murderous night is approaching
Shod with black rubber soles,
I ring your bell seeking refuge,
But you are not minded to help.

You've stuffed cotton-wool in your ears,
The ringing is muffled by sleep.
'Let him buzz on, silly sod.
Voice of the times – who cares?'

You don't accept hell or seek heaven,
Since neither exists – what's the point?

What will you say if my blood
Makes a mess of your doorstep ?

With public, friends, brothers betrayed,
How will you walk down your street,
Heading for work at eight-thirty
To pick up your four-figure pay?

Your street has been blackened by blood,
Every house marked with a cross.
You can say: 'Mind your own business,
It was hard graft earned me my sleep.'

1946 (1987)

'Air heavy with iron and rotting potatoes' [117]

Air heavy with iron and rotting potatoes,
Prison-camp dust and rank salt sprats.
Where has your name gone and where are your wings?
Vee's hackles rise in a vast, bristling horde.

Who are you now? No cross, no remembrance.
Plashing, the raft floats down the deep river.
Black sky above, and clutched in your hand
Underbaked bannock as soggy as clay.

He utters the words: 'Lift up my eyelids!' –
Points his iron finger at village communities,
Rusty earth tracts and misshapen alders
Are marked out to perish in statutory fast.

He utters the words: 'Lift up my eyelids!'
How would you not if you don't want to die?
Dyrbala – arbala – dyrbala – arbala –
What else he mutters is anyone's guess.

He twists living tendons and ties them in knots,
Plays cards, tooth and nail, with the scurvy taiga,
Sweeps over wormwood, piercing and frigid,
Chucks you down a ravine – and it's farewell, dear friend.

1946–56 (1987)

'Like Jesus crucified upon the cross' [118]

Like Jesus crucified upon the cross
The mountain crest showed black along the line
Where sky came down to meet the dust of earth,
While the sun climbed higher up the cross,
And it seemed that we were all on a stone raft,
Afloat on a stone sea.

That was what I dreamed.
　　　　　　　　　　Amid what steppes,
In what country, among what tablelands;
And whose soul, so closely bound to mine,
Was bearer of that blinding sorrow?
And from whom of all my ancestors
Did I receive that fateful heritage –
Those thorns above the slanting crosspiece,
The mauvish glint on waxy cheekbones,
The words inscribed above the drooping head?

1962 (1987)

The Russian
Golgotha
*Andrei
Rublëv*

Maria
Tarkovskaia
reflected
in a mirror
Mirror

To Youth [119]

Forgive me. It's my fault that we're apart.
The time will come when jealousy is quenched,
I'll stretch out my living hands
And what will they find? Native granite.

I built up my life and calmed my heart,
And for you I set out mirrors
Where I lived. Why did I build life?
All my hand found was native granite.

While my whole life was pulsing
In your eyes, while I built a house
In the name of work and duty,
Then you and I lived together.

You would argue, knowing all the answers,
And it wasn't easy being with you.
Don't come: now I've got a marvel,
Here with me I have a looking-glass.

And it seems as if my life is doubling,
That I am with you there, inside my mirror,
And my hand, too ashamed to touch you,
In a sombre moment meets the house.

The house is like a face with soulless eyes,
Native granite; I enter, you're not there,
But from the mirror, as if in a pit,
Stares the sleepless face of futile toil.

23 September 1938 (1990)

Psyche [120]

I remember so well that image of Cupid and tender Psyche.
A.A. Fet

A beggar am I, grovelling, sweet-tooth starveling,
A penny is brighter to me than the sun.
Do not begrudge me your nuts from the forest,
Spare an old woman a few sunflower seeds.

Just spare some biscuit for poor, homeless Psishka!
Make way, mother earth, and grant me protection,
I am harried by dogs that boys set upon me,
I have no permit to dwell on this earth.

I would climb mountains, but slopes are too steep,
I would blame others, but who is to blame?
I'd let down my grey hair, old fool that I am,
But I cannot remember my own lover's name.

The wings of my loved one I'd wash with my tears
With swans' flight lines to guide me I'd follow my love,
High above forests he'd feed me with honey,
Over mountains regale me with choice mountain wines.

As his wings spread I knew – but already too late:
A fierce blizzard blew where we two had lain.
So I wander the world, an old crone – no kolhoz,
Unwanted, unregistered, ungarmented, unshod.

April 1941 (1990)

To a Notebook of Poems [121]

Farewell, my writing-pad, so many years my friend.
For whom will you preserve your searing trace of prescience
And this strange glow, now barely to be seen,
That burns with fiery light above the precious rhymes?
A hundred years may pass, and still roused passions' music
Will lure playing children beneath a hail of bombs.
Yet some heir to our torment may survive ...
You are given me as surety, my keening guide and friend.
Your owner is to come, he's sleeping in my blood,
From the city's ashes give him blessing,
From the heap of rubble testifying destruction.
And to tell the truth – we need no other readers.

1 February 1947 (1990)

'I'm going to don an iron ring' [122]

I'm going to don an iron ring,
Tighten my belt, turn eastward,
Taigan, fell me with sawn-off shotgun,
Strike my heart, lay me under a bush.

Bury me under an aspen, my friend,
Veil my face with a wayside brocade,
For my nostrils to fill with the stench
Of sheepskin, wax candles, wolf piss.

I lost myself in Russia; living,
As one condemned I shamble past my door.
I shall enter Kashchei's busy realm
With a whistle made of bone.

Our worth must lie either in song,
In brotherhood with earth, or in death.
The cloistral voice of Mother-Untruth
Will ring out at our back – and pass by.

1957 (1990)

'You were such bitter stuff, so blind' [123]

You were such bitter stuff, so blind,
Stubborn, bitter almond,
With your hourglass reckoning
At the station mirror,

Opening up the holdall
Of the vast childhood station,
You saw before your eyes
Our suitcase and our table,

Making the spilled almonds
Pile up in a brown hill,
Their bitter smell pervading
The buffet with its toy cut-glass,

To go spinning, jostling, loving
In the station mirror,
So many almond facets –
And you in every one.

25 June 1928 (2009)

Multiple
reflections
of clock *The
Steamroller
and the
Violin*

Notes to the Poems

1. This is the first poem in all editions of Tarkovsky's verse. The original version, not published until 2009, was addressed to his first wife, Maria Vishniakova, mother of Andrei and Marina:

> I was alone. Only autumn remained.
> A gamut of yellows was melting outside.
> My house was alive with autumnal rustle
> Reflecting in pale blue glass.
>
> Autumn whispered behind the bookshelf
> Behind the mouse-holey plaster wall,
> And like a chill needle it slipped away
> Out of silence's cold, numb hand.
>
> Only – as soon as my eyelids are closed
> My sweetheart comes quietly towards me,
> Her hand brushes past low branches,
> As she restlessly sighs in her sleep.
>
> But have I the right in my narrow room
> To hear the leaves rustling outside,
> And the scattering fall of pink gravel
> From under her cautious heel?
>
> So – in September's troubled peace
> With all forgotten and nothing concealed,
> I can hear, but can't tell – why should she want
> My tender darkness, my memory?

2. Written for Maria, a year after Andrei's birth. Star and well recur in the poem 'Some black day I'll dream', and later become an image in Andrei's film, *Ivan's Childhood* (1962).

3. Final line of earlier version: 'The child is singing: "*I shall grow up, grow up!*"'

    The Sugakleia is a tributary of the river Ingu, near Elisavetgrad, Kherson province, the poet's birthplace; in the intervening years it has in fact all but 'run dry', and is now known as 'Reedy Sugakleia'.

    In Andrei's 1961 film *The Steamroller and the Violin* a child floats a paper boat in the rainwater flowing in the gutter; in Iranian film-maker Hana Makhmalbaf's *Buddha Collapsed Out of Shame* (2007), little Bakhtay is told by an old man that if she follows the paper boat he has made as it floats down the stream, she will find the school she longs to attend; and the child with Down's syndrome in Jean-Marc Vallée's *Café de Flore* (2011) sails a paper ship in a street puddle, though most of the Tarkovsky echoes in this film refer to *Nostalghia*.

4. In an earlier version the first line of the last stanza ran: 'You know that love is like a threat'.

This poem was going to be included in *Mirror*, and would have been the one poem in the film actually addressed to Maria Tarkovskaia; it was replaced by 'First Meetings', addressed to the poet's first love, Maria Falts.

It was written in summer 1935 at the Gorchakov farm near Ignat'evo, where *Mirror* was filmed in 1973 with 'Uncle Pasha', the farmer, playing himself in the burning barn scene.

5. Recited in *Mirror*. See also 'Appendix II: The Process of Translation'.

6. An elegy for childhood: the poet's eye is wandering into a scene that now exists only in his memory.

7. It is typical of Tarkovsky to seem to be looking at nature as if in the dawn of creation, like Adam; his intimacy with nature makes him a poet and therefore a prophet. Osip Mandelshtam compared Walt Whitman to a 'new Adam', who 'began to name things ... like Homer himself, offering a model for a primitive American poetry of nomenclature'. Osip Mandelshtam, *Complete Critical Prose and Letters*, ed. by Jane Garry Harris, trans. and by Jane Garry Harris and Constance Link, Ann Arbor 1979, p.125. The comparison between words and light is a recurring trope, here associated with spectrum analysis: Arsenii considered that both poets and scientists have the task of discovering the world. See his article, Arsenii Tarkovsky, 'Nauka i poezia', *Khimia i zhizn'*, no.7, 1982. In this exploration the 'vague awareness' born of gazing at nature fuses with, and is transformed by, the 'straightforward' work of the mind.

    'Truth' is a word the poet uses very seldom. Its association here with 'word' and 'light' indicate that he may have had in mind the Greek word for truth: *aletheia*, unhiddenness or revelation.

    The prophet's 'fiery word' has an obvious biblical ring; the printing-works scene in *Mirror* includes a brief shot of the slogan, 'The fiery word of Leninist-Stalinist Truth'. Igor Evlampiev, *Khudozhestvennaia filosofia Andreia Tarkovskogo [The Artistic Philosophy of Andrei Tarkovsky]*, Ufa 2012, p.173, suggests that the printing-house is an image of hell.

8. The rhythm of the poem is identical to that of the description of the messenger's ride over the 'boundless steppe' in Pushkin's narrative poem, *Poltava*.

    For comparisons between the poet and Adam see note 7.

    The steppe (see 'Azov' [p.158] and 'The Steppe Reed Pipe' [p.134] included here) was rich in associations for Tarkovsky: a place of exile for both Ovid and Pushkin; Tarkovsky himself was sometimes seen as an 'internal exile' because he spent so many years unable to publish his own verse; it was the setting for Grigorii Skovoroda's philosophical wanderings (see 'Grigorii Skovoroda', p.170); and an unchanging, timeless expanse.

    Stanza (st.) 4: 'dry land' is one possible, inadequate, rendering of *materik*, which has the meaning of 'continent,' 'land mass', 'land' as opposed to sea, but also 'subsoil' and 'earth's foundations'.

    Pavel Florensky, writing of the revelation of the image of God in the human countenance, uses an analogous simile: 'Everything accidental, everything caused by things external to this essence – i.e. everything in our face which is not the face itself – is swept away by an energy like a strong fountain of water breaking through a thick material husk, the energy of the image of God.' The assonance of 'material' (*material/material'nyi*) and *materik* seems to increase the likelihood that the poet was echoing Florensky. Pavel Florensky, *Ikonostasis*, trans. by Donald Sheehan and Olga Andreyev, New York 1996, p.52. Both Arsenii and Andrei were deeply concerned with revealing the essence hidden within the accidental. The slow, intense scrutiny of heads in the films often elicits questions about who – indeed what – the person might be, and what is actually being revealed by the head and its image.

9. St. 1 refers to the rhyming aphorism, 'Better a hundred friends than a hundred roubles' (*ne imei sto rublei a imei sto druzei*).

The epigraph, which in the first published edition was the poem's title, is not in fact a quotation from Goethe; originally from Pindar, it is a much repeated phrase in Friedrich Nietzsche's *Thus spoke Zarathustra*. Tarkovsky's attribution may have been a deliberate avoidance of Nietzsche's name: in Soviet criticism Goethe was a respectable figure and Nietzsche was not. Twenty years after writing this poem the poet said of it in an interview: 'I see Goethe's injunction as pointing to the process whereby the typical is caught up in any full manifestation of individuality. The typical is so essential to every person, I don't believe it's possible to write a poem that is not going to enter the credo of some larger or smaller group of people. A person's spiritual essence, his ethical ideals, his sense of responsibility for every drop of blood – all this is typical. Sense of the world's rhythm, sense of harmony, love and lack of love, aesthetic ideal, faith in your own world vision – these belong to the personal canon. And they constitute the poet's soul. Or should do' (Arsenii Tarkovsky, *Literaturnaia gazeta*, 12 January 1977; quoted by A. Lavrin in Arsenii Tarkovsky, *Sobranie sochinenii v trëkh tomakh [Works in 3 Volumes]*, Moscow 1991–3, vol.1, p.423). This definition of the 'typical' is close to the film-maker's formulation of the artistic image: 'The unique element in an artistic image mysteriously becomes the typical; for strangely enough the latter turns out to be in direct correlation with what is individual, idiosyncratic, unlike anything else … The image signifies the fullest possible expression of what is typical, and the more fully it expresses it, the more individual, the more original, it becomes.' Andrei Tarkovsky, *Sculpting in Time: Reflections on Cinema*, trans. by Kitty Hunter Blair, London 1986, pp.111–12.

Two of Goethe's poems in particular touch on the themes of the epigraph and title. In 'The Four Seasons' (1796) he wrote:

> Let none be like another; but let each be like the highest.
> How may this be done? Let each attain fulfilment.

And the poem 'Blessed Longing' (from *West-Eastern Divan*, 1819) contains the axiom '*Stirb und werde*' ('Die and become'), in the context of a night of love and the overwhelming attraction for the moth of the candle flame which will destroy it:

> And until you have grasped
> This: 'Die and become',
> You'll be a dismal guest
> On the dark earth.

The poem opens with praise of the living being that longs for death by fire, praise which must be uttered only to the wise, for the mob will merely mock; at some level these lines may well have fed into the transfiguring fire motifs of the films.

10. The poet's soul is listening 'to itself', but the Joan of Arc simile suggests that the sounds heard come from outside: as Arsenii wrote in a draft letter to Andrei (Marina Tarkovskaia, *Oskol'ki zerkala [Fragments of a Mirror]*, Moscow 2006, p.254), artistic creation starts with submission to a superior power ('whether God or the 3rd International'), after which he is obedient to the latter's will; in that sense he is the 'fragile vessel' of a higher authority (the allusion is to A.A. Fet's poem, 'The Swallow'). Like Joan of Arc, he himself is burnt up in the fulfilment of his prophetic task.

The 'bird of the first note' anticipates the bird flying on to Asafev's hat in *Mirror*.

A cultivated Russian of Tarkovsky's generation would be likely to know the musical metaphor in Mandelshtam's essay, 'Conversation about Dante': 'If we could learn to hear Dante, we would hear the ripening of the clarinet and the trombone, we would hear the transformation of the viola into a violin and the lengthening of the valve on the French horn.' Mandelshtam 1979, p.402.

Line 28: in some rough notes about poetry not published until 1991, Arsenii wrote: 'as for actual death, we have hardly any idea what she is – when we consider her, not one iota about ourselves will be included – it is her clearly visible, rich sister [life] that nourishes us'. Arsenii Tarkovsky 1991–3, vol.2, p.205.

11. It is typical of the poet to bracket Dante and the pioneering Italian astronomer Giovanni Schiaparelli (1835–1910); the latter worked at Pulkovo Observatory near St Petersburg in 1859–60. He was the first to observe the lines on Mars that appeared to be channels; as a boy Arsenii was bitterly disappointed to learn that in fact these were not 'canals' or even 'channels' (Arsenii Tarkovsky 1982).

Again, the poet uses both a musical simile and the motif of creativity and burning; and as a poet he lives for the sake of the world of which he writes.

12. Pine resin has associations with ancient religious rituals and is an ingredient of various perfumes, and of frankincense and myrrh; on bark it has protective properties for the tree.

Like Socrates, the poet is neither king nor slave and his life is dedicated, and ultimately sacrificed, to the search for wisdom; muteness and deafness may refer to the fact that Socrates never wrote, but was always engaging others in that search.

Poetry embraces the human race and the natural world, and will fill the emptiness.

13. The poet visited Karlovy Vary in 1959, and was enchanted by it, hence the idea of its having been created by a process parallel to that of a work of art, a song. The 'space' in st. 3 refers to the way the city is enclosed within its hills. The fact that Goethe loved the town enhanced its charms for Arsenii.

In 1962 Andrei's *Ivan's Childhood* was the highlight of the Karlovy Vary Film Festival.

14. Angelo Secchi (1818–78) was a pioneer in the field of stellar classification and the first to call the sun a star. He taught briefly at the University of Georgetown, USA, and in 1848–50 at Stonyhurst College in Lancashire. He was exiled from Rome with the Jesuits in 1870, having successfully resisted the state takeover of the Roman College.

The poet brackets him and Paul Klee as individuals of unique talent, utterly dedicated to their work. Arsenii Tarkovsky, 'Hope for the Future of Russian Poetry', interview, *Voprosy literatury*, no.6, 1979.

He sees poets and scientists as colleagues, and exemplars of man's essential identification with the natural world.

15. Van Gogh himself wrote of his work: 'It teaches me, and that's what I ask of my work above all', Letter no.629, words that could have been written by Arsenii. Of the colours which were so formative for the poet van Gogh wrote: 'No blue without yellow and without orange', Letter no.622. Vincent van Gogh, *The Letters*, Amsterdam 2009.

The poet's closeness to the painter, born of the revelatory impact of his work – the unique 'angel's roughness', is deeply personal.

Ernst Gombrich observes that 'Van Gogh discovered that you can see the visible world as a vortex of lines. We tend to see stubble fields and cypress trees now in terms of Van Gogh. Representation is a two-way affair.' Ernst Gombrich, *Art and Illusion*, London 1960, p.203.

Andrei writes of Van Gogh: 'He ... saw his task as an artist as "fighting" with all his strength, to the last breath, with the material of life, in order to express that ideal truth which lies hidden within it.' Andrei Tarkovsky, *Sculpting*, 1986, p.182.

16. The word for 'refrain' in st. 3 refers to the convention in Persian and Turkish poetry of repeating the last word(s) of each line or stanza; it originally meant 'pillion rider'.

Anna Akhmatova admired 'The Translator' for its Asiatic detail. Anna Akhmatova, *Sobrannye sochinenia v 6 tomakh [Works in 6 Volumes]*, Moscow 2007, vol.5, p.261.

The poem could be taken as an allegory for the Soviet artistic scene under Stalin: the lyricism and excessive sweetness of the poems contrast with the barbaric cruelty of the society in which they were written; shah and storyteller have lost their human image; man is reduced to an object; the well-turned arithmetical lines are without substance.

In 1946 Tarkovsky had grounds for hoping that an edition of his own poems might be published, only to have such hopes dashed by draconian reinforcement of the tenets of socialist realism. In that year he wrote a poem called 'Night work', in which he sees his translation work as endless, thankless drudgery (see also note 120).

17. *Stalker* is about the craving for, and pursuit of, a life-changing miracle; in the Strugatskys' proposal of October 1975 it had the working title, 'The Wish Machine'. Andrei Tarkovsky, *Collected Screenplays*, trans. by Natasha Synessios and William Powell, introduction by Natasha Synessios, London 1990, p.375. This approach is already to be found in *Roadside Picnic*, although both the Writer and the film-maker himself suggest that the Zone's secret may be no more than an alluring fiction. In the screenplay of *Light Wind* (1972) Father Grigorius talks of belief in an ideal as a 'correct idea', even if 'the ideal itself is absurd'. Ibid., p.208. See also note 80.

When the Writer declares that we are on earth for the purpose of creating works of art, which seems to paraphrase the final stanza, it could be either aspiration or irony – or possibly both; or he could be mouthing a thought that is not his own and that he has picked up from this poem. See also note 40.

The transitions between reality and daydream are as seamless as those in the films.

The Tarkovsky family lived on Serpukhov Street in Moscow.

18. Anna Akhmatova telephoned Tarkovsky to say, 'After reading your poems, particularly "This earth", I thought – now if you were to be run over by a tram, I should not be quite so prostrate with grief.' Tarkovsky/Tarkovskaia 2009, p.292; 'What a sophisticated compliment!' he later remarked. Arsenii Tarkovsky 1991–3, vol.2, p.224.

The last stanza refers to the Elisavetgrad theatre, where high above the heads of the audience was a picture of Apollo, smiling down superciliously, playing the violin and surrounded by Muses (conversation with Marina Tarkovskaia). In a draft letter to Andrei the poet refers to Apollo's music in the context of an Olympian indifference to good and evil, and insists on the artist's essential dependence on earthly things – for 'colour, chiaroscuro, sounds, meaning', which can be taken only from 'space and time'. Tarkovskaia 2006. p.254.

There may be an echo of Pindar's injunction: 'Seek not, my soul, the life of the immortals, but enjoy to the full the sources that are within your reach.' Certainly the poem expresses Tarkovsky's acceptance of life as it is, even including the reality of death as an element of the artist's material.

19. This and the following two poems are from the 'Chistopol' Notebook' cycle, originally entitled 'Kama Notebook'. In October 1941 the poet evacuated his mother from Moscow to Chistopol', where they joined his second wife and her daughter. He spent two months there, working on a collective farm and unloading timber from barges, while sending repeated applications to be sent to the front; he returned with other writers to Moscow in December and at the end of the month, after his tenth application, he was accepted for active service. 'Around the threshold of the Lord' seems to echo Lermontov's 'Angel of Death', one of Tarkovsky's favourite poems in his childhood.

20. 'Marina' is Marina Tsvetaeva, after whom Tarkovsky named his daughter. He had always deeply admired Tsvetaeva, and the two poets first met in 1939, shortly after Tsvetaeva had returned to the Soviet Union from Paris. Tsvetaeva's husband and daughter were arrested that summer. For KGB archive material see Vitali Chentalinski, *Les surprises de la Loubianka*, Paris, 1996, pp.256–300. In 1941 she and her young son left Moscow with the evacuation and found themselves in Ielabuga on the river Kama. She hanged herself there on 31 August. Tarkovsky did not hear of her suicide for some weeks.

    In the last line the adjective 'piny' is a literal translation of the Russian '*ielovaia*'; the English word loses the insistent assonance with the place name, suggestive of an evil spell.

21. Addressed to the poet's second wife, Antonina Bokhonova, for whom the poet had left Maria and the children in 1937. His family grew very fond of Antonina, indeed she and Maria became close friends; the latter recognised that Antonina and Arsenii truly loved each other.

    While serving on the front line the poet edited an army newspaper called *Battle Alert*, made up of sketches and poems about army life. He would sign his own pieces 'Ia.Tonin – I am Tonia's [Antonina's]'. In 1943 an injury to his leg from an explosive bullet led to several operations and gangrene (see the poem 'Field Hospital', p.98). The last stanza seems to foresee his injury. In 1944 Antonina organised her husband's transfer from an army hospital to a Moscow clinic, where his leg was amputated to the hip; she then nursed him through convalescence and depression. See also note 30.

    St. 2: Iaroslavna was the hero's beloved in the twelfth-century *Lay of Igor's Campaign*, the story of the defeat of Prince Igor by the Polovtsians in 1185. The lay is set in a nature filled with signs and portents, and which participates in human affairs. Iaroslavna, alone on the city walls, utters a lament for Prince Igor, singing of herself as a cuckoo who will fly to the battlefield, dip her long sleeve in the river and wipe the blood from his wounds. The thirst in the final stanza again echoes the lament, which ends with images of dying warriors parched with thirst and a plea to the sun to stop adding to their torment: a realistic enough picture of a battlefield in any century. In 1921 Marina Tsvetaeva wrote a hauntingly tragic new version of the lament.

22. The poet is cast as 'wizard' (*volkh*) and political power as 'wolf' (*volk*). '*Volkh*' is the word used in Russian for the Magi, subject of Leonardo's picture that Andrei uses in *Sacrifice*, and which frightened Otto by the mystery the painting seems to contain.

23. The scene in *Ivan's Childhood* with the ruined house and the crazed old man is reminiscent of this poem, with a rooster instead of the eagle.

24. In this picture of sounds recorded and movements imprinted in the air, there may be an echo of the 'frozen words' episode in Rabelais's *Pantagruel*, Book IV, ch.55–6, where the companions hear the cries of a fierce battle fought the previous year, a scene which Michel Chion cites as a 'cinematographic phenomenon': an example of the dissociation of body and voice, as between celluloid image and soundtrack'. Michel Chion, *Voice in Cinema*, New York 1998, p.123.

    In the poem time-layers shift, the real and the phantom overlap. 'We' are tuned in to past sounds and sights experienced by the dead, and they in turn will hear the actual spring song of the bullfinch.

25. A and O can be read as Alpha and Omega, the beginning and the end; or as the patterns made by the butterfly's wings in flight, visible but inexpressible. As the butterfly is a classical image of the soul, the poem may also be about the poet's life, which could leave him at any moment.

    The tiny looking-glass may be associated with the myth of Mother Earth, who holds a little mirror in her hand: the universal soul perpetually reflected in Nature.

Certainly, the poem is about the poet's delight in the visit of a butterfly, a delicate, elusive vision of beauty.

26. The English loses the rhyme-scheme aaaabbaab, and the repeated liquid sounds ee, l, r.

27. Section I: See the poem 'Field Hospital' for another account of the poet's experience after he was gravely wounded. See also the poem 'Joan of Arc's Tree' (p.85) for music as a metaphor for poetry, as opposed to emotion, as here.

     Section II: Marsyas was flayed because he dared to challenge Apollo to a contest of skill – Apollo playing the lute and Marsyas the flute – which he lost.

     Section III: Tarkovsky sometimes uses a needle simile or metaphor to suggest a startlingly sharp new awareness.

     Section IV: Lazarus, 'lover of life', seems to be Lazarus of Bethany, who was resurrected, John: 11–12, but the sleeping Lazarus seems more like the beggar who lay at the rich man's gate, and after his death rested on Abraham's bosom, Luke: 16, 19–21. However, Lazarus also harks back to Russian oral poetry, with origins in Byzantium and the Apocrypha: one tale (in many versions) tells of how Lazarus, briefly in hell but about to be brought back to life, is begged by Adam to intercede with Christ for him and for all the righteous people who throughout history have had to go to hell after death, pending Christ's own resurrection; it is David, poet and singer, who is first aware that Christ is on earth and tells Adam to address him through Lazarus. Tarkovsky often equates Adam with the poet.

     Section V: The poet moves from Lazarus to his child, and in terms reminiscent of 'Testament', written thirty years earlier when Andrei was an infant, he offers him all he has. But the 'disconnection' which in the parable was 'a great gulf fixed', which no one could pass over in either direction, here becomes the gulf between the poet who feels that life is already largely behind him, and the child who has infinite potential and is himself 'a song'; the poet can merely write songs and is bound to lose any contest – as Marsyas did to Apollo.

28. The plant mare's tail is an equisetum, a 'living fossil', that abounded for over a hundred million years in Palaeozoic forests; the Silurian period is the third period of that era, from about 435 million to 408 million years ago.

     Apocalyptic and post-nuclear nightmares, frequent in his son's films, are very rare in the poet's work.

29. Titania: Ovid's name for the daughters of Titans (powers of the subterranean world) including Diana. Ovid, *Metamorphoses*, Harmondsworth 1961, Bk III, p.173.

     Curiously, in *Andrei Rublëv* Kirill utters virtually the same words as those in the last two lines of the poem when he begs the Abbot to take him back.

30. Written after the death of the poet's second wife, Antonina Bokhonova. The marriage was destroyed when the poet fell in love with Tatiana Ozerskaia in 1947. Antonina then worked as a professional retoucher of photographs, mostly of people who had died, including many who had perished in the war. Only two months after the divorce she was diagnosed with terminal cancer. See also note 21.

31. This must have been written very shortly after the poet heard of Maria Falts's death on 7 December 1932. She had died on 5 August.

32. The first of many poems in which the poet sees his dead love; here, three years after her death, there is little to suggest that she is not alive. Her spectral presence in the poems written after her death is oddly reassuring in that it evinces the fathomless pain and love of bereavement; it is thus in sharp contrast to the disquieting relationship between Kelvin and Hari in *Solaris*. The dead Maria is present as herself, albeit not physically; the regenerated Hari is a copy, potentially capable of any number of reproductions.

33. The epigraph was originally one stanza of the poem.

     Maria Falts was born in Slaviansk and died there. The poem was written a few days before the eighth anniversary of her death on 5 August 1932.

This gathering of people dear to the poet, who have died at intervals of several years – his brother in 1919, his father in 1924, Maria Falts in 1932 – has obvious parallels with the meetings between the dead and the living in the films. However, whereas both Ivan (*Ivan's Childhood*) and Kelvin (*Solaris*) talk with their dead mothers in dreams, this scene in the poem is not presented as a dream; the mysterious woman in *Mirror* appears only in waking scenes, but she is not emotionally close to either Ignat or his father; and the dead son in Otto's story in *Sacrifice* appears only in a photograph, there is no meeting. Here the departed brother and father communicate wordlessly with the lyric hero, respectively with a smile and by pouring wine. The dead woman only addresses the hero, there is no dialogue. The plural 'we' in the fourth stanza recall the poet's young friends who had sighed for Maria Falts, and their words are written between clear inverted commas, rather than being preceded by the more usual (and sometimes ambiguous) dash, like the one that introduces her words in the final stanza. This punctuation contributes to the sense that the young men's words are heard coming from somewhere else, as it were acousmetrically. Their love had remained unrequited, but it is still intensely felt in recollection, and therefore they seem to be in the same timeframe as the poet, although 'offscreen'. Their words are not only in the protagonist's memory: they are physically carried in wine poured by a beloved brother, who always remained present to Arsenii; and in the music of glasses on a table that symbolises undying closeness between the poet and those dearest to him both before and after their death.

Although it remained unpublished until 1966, Marina Tsvetaeva knew this poem, having been present when the poet read it aloud for a gathering of friends – she would remember a poem from a single hearing. In March 1941 she wrote the following rejoinder, which was to be her last work; she hanged herself five months later. Tarkovsky did not know of its existence until it was published for the first time in *Neva*, no.4, 1982, forty-one years after she had written it. 'It was like a voice from the grave,' as he said. Arsenii Tarkovsky 1991–3, vol.2, p.243.

Tsvetaeva deliberately changed the title, and instead of the ballad or song rhythm of the original, with its feminine-masculine rhyme scheme, used the more dramatic masculine-feminine pattern (which I have not attempted to reproduce). She appears not to have wanted to recognise that the poet's unexpected guest was his dead beloved; and she adds a second brother.

    I've set the table for six

    I keep repeating that first line,
    And keep correcting what is said:
    'I've laid the table for six people …'
    You've forgotten the seventh.

    It's cheerless for you, being six,
    All those faces streaked with rain.
    How, with a table such as this,
    Could you forget the seventh.

    And it's cheerless for your guests,
    The crystal decanter's unused,
    They are as downcast as you,
    Above all the unbidden one.

    It is cheerless and it's dark.
    Oh! You're not eating or drinking!

How could that number slip your mind?
How could you get the total wrong?

How could you, how did you dare
Not see that six (two brothers, you –
That's three, wife, father, mother)
Make seven – with me in this world.

You laid six places on the table,
The world did not die out on six.
Rather than scarecrow to the living,
I must be a ghost with you and yours.

(With mine) ...
     Timid as a thief,
Oh – careful not to touch a soul! –
Unbidden seventh, I shall take
The place that was not set.

There! Now I've upset a glass!
What was yearning to pour out,
Pent-up salt from eyes, of pain from wounds,
Drips from tablecloth to floor.

And there is no grave! No parting!
Table unbewitched and house aroused.
Like death appearing at a wedding feast
I am life and I have come to dine.

... Nobody: not brother, husband, son,
Or friend, yet I make this reproach:
'You who set the table for six souls –
You did not seat me at the very end.'

           1941

34. This poem is associated by the poet's daughter with Maria Falts. The dedication
to his third wife was a gift to the latter; in 1944 the two had not met.

35. The description of the house and garden, and mention of piano playing, link
the poem clearly with Maria Falts. The last line encapsulates one of the poet's
important themes, which also runs through his son's films: death as part of life
and a source of poetry.

36. The repeated well scene in the film *Ivan's Childhood* seems to recall the well image
in st. 1, 3 and 6.
  St. 2: they were released from prison by the fact of meeting each other,
and, as in 'First Meetings', they were 'alone in the world'. Her bright sleeve echoes
references in Russian oral poetry to the hanging sleeves on medieval dresses,
associated with womanly grace; see also note 21.

37. Reviewing the collection in which this poem first appeared, Anna Akhmatova
singled it out for particular praise in what was altogether a laudatory notice: 'One
of the most poignant poems ... the heroine is portrayed with reverent awe ... A high
point of contemporary verse.' Akhmatova 2007, vol.5, p.262.
  The banks of the river Ingu, which runs through Elisavetgrad, were
traditionally a place of gypsy camps; the river flowed with oil-like slowness.
  As in the poem 'Song', the poet mentions his love's name but does not write
it. Also see references to 'Eurydice' in the introductory essay, 'The Poet's Voice'.

38. Andrei considered using the first stanza as an epigraph to *Mirror*.

    N. Synessios suggests that the willowy white hands may have inspired the hair-washing scene in the 'weeping room'. Natasha Synessios, *Mirror*, London 2001, p.12. In Russian there is one word for 'hand' and 'arm', and while in the poem 'hands' seems more appropriate, the hair-washing scene would suggest 'arms'.

    This picture of an unattainable beloved on the far bank of a river may well have conflated in Andrei's imagination with his reading of *The Lives of the Fathers*. He quotes in his diary entry for 28 February 1982 the sentence: 'If a woman came to talk to a monk, or if a monk found it necessary to talk with a woman, they would sit at some distance from each other on opposite banks of a stream, and their conversation would take place in that way.' Layla Alexander-Garrett tells us that the film he hoped to make about St Antony, exploring 'the conflict between spirituality and sin', would culminate in a declaration of love between a monk and a woman standing on either side of a smoothly flowing river. The water would be a medium of contact between them. The monk would bathe his bleeding feet, and she would wash her delicate, wing-like arms, and she would stroke and kiss the water, as if it were her unattainable beloved. Layla Alexander-Garrett, *Andrei Tarkovsky: The Collector of Dreams*, London 2012, pp.220–1.

39. Perhaps the 'riddle' in st. 3 is an echo of Nietzsche's dance-floor image: 'Where all becoming seemed to me the dancing of gods ... Must there not exist that which is danced upon, danced across?' Friedrich Nietzsche, *Thus Spoke Zarathustra*, Harmondsworth 1961, p.215. If so the child in the poem could be seen as Zarathustra's 'the nimble, the nimblest'. Also see references to 'Eurydice' here in the introductory essay, 'The Poet's Voice'.

40. Since 'meetings' is already the established English rendering of the Russian title, it has been kept as the most satisfactory of various options. 'Trysts' would be close, but is too poetic. Such phrases as 'When we first used to meet' or 'The first times we met/were together' are too long, but accurate.

    Geoff Dyer points out the similarity between the two first lines of st. 3 with the Writer's suggestion in *Stalker* that we are here on earth for the purpose of creating works of art, and draws a parallel with the ninth *Duino Elegy* by Rilke:

> Perhaps we are <u>here</u> to say: house,
> bridge, spring, gate, jug, fruit-tree, window –
> at most: column, tower ... but to say them, you must grasp them,
> oh, to say them in a <u>way</u> that the Things themselves
> had never dreamt of being.

'The poet *says* these things, Tarkovsky *shows* them, enables us to see them more intensely than we can with the naked, non-cinematic eye.' Geoff Dyer, *Zona*, Edinburgh and London 2012, pp.132–3. Also see references to 'First Meetings' in the introductory essay, 'The Poet's Voice'.

41. Both poems titled 'Just like forty years ago' make the memory of the lovers' last parting into a present experience: forty years earlier, in 1929, Arsenii Tarkovsky had visited his parents in Zinovievsk (formerly Elisavetgrad) and seen Maria Falts. The circumstances are detailed with precision, as if to preserve the reality of that final meeting perpetually, in the here and now.

42. The last Maria Falts poem is a hymn of thanks for all that she has given him as a poet, even since her death. Again her name is referred to, but not written (see references to 'Eurydice' in the introductory essay, 'The Poet's Voice').

    Sadly, the English has lost the tight rhyme scheme, and much of the rhythm, of the original, and also a powerful alliteration in st. 3, in which the vowel 'u (oo)' is repeated ten times; line 3 ends '*glukh i grub*' and line 6 '*grud' o srub*'.

43. 'Sectarian' snow refers to his nonconformist status.

    Holy bread: not the communion host, but blessed bread, given out at the end of the liturgy.

Kerensky-penny: currency under the Provisional Government, 1917–18.

Mathilda Kshesinska, prima ballerina of the Imperial Marinsky Theatre, was mistress of three grand dukes, including Nicholas II before his marriage.

Lena: in 1912 miners at the Lena goldfields, striking in protest against appalling working conditions, were fired on by government troops and over 100 were killed.

The poem was based on a childhood memory (Arsenii Tarkovsky 1979).

44. Achaea: Greece.

St. 4: formal and informal poetry readings were frequent in the early years of the revolution, and the readiness of groups of sailors (who often formed the vanguard of the Red forces) to listen to poetry was witnessed by many people recalling that period.

St. 6: an echo of the 'flinty path' in Lermontov's poem, 'I set out alone on the road'.

St. 7: General Budionny commanded the famous Red Cavalry in the Civil War; the helmet, modelled on the headgear of ancient Russian warriors, was adopted from the pre-revolutionary army. Young Arsenii got a job distributing the *Trade Gazette*, and was paid according to the number of people whom he could persuade to take out subscriptions; with the proceeds he bought himself a pair of boots – for some time he had been going around barefoot. The newspaper kitted him out with a Budionny helmet, for which he incurred as much dislike from members of the public as he did for his actual mission. His mother was so horrified when she heard of what he had been up to, particularly by the shameful fact that he had bought himself boots with his ill-earned gains, that he had to take the helmet back and give up his job. Arsenii Tarkovsky 1991–3, vol.2, p.174.

45. Ol'ga Grudtsova was the daughter of famous photographer M. Nappel'baum. Photographs are important in Andrei's films: in the last episode of *Ivan's Childhood*, when we learn of Ivan's fate at the hands of his Nazi captors; in *Solaris* they contain fragments of Kelvin's earlier life which are still a living part of him; in *Mirror* actual Tarkovsky family photographs are set alongside fictional portraits; and in *Sacrifice* a photograph seems to be possessed of its own life force in Otto's mysterious story.

46. St. 1 contains clear echoes of Gavriil Derzhavin's ode of 1784, 'God'.

In an interview (Arsenii Tarkovsky 1982) the poet spoke of man's central place between the macro- and micro-worlds, and the common ground between poets and scientists, referring to Einstein's statement that Dostoievsky had helped him to discover far more than any scientific thinker, including even the mathematician Karl Gauss. Andrei takes this line of thought further: 'Science involves the discovery not so much of objective laws of nature, as of the laws which govern the functioning of our consciousness. A kind of music; symbol; sign. A mathematical symbol of truth, corresponding to our capacity for knowing it with our brains.' Andrei Tarkovsky, *Time within Time: The Diaries*, trans. by Kitty Hunter Blair, Calcutta 1991, 2 April 1982. His scientific knowledge was considerably less than his father's – Arsenii had written radio plays on sphagnum moss and on glass manufacture, and constructed his own astronomical telescope – but for both father and son the world was full of 'music' and 'symbols'.

47. The word for 'grasshopper' is related to 'forge' and 'blacksmith'. Its song is often associated with music and poetry, both in folk verse and in the classical tradition, where it is seen as related to the cicada, dedicated to Apollo and the Muses. The cicada was the emblem of Attica.

St. 2: the centaur Chiron, wise and benevolent, taught music, medicine and hunting. Anacreon, singer of the simple idyllic life, wrote a poem 'To the Cicada'.

St. 3: Gavriil Derzhavin (1743–1816) and Velemir Khlebnikov (1885–1922) both wrote poems to the grasshopper. The grasshopper produces its music by 'sawing' on its wing with its serrate leg; the archery bow metaphor relates to the leg's capacity for propulsion.

St. 6: the Ionic mode in music – the major key (see also the poem 'Paul Klee').

48. Andrei wrote: 'Certain things are more cinematic, more photogenic than others. Water is very important to me in this respect. It is alive, is has depth, it moves, it changes, it reflects like a mirror, you can drown in it, you can drink it, you can wash yourself. You probably know that the entire mass of water on earth is made up of one molecule. Water is a monad.' *Russkaia Mysl'*, Paris, 1 April, 1986, pp.12, 14. Quoted in Synessios 2001, pp.66–7.

49. The nightmare fear of the dark forest leads into a homely picture reminiscent of the fan-letters about *Mirror* received by the director, in which correspondents thank him for showing scenes and objects that seem to belong to their own childhood. Andrei Tarkovsky, *Sculpting*, 1986, Introduction.

50. Tarkovsky first met Anna Akhmatova in 1946 at the home of his friend and mentor, Georgii Shengeli, and they became firm friends; at the time she was under a heavy political cloud. In a volume of her verse published in 1961 she wrote: 'To Arsenii Tarkovsky, great poet and dear interlocutor'. Over thirty years later he wrote: 'Both humanly and artistically I was always captivated and amazed by Akhmatova … There was nothing haughty, or grand, or unapproachable about her … even though some memoirs have asserted the contrary. In fact she was extraordinarily modest. Unforgettably clever and witty. And in poetry she revived the half-forgotten tradition of lofty verse.' Arkadii Khvoroshchan, 'Derzhava knigi' ('The Realm of the Book', interview with Arsenii Tarkovsky), *Almanakh bibliofila*, Moscow 1979, vol.7, p.7.

In her review of the slim volume where this poem appeared, Akhmatova called the publication 'an unexpected and precious gift for the reader'; the poet was still almost unknown except as a translator. She singled out the four lines starting, 'I am he …' as an example of Tarkovsky's way of making 'words we use every moment of the day unrecognisable, wrapped in mystery'. For her the lines were at once timeless and contemporary. The poet had 'come to life at the feast of the living, and told us a great deal about himself and about us'. Akhmatova 2007, vol.5, p.263.

St. 1: insofar as the poet is the 'double' of his work, he is changed by the writing of a poem. Marina Tarkovskaia chose line 3 as the subtitle of her 2009 book of her father's poems with commentaries.

St. 2, line 4: a reference to Jacob, who wrestled with God's angel and would not let him go, and so remained forever in God's presence (Genesis 32:28–9). See also note 115.

In the screenplay of *Light Wind* the scientist, Dekker, mockingly asks the monk Iakov (Jacob): 'And have you never fought with the angel, eh, Iakov?'

St. 3: the poet was almost certainly referring to the impossibility of having any appreciable amount of his own work published.

51. The final line seems to refer to Adam (see note 77); King David (see notes 23, 56, 86), and Christ, a carpenter's son. N. Reznichenko sees Adam, David and Jesus as 'protopoets' in Tarkovsky's 'mythopoetic schema: at once the precursors, contemporaries and perpetual companions of the poet, who has to walk a prophet's way of the cross, and to write his own Book of Genesis' (in Russian: the 'Book of Being'). N. Reznichenko, 'Slovar' tsaria Davida', *Voprosy literatury*, no.4, 2012.

According to A. Lavrin, editor of the 1991 three-volume edition of Tarkovsky's poetry, the censors objected to an earlier version of the second line of the third stanza: 'So why do you seem to be there in the dust-cloud' (Andrei Tarkovsky, *Screenplays* 1990, p.201). All published versions are as printed here.

52. In all editions published before 2006 this poem appeared without the last stanza. It was written the day before Tatiana Ozerskaia (who was to become the poet's third wife) was due to join him in Turkmenia, and he anticipated her arrival with

dread: 'It's painful to think of her capacity for betrayal,' he wrote in his notebook. 'I'm frightened, but not of losing my freedom, which I don't have and which anyhow I wouldn't appreciate even if I felt I had it ... What I'm doing is something approaching suicide.' Tarkovskaia 2006, pp.290–1. His despair seems to have driven him almost to the point of repudiating his poetic calling.

53. Prometheus, son of Earth (prime source of foreknowledge and prophecy), was responsible for giving humanity fire, stolen from the gods; and, according to some accounts, writing, mathematics, agriculture, science and medicine. Aeschylus's tragedy *Prometheus Bound* ends at the point where the hero, after years of being fettered to a rock, is about to endure the daily torment of having his liver torn out by an eagle.

St. 3 is clearly based on the hero's defiance of the 'lickspittle' Hermes: 'I would not change my painful plight/On any terms for your servile humility.' Aeschylus, *Prometheus Bound*, Harmondsworth 1961, pp.48–9.

Although in the play the hero's last words are: 'O Earth, my holy mother, ... You see how I am wronged!', Aeschylus's hero knows that he is 'one whom he [Hermes] cannot kill'. Nor, ultimately, can poetry be killed. But Tarkovsky recognises the high price of writing poetry that is not merely for the passing moment.

54. St. 1: 'There are times when poetry doesn't merely anticipate fate, it influences it', the poet observed in an interview (Arsenii Tarkovsky 1979).

St. 4: this seems like a discussion of Zarathustra's contention that the 'imprisoned will' cannot 'roll away the stone called That which was'. Nietzsche 1961, p.161. The only force capable of 'rending rocks', he claims, is 'my will'. Ibid., p.135. If so, the poet is casting doubt on Nietzsche's 'new god', the Overman. The film-maker resolved the argument quite differently in *Sacrifice* when he had Alexander apparently undo time.

55. For comments on the epigraph, see the introductory essay, 'Affinities'. For the text of Pushkin's poem, see Appendix I.

Although the physical detail of st. 2 identifies the subject as Osip Mandelshtam, the title *Poet* (with or without definite or indefinite article, since neither exists in Russian) suggests a portrait of a poet as such, and it is one that could have been drawn by Andrei.

The pauper knight was possessed by his vision of womanly beauty and goodness to the point where he could not participate in human affairs, even his crusading was undertaken for the sake of his ideal beloved. Prince Myshkin, born of Dostoievsky's aspiration to create an 'utterly beautiful human being' (who recites the poem in the Epanchins' drawing-room and then accidentally breaks a precious vase) finishes his days insane. The epigraph points towards the tragic divide between a poetic vision of beauty, goodness and truth, and worldly reality, the latter (as the poem tells us) being the actual material of the poet's work. In a letter to Anna Akhmatova, Tarkovsky writes of the Virgin Mary in the Knight's vision as both the archetypal mother and the eternal feminine. Arsenii Tarkovsky 1991–3, vol.2, p.266.

The figure of Don Quixote stands behind Pushkin's Knight and Arsenii's Poet. In *Solaris*, Don Quixote is declared by Snaut to be worth far more than the 'rubbish' that is science, and he has Kelvin read Sancho Panza's ambiguous words in praise of sleep, that infinitely desirable escape from the body which, however, resembles death.

When as a very young man Arsenii had asked Mandelshtam for his opinion of his work, the latter had been rather dismissive. However, he clearly acknowledged Tarkovsky as a fellow-poet, since he gave him a copy of the second edition of his collection *Stone*, published in 1916. Tarkovsky was delighted and deeply touched. This is unlikely to have happened earlier than the 1930s, by which time any book of Mandelshtam's verse was rare and precious.

Although the English version has reproduced something of the rhythm of the original, virtually no trace is left of rhyme, the most regrettable loss being the final open -a (some stressed, some unstressed) repeated over the last eight lines of the poem, the final line sounding: '*naplela sud'ba sama*'. This open, vacant vowel creates a sense of yawning void.

56. Written to Marina Tsvetaeva (see note 20). Many people shunned Tsvetaeva because it was dangerous to associate with someone who had lived abroad, but such caution was alien to Tarkovsky. Their friendship was strained despite his genuine affection, for she was extremely demanding. 'She was dreadfully unhappy,' he recalled, 'lots of people were scared of her. I was a bit scared myself. There was a touch of black magic about her.' Arsenii Tarkovsky 1991–3, vol.2, p.243.

57. The poems were not published as a cycle until after Arsenii Tarkovsky's death; this first poem, written shortly after he heard of Tsvetaeva's suicide, did not appear until 2009, in *Sud'ba moia* (Tarkovsky/Tarkovskaia 2009).

   The sea metaphors in this and the preceding poem suggest the assonance of the name Marina with '*more*', sea.

   'Hallowed' ('*zavetnyi*' – hallowed, cherished, secret) in the last line is a word suggested by Tsvetaeva to Tarkovsky in place of 'funeral' or 'funereal', in his poem 'The Cricket':

> Truth to tell – by birth
> > I'm a domestic cricket,
> I sing a hallowed song
> > over ashes in the hearth.
> And one will prepare for me
> > deadly boiling water,
> While another makes
> > a golden perch.

Both this and the previous poem speak of the generosity of her talent: Tarkovsky saw how totally she gave of herself in her poetry.

58. There is an urgency in the poet's grief in this second poem of the 'In Memory of Marina Tsvetaeva' cycle, written some five years after Tsvetaeva's death, when Tarkovsky was slowly and painfully recovering from his wartime injuries. He responds to her call by relating his tragedy to biblical images of war: the dead left out on walls, recovered by devoted survivors (1 Samuel 31), which now reminds us of the recovery of the bodies in *Ivan's Childhood*, and King David's lament for his sons (2 Samuel 1). Her bitterness is sacrificial and has meaning not only for her: she will take 'our' poisoned bread. Her prophetic voice will still be heard. Deeply personal pain is put into archetypal images. King David is also referred to in 'Field Hospital', 'A star dances before stars' and as 'psalmist' in 'Poets'.

   The first sentence covers eight lines, one image driving on to, and overlapping with, the next. In the last three lines the poem returns to the physical sense of Tsvetaeva's voice.

   The opening line might well evoke for the Russian reader Pasternak's well-known quatrain, quoted by the film-maker in *Sculpting in Time*: 'Stay awake, stay awake, artist,/Do not give in to sleep,/You are eternity's hostage,/Imprisoned in time's keep'. Andrei Tarkovsky, *Sculpting*, 1986, p.181.

59. After an interval of twenty-one years the poet can bring himself to consider the actual circumstances of Tsvetaeva's funeral, of which at the time he had been unaware, and wonder about her last thoughts.

   St. 5 refers to 'strangers' evacuated to Chistopol', perhaps also to the German prisoners of war whom the poet saw there.

60. Washing, soap-suds and river-beds are all recurring images in Andrei's films. In the final line 'out-stubborn' is a literal translation of the Russian verb '*pereupriamit*', to

outdo in stubbornness, but because the latter contains the word '*priamo*', straight, it here has a chilling hint of 'straightening out'.

61. Despite his love of Marina Tsvetaeva and her poetry, it is clear that he felt the roots of her writing to be very different from his own. He could not accept what he called in a draft letter to Andrei her 'Olympian indifference to good and evil', which he saw as the cause of her 'irreligious suicide', as it had been for the poets Sergei Esenin and Vladimir Maiakovsky, who killed themselves in 1925 and 1930 respectively. Tarkovskaia 2006, p.255.

    The phrase 'it doesn't matter' is close to Zarathustra's axiom that in a world without meaning 'it is all one' (Nietzsche 1961, p.256).

62. Komitas was the priestly name of Soghomon Soghomonian (1869–1935), the Armenian composer and musicologist, who dedicated his life to the notation of traditional Armenian folk and sacred music. He studied, lectured and performed in Europe and the Ottoman Empire. In 1915 he was arrested in Constantinople, and though he survived the Armenian massacre, he suffered a severe mental breakdown. He died in a mental institution in Paris.

    St. 5: regarding Lazarus, also see the poem 'After the War'. In the earlier screenplay of *Mirror*, still entitled *The White, White Day*, the film was to open with a resurrection scene in a cemetery. A coffin would rise from the grave and the mourners would walk away, 'their tears dried'. Andrei Tarkovsky, *Screenplays* 1990, p.266.

63. 'The Steppe Reed Pipe' was first published as a cycle in 1966 without the first poem, which first appeared in 1969.

    A significant 'echo' in this cycle is of Pushkin's narrative poem *The Gypsies*, in which a world-weary young Russian, Aleko, falls for a gypsy girl, Zemfira, only to kill her later when she falls for someone else. Her old father talks to Aleko about Ovid (who was exiled to Tomi on the Black Sea where he died in AD 17); the old man can't remember the poet's name, only that he had had 'a wondrous gift for song', could not cope with the primitive life and longed for an end to his exile.

    Mariula was the old man's wife, but had deserted him after only a year. Still in her cradle, Zemfira had heard Mariula's song of defiance against her 'old husband': 'Slash me or burn me,/I shall not flinch,/I fear no knife and no fire!' Pushkin had heard the song in a gypsy camp. For a long time thereafter he – or his lyric hero – would 'repeat Mariula's tender name'. Pushkin says of his hero: 'But – God! – what play his passions made/With his compliant soul!' – words equally apt for both Pushkin himself and Tarkovsky.

    Without the mention of Mariula, these poems would be about the poet's love of the empty steppe, its beauty and the way of life it imposes; and of Ovid, to whom he relates as to a contemporary colleague. Mariula's name opens up Pushkin's uniquely beautiful poem and themes of passion, freedom and fate.

    Whereas Ovid had longed for the city, for Tarkovsky 'ill-fortune' had made the steppe a place of respite.

    The expression rendered here as 'black sheep' has complex connotations. Literally it runs: 'a family is not without its runt', but this word, '*urod*' – a monster, or person with a defect – originally meant 'first-born'. The implications thus are of one who does not fit the common mould, but perhaps with a particular role, such as may indeed entail the kind of fierce self-assertion that is expressed in Mariula's song, which transcends gender and circumstance.

64. 'World' is one of several less than satisfactory possible translations of '*iav*' (see also notes 70 and 71). I have opted for 'world' to convey the idea of 'everything we see'. In 'Dreams', where the word is used in opposition to dreams and death, I have translated it as 'waking', which is its most common meaning.

    This is one of Tarkovsky's most important poems about poetry. He starts with the poet as subjective centre: the retina – sensitive part of the eye, physical mechanism allowing sight; throat – site of voice, conduit of both food and breath;

reason – mind, thought, intellect; and heart – seat of both life-blood and emotion. Each time the ranging vision, speech, thought or feeling is brought back to its physical starting-point. But for the poet to aim at capturing what is already visible is to do violence to his art: there is no need to teach the bow to curve. (One is reminded of Paul Klee's axiom about making visible what is unseen.)

The poet has been created from language, as God made Adam from earth – indeed in Hebrew the name 'Adam' means red clay. It is not for the poet to doubt the reality of the world as Thomas doubted the resurrected Christ; experience and appearance are borne in upon him by the very flow of life. The poet is of the essence of the wounded world, which is alive and perpetually becoming.

All that is present, all that is, in combination with language, can stretch open his pupils to let in more light (as in a camera, but this also echoes Pushkin's 'The Prophet' – see Appendix I: Pushkin Poems). He yearns to partake of the transcendental power born of reality and speech. No longer throttling his art, he will be the onlooker as a miracle takes place: the great ship will take flight, beyond gravity, limitless in its trajectory, propelled by wings that are like the vanes of a stronghold or bastion (the word is rhetorical in register). The creative miracle happens when phenomena and language come together, the image of the soaring ship is reminiscent of both dreams and science fiction, and may echo Osip Mandelshtam's 'flying machine' analysis of Dante's imagery (Mandelshtam 1979, p.414). Inevitably it brings to mind the ending of *Solaris*.

The repeated 'Oh' is exceptional; ejaculations occur very rarely in Tarkovsky's poems.

In an interview Tarkovsky talked of the importance for him of this poem (Khvoroshchan 1979). It may have influenced Andrei's decision to use the speech therapy session as the prologue to *Mirror*. Certainly there is a parallel: the boy's whole body is used to produce fluent speech. The therapist specifies how he must stand; her hand 'pulls back' his head (interestingly, Andrei wrote that he could feel God's hand on the back of his head, Andrei Tarkovsky, *Time*, 1991, 10 February 1979); his eyes and his will are concentrated in his hands, which are then released by the touch and movement of her hands: the gift of speech emerges from precise, scientifically informed use of hands, head, eyes and stance.

65. The last stanza may be an allusion here to Mandelshtam's poem, 'I've forgotten the word ...' in which 'the swallow, sweet girl, Antigone', 'unbodied thought', will return on clipped wings to the 'hall of shades'.

66. Almost certainly an image of the loneliness experienced during the forty years of the poet's third marriage. The last stanza reminds us of the cross-purpose exchanges between Aleksei and Natalia in *Mirror*, and the rainbow wheels of the play of light in Andrei's films generally.

67. The poet was in Daghestan in 1939 and probably also in later years. Azrael is the angel of death in some Eastern traditions.

68. The poet's lifelong passion for astronomy is less evident in his poetry than one might expect; this poem is almost the only example. He would certainly have known Goethe's essay on Johann Winckelmann: 'What end is served by all the expenditure of suns and planets and moons, of stars and Milky Ways, of comets and nebula, of worlds evolving and passing away, if at last a happy man does not involuntarily rejoice in his existence?' Quoted in R.J. Hollingdale, 'Introduction', in Nietzsche 1961.

69. In Pushkin's *Mozart and Salieri* Isora had given Salieri the poison with which he murdered Mozart.

In a draft letter to Anna Akhmatova of November 1958, Tarkovsky posits that Salieri's condemnation of Mozart's flippancy chimes with the views of the average reader, who will be on the side of rules and scrupulous study, and for whom inspired genius is incomprehensible and disturbing; Salieri killed Mozart because he was 'a god in a fragile vessel'. Arsenii Tarkovsky 1991–3, vol.2, p.265.

The poet seldom writes of wickedness, but here Isora is essentially both evil and feminine, and in st. 3 takes on the guise of a baneful spirit who travels through the world depriving people of their physical senses: a grotesque counterpart to the artist, who opens eyes and ears.

70. St. 1, line 7: see Ovid 1961, Bk III, 'There is no death – no death but only change/ And innovation'.

'Reality' (*iav'*) = *phainomenon*, the Greek word being related to '*phaos*', light, and 'apophansis', statement, speech. See also note 64.

The last lines of the stanza seem to echo Christ's words to the apostles that they will become 'fishers of men'.

St. 3, line 3: for the association of the grasshopper with poetry and prophecy see note 47.

71. St. 4, line 2: see notes 64 and 70.

72. The poet had a photograph in his room of a bust of Kore, queen of the underworld, who carries into effect the curses of men upon the souls of the dead.

73. The dedication to the poet's third wife was chosen after first publication by Tatiana herself at Tarkovsky's invitation.

In her review Akhmatova praised the delicacy of the last two lines (Akhmatova 2007, vol.5, p.264).

74. Marina Tarkovskaia chose the dedication when invited by her father to choose a poem. In the documentary *Marina's House* this is the one poem she recites. The poem is set in Ashkhabad, a region of olive trees.

Originally the last line of st. 2 read 'the iron bolt was closed'; the poet altered it in order to avoid the possibility of association with 'iron curtain'.

75. The words of the epigraph, originally 'So I've locked my house and come on' (H.G. Wells, *The War of the Worlds*, London 1975, p.86), are spoken by a nameless man in the crowd, in the context of rumours that various Surrey towns had been destroyed, though all he personally had seen were clouds of smoke to the south; the words sum up the unawareness and futility of the populace in the face of cataclysm. H.G. Wells was much read in Russia.

St. 7: 'God is dead': a Nietzschean premise.

Every Russian reader will be reminded of the 'glum' priest, whose gold-adorned fat belly used to shine above the people, in Aleksandr Blok's poem *The Twelve*.

St. 11: crucifixion is the archetypal image of cruelty done by the crowd, or the powerful, to the 'outsider' individual, in this instance to the prophet-poet.

Aliens and flying-saucers were much talked of in Soviet Russia in the 1950s. In a diary entry, Andrei quotes Montaigne: 'We do not move in one direction, rather do we wander back and forth, turning now this way and now that. We go back on our own tracks', and he reflects: 'That thought of Montaigne reminds me about something I thought of in connection with flying saucers, humanoids, and the remains of unbelievably advanced technology found in some ancient ruins. People write about aliens; but I think that in these phenomena we are in fact confronting ourselves; that is, our future, our descendants who are travelling in time.' Andrei Tarkovsky, *Time*, 1991, 23 June 1981.

76. Originally published with the title 'Willi Schnell' in order to screen Klee's name: in those days he was officially regarded as a bourgeois-reactionary painter.

St. 4: grasshoppers are said to sing in a major key; see note 47.

St. 5: in *Andrei Rublëv*, Feofan declares, 'Soon I shall die. Two days ago an angel appeared.'

77. 'Anka' is a familiar form of Anna.

78. St. 4: see Genesis 22 for the story of Abraham and Isaac.

Igor Evlampiev considers that the title and argument of Andrei's *Sacrifice* are based not only on Nietzsche but also on the work of the émigré philosopher Lev Shestov, for whom Abram, or Abraham, is a pivotal figure. Evlampiev sees

Alexander's sacrifice of what is most dear to him not as an act of utter obedience to an omnipotent and loving God, but as a galvanising of the hidden forces of being, capable of transforming the world through the concerted effort and will of individual people. Evlampiev 2012, p.445. It is very likely that both father and son had read Shestov; the early twentieth-century Russian thinkers were avidly studied by a minority of Soviet intellectuals.

In the poem, however, the separations in the first two stanzas echo those in the opening of Genesis. Through working in and with matter, the poet reveals the light of the word. The poet, here cast as Abraham's son and joy, is not to be sacrificed as he is needed by his times. The poet's 'cup' is one of sacrifice; yet life, the raw material of his verse, is the sweetest of cups.

79. The poet's search for his own language takes him back to Adam and the very beginnings of naming. As a poet he is at once reaper, scythe and basket – 'subject, object and creative tool.' Reznichenko 2012.

See also the poems 'Opening my notebook I studied the grass', 'The Steppe' and 'For my daily bread, for every drop of water', and notes 51 and 64.

The last line seems to refer to the Bergsonian notion of a consciousness which 'would take itself as object, and which, spectator and actor alike, at once spontaneous and reflective, would bring ever closer together – to a point where they would coincide – the attention which is fixed, and time which passes.' Henri Bergson, *The Creative Mind*, New York 2007, p.3.

80. St. 2, line 1: the 'straightness' of Isaiah's staff does not refer to any passage in the Book of Isaiah, but connects clearly with the gift of direct, straight utterance in the poems 'The Steppe' and 'Pushkin Epigraphs' ('I was given short change in the shop') and the *'true'* (in Russian – 'direct, straight') lexicon in 'The Manuscript'.

St. 2, line 2: tympanum – rereading Beckett's *The Unnamable* at the time when I was puzzling over this poem, I was struck by the following passage: 'I'll have said it, I'll have said it inside me, then in the same breath outside me, perhaps that's what I feel, an outside and an inside and me in the middle, perhaps that's what I am, the thing that divides the world in two, on the one hand the outside, on the other the inside, that can be as thin as foil, I'm neither one side nor the other, I'm in the middle, I'm the partition, I've two surfaces and no thickness, perhaps that's what I feel, myself vibrating, I'm the tympanum'. Samuel Beckett, *Molloy, Malone Dies, The Unnamable*, London 1959, p.386. The Russian word *'plënka'*, which I had translated as 'film', also means drum and eardrum, tympanic membrane and middle ear – the organ that catches sounds. One would not readily equate Samuel Beckett with Arsenii Tarkovsky, but here it seems that they are both talking of the same phenomenon: the self as the finest of sensitive films.

We know that Andrei was aware of Beckett: he mentions him in the context of Theatre of the Absurd, observing that such plays 'produce an impression almost of naturalism; or at any rate of total truth'. Andrei Tarkovsky, *Time*, 1991, 4 February 1974. He writes down the title *Molloy* on 25 December 1974, then notes in parenthesis: '(Take *Molloy* for the Strugatskys).' Robert Bird with characteristic insight draws a parallel between Kelvin's last monologue in *Solaris* and the end of *The Unnamable*. Kelvin asks: 'Do I have the right to refuse even the imaginary possibility of contact with the Ocean, to which my race has for decades tried to extend a thread of understanding, and remain here among the things and objects which we both touched? ... For the sake of my hope for her return? But I have no such hope. All that remains for me is to wait. For what? I don't know. New miracles?' The very end of Beckett's novel reads: 'I'll go on, you must say words, as long as there are any ... I don't know, I'll never know, in the silence you don't know, you must go on, I can't go on, I'll go on.' Beckett 1959, p.418. Bird sums up the 'thrust' of the two passages thus: 'between our intuitions of a transcendent source (i.e. the Ocean) and the insecurity of corporeal life we erect systems of representation – threads of understanding – which never form themselves into a

clear design, yet comprise the very fabric that weds consciousness to corporeality'.
Robert Bird, *Andrei Tarkovsky, Elements of Cinema*, London 2008, p.162.

81. St. 1: an allusion to Lermontov's poem, 'The Three Palm Trees'.

St. 3: Alexander Tarkovsky had been exiled to Siberia, 1887–92, as a member of the group 'The People's Will'. He always read the journal *The Bell*, published in London by Alexander Herzen and available in Russia despite being banned.

82. Written following his last visit to the town of his birth, which saddened him because the place was so changed. He wrote to his friend Nikolai Stanislavsky, also a native of Elisavetgrad: 'I realise that one must often visit the place one was born, otherwise one's heart dries up, and your birthplace, our town, is a good reason for tears.' Tarkovskaia 2006, p.141.

83. Tarkovsky had scarlet fever in 1914.

84. St. 1, line 4: a reference to the Greek expression, 'Swallows speak the language of the barbarians', i.e. Latin.

St. 2: Bagrat's church in Kutaisi, in ruins since the seventeenth century (and now to be restored by UNESCO).

Simon Chikovani (1902–66) was boldly experimental as a young poet, more mainstream later on, always graceful and vivid. Tarkovsky first met him in 1945 and considered him 'generous and wise ... one of the most admirable people I have ever known'. Arsenii Tarkovsky 1991–3, p.191.

85. Andrei Tarkovsky thought of writing a short story, based on this poem and 'Song', in the hope of freeing himself from a recurring dream about the house of his childhood. Synessios 2001, p.12.

The White Day was one of several possible titles for *Mirror*; early in the version of the screenplay still called by that title, there is a scene in a cemetery during which the director-narrator's voice is heard saying: 'Nobody believes me when I say I can remember being one and a half years old ... The steps from the verandah, the lilac bush ... And it's such a sunny, sunny day.' Andrei Tarkovsky, *Screenplays* 1990, p.265.

I have finally opted for 'white' here, rather than 'bright', as this usage is also uncommon in Russian.

86. Written on a visit to Lithuania. The poem has been set to music several times, sometimes changing the meaning, much to the indignation of the poet's friends. He himself was usually unconcerned: 'Never mind, it's not important, let them sing it.' Tarkovsky/Tarkovskaia 2009, p.308. See also 'Appendix II: The Process of Translation'.

87. See the introductory essay, 'Affinities'.

88. Metaphors here seem to echo a passage in Bergson about the impotence of speculative philosophical systems, disillusionment in which lead us 'to acknowledge the fragility of every edifice we've built'; the 'infinitely small elements' of human experience become 'a curve stretching out into darkness behind them'. Henri Bergson, *Matter and Memory*, trans. by N.M. Paul and W. Scott Palmer, New York 2004, pp.240–2 .

89. Phaethon insisted on driving the chariot of his father, the Sun, and could not control the horses; he was killed by Zeus to prevent further destruction.

In 1966 Tarkovsky entitled his second collection of verse *Earth to Earth* (or, literally, *The Earthly to Earth*) – as in this poem he was evoking the words of the Orthodox funeral service: 'Out of earth were we mortals made and unto the earth shall we return.'

The flying peasant episode in *Andrei Rublëv* is now referred to as the 'Russian Icarus'.

90. In the screenplay of *Stalker* this was to be the poem recited by the hero. By changing to 'Now summer is gone' the director moved from the themes of strength in weakness and human beings as children of the earth, both of which are demonstrated in the person of Stalker, to a more personal, and more open-ended,

expression of spiritual search.

91.   See note 50.

92.   St. 3: 'homeless': like many writers, and for some periods Tarkovsky himself, Akhmatova had no permanent place to live.

93.   The poet was in charge of the funeral arrangements and one of three who spoke at the service; he was so affected that he could barely utter a few unhappy phrases. V.I.A. Vilenkin and V.A. Chernykh (eds.), *Vospominania ob Anne Akhmatovoi*, Moscow 1991, p.611.

94.   Recollection of being wounded in the war conflates with the legend of Phaethon, whose mourning sisters were turned into poplars that wept tears of amber.

95.   See the introductory essay, 'Affinities'.

      The poem addresses a plural 'you', i.e. readers, or, by extension, humanity at large. As in 'Life, Life', the poet personifies poetry, or art generally, and in that sense is immortal.

      The phrase 'alone amid mirrors' sounds very like an image in Grigorii Skovoroda's *Disputation on the Ancient World*, in which he writes of the world as shadows: 'Were you to stand in the middle of a chamber of which all four walls and the door were covered with some sort of varnish, like mirrors ... You would see that your own bodily frame is possessed of hundreds of views, all dependent on it alone ... However, our bodily frame itself is but a single shadow of the one true one.'

      The weeping mother echoes the picture of Icarus's mother in the poem 'Our blood does not yearn after home', who dreams (either before or after the event) of her son's destruction. This archetypal image of maternal grief may hark back to the poet's memory of his own mother as she mourned the death of her elder son Valerii, killed at the age of fifteen (see note 102).

96.   St. 3: I have translated the archaic Russian '*blagostynia*' not as 'good works', but in the specific Greek sense of which Pavel Florensky writes in *Ikonostasis*. Quoting Matthew 5:16, 'Let your light so shine before men that they may see your good works, and glorify your Father who is in heaven', he goes on: 'this is not "good works" in the Russian understanding of the words – i.e. not philanthropy and moralism – but rather it is [in Greek] literally "the works of your beauty", i.e. the lightbearing and harmonious manifestations of spiritual personality, and above all the illumined face whose beauty arises from the dispersal of inward light into the outward appearance.' Florensky 1996, p.57.

      St.4: as in English, 'jealousy' can also have the sense of 'zeal'.

97.   These four poems illustrate Osip Mandelshtam's dictum that 'a quotation is a cicada' ('*tstitata iest tsikada*'). 'Its natural state is unceasing sound'. Mandelshtam 1979, p.401. Each of the epigraphs, familiar to the Russian reader, resonate steadily from inside the poem.

      In 'Winter Evening' (1825) the poet is alone with his aged Niania, from whom he had heard so many folk-tales and songs, and he asks her to sing, suggesting that it will be more fun to drink together as the storm rages outside. The song tells of a maiden going for water in the morning and seems to contain a promise of love. Whereas Pushkin asks Niania to sing a specific song, Tarkovsky asks his 'soul' to 'sing ... sing ... sing', the imperfective verb being repeated seven times; singing even to the end of time is the very meaning of 'her' being. Pushkin invites Niania to drink and be merry; Tarkovsky asks his soul to sing because of all the pain in the world.

98.   The Pushkin lines are from a poem to Anna Kern, 'I remember the wonderful moment', written in 1825, which tells of how, after dark years of despair during which the poet did not see her or think of her, a new meeting renewed his 'inspiration, life, tears and love'. Pushkin himself had taken the phrase 'genius of pure beauty' from a poem by his friend Vasili Zhukovsky (written a year earlier) whom the Muse seems to have deserted, but in whose return, at some future moment, he ardently believes. The first line of Tarkovsky's poem makes the reader

think of Pushkin's narrative poem *The Prisoner of the Caucasus*, but lines 3 and 4 make it clear that the prisoner in question is the hero of Tolstoy's story for children of the same title, who was kept in a pit by his Tartar captors and made toys for the children, until he eventually escaped. The epigraph thus evokes one of several shadowy presences.

However, the poem is written unmistakeably, and scrupulously, in the rhyme scheme of Pushkin's poem to Anna Kern, and where Pushkin's poem repeats in the penultimate stanza lines 3 and 4 of st. 1, Tarkovsky, also in the penultimate stanza, repeats the first line of the epigraph. The 'cicada' voice is that of Pushkin, though Tarkovsky writes in a conversational register except where he quotes Pushkin, and whereas the latter's 'thou' was a specific woman, Tarkovsky's 'other' is the Muse, in the third person; this is the only poem in which the Muse is mentioned.

A further Pushkin echo is woken by the image of his moral recovery: in a draft of 'Once again I visited' Pushkin wrote the much-quoted lines: 'Poetry saved me like a guardian angel/And my soul came back to life.' Yet Tarkovsky inserts into the rather lofty last two stanzas the lines about the ladder, which take us back to the escape of Tolstoy's hero from the pit by means of a pole.

This complex series of allusions can be compared with the film-maker's literary references, which often lead off in several different directions at once.

99. In 'Lines written during a sleepless night' of 1830, Pushkin wants to know the meaning of the clock's ticking: is it the Parcaes's womanish prattle, a reproach for his wasted day, a summons, a prophecy? Tarkovsky ends his poem with an urgent rhetorical question which, however, takes the reader to Pushkin's 'Elegy', written a little earlier in 1830, which contains the line 'I want to live, that I may think and suffer', and ends with the hope of future love.

100. The epigraph is from the Baron's first monologue in the verse drama, *The Covetous Knight*. The Baron has gained enormous wealth through obsessive greed, and the speech is about his quasi-erotic pleasure in the moment before he opens his coffers. The play raises questions about social symbols and hollow worldly values, psychological imprisonment and loss of humanity. Tarkovsky's lyric hero is a victim, his coffers empty; but such is the price of his capacity to speak. The poet spoke of Pushkin's sense of the prophetic power of poetry and contrasted the 'kopeks' of worldly success with the epic task of poetry, of which the price is life or death (Arsenii Tarkovsky 1979). Andrei Tarkovsky equally derided the practice of 'trading' art.

101. Grigorii Skovoroda (1722–94), known variously as a 'Russian Socrates' and a 'versifying Diogenes', was a highly educated Ukrainian, fluent in Greek, Latin, Hebrew and German, and a chorister. Despite his father's urging he decided against ordination and soon gave up the academic career that was open to him because he wanted only 'to teach people virtue'. He spent the rest of his life as a wandering teacher, homeless, unwashed, living off the hospitality of his numerous followers, mostly in the Ukraine. His doctrine was a jumble of the Bible, which he called 'God's very word', while insisting that it must be understood allegorically because of its contradictions (which he enjoyed); the ancients, his heroes being Socrates, Seneca and Marcus Aurelius; and the teaching of the German mystics. Throughout his wanderings he always carried the Bible and his flute, and he would speak of the 'marvellous melodiousness' of King David's singing: 'he strikes all the strings'. (See also the poems 'Field Hospital', 'Poets', 'I can hear, I'm not asleep, you're calling me, Marina' and 'A star dances before stars'). He was outspoken in his criticism of the faults of the powerful, and held superstition, alchemy and much of the clergy in varying degrees of contempt. In winter he slept in a shed, in summer in the open, whenever possible near bee-hives.

One day in 1794 he arrived at a friend's house and announced that he had come there for good. For the next three mornings he left the house with a spade and spent that time digging his grave. He then told his friends that his time had come, asked for the words, 'The world tried to trap me and failed' to be inscribed on his headstone, lay down and breathed his last.

He wrote in a ponderous amalgam of Church Slavonic and bookish Ukrainian, and the bulk of his writings were not published until a hundred years after his death; several writers were influenced by him, including Fëdor Dostoievsky and Vladimir Soloviev, and in the twentieth century, Mikhail Bulgakov.

Tarkovsky was introduced to Skovoroda's writings by a doctor friend of his father at the age of seven, and acknowledged that he had an enormous influence on him as a child; Skovoroda's philosophy developed in Arsenii's mind in parallel with his poetic sensibility. He quotes approvingly the thinker's axiom that everyone must dedicate himself solely to the one thing to which he truly feels drawn, and he too saw self-knowledge as central to philosophy. The first of Skovoroda's works to be published, which appeared only after his death, was entitled *Narcissus, or Know Thyself*. The Narcissus image chimes with a recurring reflection motif in his work (see also note 95).

Arsenii's juvenile attempts to write verse in the manner of his hero provoked mirth from his family, but as they also laughed at Skovoroda's own poems the small boy did not find their reaction too discouraging.

The alphabet image in the last stanza seems to allude to Maximus the Confessor's exegesis on the incarnation: 'The Word ... hides himself mysteriously in the spiritual essences of created beings, as if in so many individual letters, present in each one totally in all his fullness ... He has deigned to use these letters to express the syllables and sounds of Scripture'; 'The Logos ... shows himself to our minds ... through visible objects which act like letters of the alphabet, whole and complete both individually and when related together.' Maximus the Confessor, *Ambigua*, quoted in Olivier Clément, *The Roots of Christian Mysticism*, New York 1993, pp.36, 227.

102. Valerii (Valia) Tarkovsky had welcomed the revolution with youthful ardour and joined the revolutionary anarchists. He was killed in 1919 at the age of fifteen, fighting against Ataman Grigor'ev. The pain of losing his talented elder brother never left the poet. Many of Valerii's friends were arrested and shot by the Bolshevik administration in Elisavetgrad.

The poet's notes include mention of how he and his brother enjoyed sitting on these cannons in 'the town now known as Kirovograd. Earlier it was called Zinovievsk ... while that person was still resident on earth. Then after he had been ... "decommissioned", the town was renamed in honour of Kirov ... Every period has its names.' Arsenii Tarkovsky 1991–3, vol.2, p.240. Grigorii Zinoviev was executed in 1936 for participation in the plot to assassinate Sergei Kirov, who had been killed in 1934, probably on Stalin's orders. Political events rarely figure in Tarkovsky's poems, or in his published notes, but they were of course always present in his life.

Milk had an almost sacred significance. The dream scene in *Mirror* of the small Aleksei with the glass jug full of milk strongly conveys this sense, in contrast to the scene in the doctor's house, where spilt milk was dripping on to the floor; in *Andrei Rublëv* the spoilt little princess splashes milk at the painter as if it were a plaything.

103. St. 5: Grisha is Grigorii Rasputin.

St. 7: this 'first poem' was not in fact his first, he had been writing since his early childhood – writing poems was a family pastime. At the age of six he wrote: 'Papa came home from Odessa,/He brought me water from the sea' – a little bottle of seawater was the one present he had asked his father to bring him.

104. See the *Nostalghia* section of the introductory essay, 'The Poet's Voice'. The first person to whom he read this poem was his daughter Marina, who happened to visit him the morning after he had written it late at night. Tarkovksy/Tarkovskaia

2009, p.316.

105. In a draft letter to Andrei, the poet writes of Peter's betrayal as 'a moment of human weakness; Peter is the founder of the Christian church, a martyr, he redeemed his fault (not a sin) by his righteous death'; the letter was presumably written in the mid-1960s (Tarkovskaia 2006, pp.254–5). This poem and the reflections in the letter indicate how far the poet was from making hasty judgements at a time when questions about people's past actions lay heavily on many minds.

106. Lines 5–6 of st. 2 could also mean: 'throwing tiny beads to and fro between them and their leader'.

107. When Pushkin died, the poet Vasili Zhukovsky, who had been at his bedside for many hours, said that the expression on the dead poet's face made him long to ask, 'What do you see, my friend?'

108. Addressed to both his children at the time when Marina was still in the womb.

     Section I, st. 4: see introductory essay, 'Affinities'.

     Section I, st. 6: the lofty register 'tormented' echoes the first word of Pushkin's 'The Prophet'.

     Section II, st. 1: aul (a-ool) is a Turkic word for a fortified Caucasian village.

     Section II, st. 3: in 'My Shengeli' the poet writes of how as boys he and his contemporaries were 'nurtured by the romance of civil war', dressed in rags (often made up from army uniforms) and armed with whatever weapons they happened to find lying on the ground (Arsenii Tarkovsky 1991–3, vol.2, p.183).

     Section II, st. 7: see introductory essay, 'Affinities'.

     Section III: Maria Tarkovskaia was particularly fond of this section of the poem; when she read it aloud to the children it reduced her to tears (conversation with Marina Tarkovskaia).

109. The image of the magic grove seems to anticipate the Zone in *Stalker*, though the film is based on the Strugatsky brothers' *Roadside Picnic*.

110. Mikhail Petrovich von Medem, exceptionally talented graduate of the Berlin Conservatoire, Baltic baron and Russian patriot, Marshal of the Nobility for Elisavetgrad; after the civil war he avoided arrest by immediately registering as a piano teacher. He gave at least half his lessons free of charge (Tarkovskaia 2006, p.274).

     Arsenii's first teacher had held sharpened pencils under his wrists to prevent him from dropping them (Tarkovskaia 2009, p.54); the grim-faced music teacher in Andrei's *The Steamroller and the Violin*, who so disapproved of Sasha's imagination, may well be based on what the director knew of his father's childhood experience. Later, Arsenii was expelled from the music school for attending with no shoes.

     St. 1: Ganon was the author of study books for piano. The forest hunting scene conjured up by the music is echoed in the much later poem 'Joan of Arc's Tree'.

111. 'Fluffy-fine shawls': a descriptive rendering of 'Orenburg shawls', which normally are crocheted out of spun kid's wool, very fine and fluffy; however, camel down was the warmest, softest down of all.

     'Tyke Mongrelich' is a 'translation' of 'Barbos Polkanych': both 'Barbos' and 'Polkan' are derogatory words for dogs, similar to 'cur', 'tyke' and 'mongrel'.

112. Marc Augé talks of 'the continuity of the figure behind the return': 'it is not altogether the "deflagration of remembrances" of which Proust speaks that is at work here: it is a short-circuit of the same order, in the sense that it passes through the body from the contact made between two separate periods but produced in the very places themselves, associating them with the evidence of a time retained more than regained'. Marc Augé, *Oblivion*, trans. by Margolin de Jager, Minneapolis 2004, p.71.

113. The poet's father died in 1924; he had started to lose his sight (from grief, as his family believed) after the death of his young son, Valerii, and became completely

blind; the last line may refer to his blue eyes. The poem expresses the poet's sadness that his father had not lived to see his grandson: Andrei was born in 1932 in Zavrazhe, on the other bank of the river from Iurovets.

It is clear how deeply the sound of the church bells was imprinted in the poet's imagination. Before the revolution there were about a dozen churches in Iurovets, so the resounding chimes would have been heard far down the river.

During the war his son witnessed the demolition of the cupolas of the Simon Church, of which the screenplay of *The White Day* includes a detailed account; this was kept in almost all versions but dropped before *Mirror* was actually filmed. The demolition was to be accompanied by a voiceover of extracts from Leonardo da Vinci's description of how to paint the dust-filled air of a battle scene (Synessios 2001, p.13; Andrei Tarkovsky, *Screenplays* 1990, p.272).

A cupola is brought down in *The Steamroller and the Violin*, although its actual fall is not shown in full. Sasha finds the demolition exciting; the cut from falling stonework and dust to a towering Stalinist building, made visible by the destruction, highlights the contrast between different eras and styles in a well-tried Soviet manner – this was after all a degree film made in 1960 – but the aesthetics speak for themselves. In *Ivan's Childhood* a bell is seen lying on the floor as Ivan is talking of how the Germans (whom he equates with the horsemen of the Apocalypse in Dürer's engravings) burn books. He hoists it up to the ceiling, then launches into an imagined avenge attack on enemy soldiers, and the beam from his torch falls on to messages scratched on the wall by teenage prisoners who are about to be shot: an association is made between the bell, of which the function is to announce good or ill tidings, and those tragic words; finally Ivan rings the bell furiously. Later, it hangs above the table in the crypt, more or less centre-screen, where it is first seen as the gramophone starts to play: it can thus be read as a symbol of voice, a suggestion that the story of the protagonists and the voices of the murdered children will eventually resonate. The creation of the bell in *Andrei Rublëv* may be seen as a redemption of earlier destruction, both in the narrative and in Russian experience; and the boom of the new bell, forged from earth and fire by the concerted effort of the whole community, is like an aural preface to the ikons that will shortly be seen in all their glory. In the opening scene of Andrei Tarkovsky's production of the opera *Boris Godunov* a huge bell has a central position above the stage.

114. The poem takes its title from Baudelaire's 'L'Invitation au voyage', but in tone and feeling is very far from the '*ordre et beauté, luxe, calme et volupté*' promised by the French poet to his fickle mistress.

The lottery win may be as I have translated it, or it may contain a further level of unpredictability because of the Soviet habit of joining a queue without necessarily knowing what you might acquire or whether the window will slam shut before you reach it.

St. 2: 'Butterflies that grace a grave', Ovid 1961, Bk III. p.363; souls of the departed are a recurring Tarkovsky image. See also note 120.

St. 3: Lefaucheux was a nineteenth-century French gunsmith. Clementi Muzio (1752–1832), composer and teacher, developed the piano sonata, a form which Tarkovsky saw as akin to that of the sonnet.

115. St. 1, line 4: the reference is to John the Baptist.

St. 2, line 1: after wrestling with the angel, or with God, Jacob was given the name Israel and received an injury to his thigh (Genesis 32:28–9; see also Isaiah 4, about Jacob, still alive after confronting God; see also note 50).

116. St. 2: the rubber soles remind the Russian reader of 'Introduction' in Anna Akhmatova's cycle, 'Requiem':

Stars of death hung above us
And innocent Russia writhed

Beneath boots wet with blood
And black prison-van tyres.

St. 6: the marking of every house reverses the biblical account of the
Passover, Exodus 12; far from being a protective sign, it signals doom for every
household.

117. Apparently Tarkovsky's only poem about the Gulag, in which many of his
friends had done time. Only after the poet's death did his daughter Marina
discover that he had been a friend of Varlaam Shalamov (1907–82), a writer of
outstanding talent who spent seventeen years as a political prisoner and who,
after he eventually returned to Moscow, found it virtually impossible to have
his work published; he died in a hostel. Tarkovsky helped him with advice and
recommendations, and in 1972 Shalamov gave him a copy of his first published
book of poems, *Moscow Clouds*, with the inscription, 'with deep respect and
affection'. It was typical of the times that even in the 1980s Marina knew very
little about Shalamov, though she had read his *Kolyma Tales*, short factual stories
about the camps, 'which, like the Bible, everyone in the world ought to read'
(Tarkovskaia 2006, p.309).

Vee is the fiendish monster in a tale by Nikolai Gogol, who is able to see
the victim of the evil spirits whom prayer and incantation render blind; his huge
eyelids only have to be lifted for him to point a lethal iron finger at the hapless
figure who until now has been safe within the ring drawn around him.

Osip Mandelshtam uses Vee as a metaphor for Stalin towards the end of
his *Fourth Prose*, written in 1930: 'On Red Square Vee is reading the telephone
directory. Lift up my eyelids. Give me the Cheka ...[political police]' (Mandelshtam
1979, p.325).

118. Most of the poet's biblical references lead to the Old Testament, the obvious
exception being Lazarus ('After the War', 'Komitas'), associated above all with
resurrection. On the other hand images of crucifixion, themes of sacrifice and of
the artist/poet as victim recur in many different forms, as they do in the films.
This one poem where Jesus Christ is named is deeply contemplative: the dream
is strangely static – stony – but the sun is rising. The vividly physical figure,
reminiscent of countless ikons and other paintings, is set in the context of two
urgent, open questions about why this image is so essentially a part of the poet's
consciousness.

The comparison of mountain crest and crucifixion reads like an echo of the
words of Maria Lebiadkina (to whom Lisa compared Maria in *Mirror*) about the
Pointed Hill beside the monastery that casts its long, slim shadow across the lake
and, on hitting the island, becomes a sign of the cross. Fëdor Dostoievsky, *The
Devils*, Pt.1, ch.4. Viacheslav Ivanov has an interesting analysis of this passage
(Viacheslav Ivanov, *Freedom and the Tragic Life*, London 1952, pp.43–4).
See also note 75.

119. The poem's 'you' is the poet's youth, which he feels is already over, but it also
seems to address Maria Tarkovskaia.

Elisavetgrad/Kirovograd is built on granite.

In 1938 the poet was building a family home and also the house of poetry.
He was torn between two loves, already married to his second wife; and although
still young, wrote this farewell to his youth.

120. In the romantic, subtly erotic poem of 1857 by A.A. Fet from which the epigraph is
taken, the poet writes of a beautiful young girl in a garden, on whose knee sits an
equally beautiful, 'wicked' little boy whose fidgeting causes her hair to fall down in
a bewitching cascade. The poet suspects the child of being a minion of Aphrodite,
whom he accuses of bearing his soul away to her domain. A white butterfly has
long been fluttering nearby, an image of the soul and of Psyche. (In Apuleius'
tale Cupid could only visit Psyche in the dark, and she lost him because she lit a

candle and looked at him). The themes of doomed love and inexorable fate are present in both poems, but here Psyche is a Russian beggar-woman, of the kind that existed both before and after the revolution, as pilgrim or vagrant. The word '*bezkolkhoznitsa*', 'without a kolkhoz', portrays her as an outcast from the collective system that had been destroying village life for over a decade. This is the only poem about Psyche, though there are many with butterflies, and the only one that refers to collectivisation, here juxtaposed with nineteenth-century Romanticism and Greek legend.

The images are reminiscent of Bergson's reference to the fable of Cupid and Psyche. The latter was guilty of 'an unholy curiosity to know, otherwise than through God, how to tell good from evil', for which she was punished by Love, 'but only in order that she may anew be worthy of his choice ... Soul and butterfly, the symbol of resurrection, have always been synonymous' (Bergson 2007, p.215).

121. Written in Pushkinian Alexandrines, this is one of only a few doom-laden poems; it contains a strong echo of a poem by Evgenii Baratynsky about his work being found by some distant descendant who will hear his 'poor voice' and with whom his soul will be in concord – 'As I have found a friend in this my generation,/So shall I find a reader among my distant heirs'. Tarkovsky wrote for years in the knowledge that his poems were unlikely to be published: 'I wrote with no idea of my reading public, but still trusting that my voice would not be lost, because it was not born of impenetrable darkness' (Arsenii Tarkovsky 1991–3, vol.2, p.199). Mandelshtam (Mandelshtam 1979, p.68) writes about the same Baratynsky poem, comparing its central image to the experience of finding a bottle with a message cast into the sea. He contrasts this 'providential reader' with the addressee of civic verse, the Russian man-in-the-street of a specific decade.

Andrei's position was also uncompromisingly un-civic: 'I have never thought of the viewer. How could I? What should I think? Should I educate him? Or will I find out what one John Smith in London or a certain Ivanov in Moscow thinks? ... If I want to do anything at all I can only do it my way and take the viewer as my equal' (Andrei Tarkovsky, *Interviews*, 1986, p.121).

The poem was written just under six months after the infamous speech by Andrei Zhdanov (secretary to the Central Committee in charge of ideological affairs) in which he berated Mikhail Zoshchenko and Anna Akhmatova (referring to the latter as 'half harlot and half nun'), and the decree insisting on strict observance of the tenets of socialist realism. This put an end to the mood of optimism that followed the victory of 1945. During that brief period a volume of Tarkovsky's verse had actually been accepted for publication, even though it contained no mention of Stalin, and only a statutory mention of Lenin: 'happy that I've read Lenin/Not in translation, but in his native tongue'. This line the poet called his 'engine' which would pull the train of poems through; the only occasion, says his daughter, when he 'twisted his soul' (Tarkovskaia 2006, p.312). After Zhdanov's speech there was no question of publication and his first collection did not appear for another seventeen years.

122. Kashchei: a sinister, bony, predatory figure in Slavic folklore, immortal unless the egg in which his soul is kept can be found and broken; he figures in the ballet *The Firebird*.

123. Written at a time when his wife Maria often used to visit her divorced parents: her mother in Kineshma, her father in Maloiaroslavets (when his second wife died, he was left with three young children, and, having been a judge under the old regime he had no right to work). At the same period the poet often went to visit his mother in Zinovievsk (Elisavetgrad/Kirovograd) or on work assignments. Thus railway stations and partings punctuated their lives. The poem plays with the multiple reflections in an actual mirror and in the tiny facets of different cut-glass objects in the station buffet.

Appendix I: Pushkin Poems

The Prophet

Tormented by my spirit's thirst
I dragged myself through gloomy wastes
And at a place where two paths crossed
A six-winged seraph came to me.
With fingertips as light as sleep
He touched the pupils of my eyes
And with a startled eagle's gaze
My mantic pupils opened wide.
Then his fingers touched my ears
And they were filled with roar and clang,
I heard the shuddering of the sky,
And celestial angels' flight,
Sea-beasts moving in the deep,
And grape-vines growing in vales.
And he pressed against my mouth
And out he plucked my sinful tongue
With its guile and empty words,
And taking a wise serpent's tongue
He thrust it in my frozen mouth,
With his blood-soaked right hand.
He cleft my breast with his great sword
And removed my quivering heart,
And swiftly in the yawning hole
He placed a flaming coal.
I lay in wasteland like a corpse,
And the Lord's voice called to me:
'Rise up, prophet, see and hear,
Be thou charged with my will,
And going out over seas and lands –
Fire men's hearts with the word.'

1826

'What can my name be for you?'

What can my name be for you?
'Twill die as will the mournful thud
Of splashing wave on distant shore,
Or night-time noise in deepest woods.

'Twill leave upon the keepsake page
Dead traces like the pattern made
By lines cut in a burial-stone
In some mysterious tongue.

What is my name? Long since forgotten
In tempestuous new emotions,
It will offer to your soul
No pure or tender recollections.

But on some mournful, silent day
Pronounce it, even as you grieve;
You will say: 'I am remembered,
A heart exists where I'm alive.'

1830

'Once there lived a pauper knight'

Once there lived a pauper knight,
A simple man who rarely spoke,
Pale and gloomy was his mien,
His spirit bold and frank.

Long ago he'd had a vision
Beyond mind's comprehension,
And its profound impression
Cut deep into his heart.

Travelling to Geneva
Close by a roadside cross
He had seen the Virgin Mary,
Mother of the Christ.

From that time, his soul aflame
He would not look on women,
Nor would he ever talk with them
Until the very grave.

His steel visor from that time
Was never raised again,
No scarf adorned his neck, instead
Rosary beads were hung.

No prayer to Father or to Son
Or Holy Ghost was offered
By that paladin, he was
Outside the common mould.

He would spend long nights awake
Before the sacred visage,
On which he fixed his mournful gaze,
His silent tears flowing freely.

He was filled with faith and love,
True to his pious dream,
In letters of blood his shield proclaimed
Ave, Mater Dei.

When sallied forth the paladins
To face the trembling foe
On Palestinian plains,
Pronouncing ladies' names,

Lumen coeli, sancta Rosa!
He would cry, transported,
And at his threat Mahomedans
Would scatter on all sides.

Retiring to his distant keep
He lived in stern seclusion,
Never speaking, ever sad,
Until he died, unhouselled.

When he was on the point of death
The evil spirit came
To carry the knight's soul away
To his infernal realm.

'He didn't ever pray to God
He never observed fasts,
He wasn't up to any good
Chasing the mother of Christ.'

But She, the Most Immaculate
Interceded for him,
And let her paladin come in
To the eternal kingdom.

1829

Appendix II: The Process of Translation

Verse translation took up much of Arsenii Tarkovsky's time and fills most of this book; here are some examples of the kind of problem that can face the practitioner.

Some earlier versions of 'Yesterday from early on I waited'.

The Russian original and the 1986 version published in *Sculpting in Time*:

С утра я тебя дожидался вчера,	From morning on I waited yesterday
Они догадались, что ты не придёшь,	They knew you wouldn't come, they guessed.
Ты помнишь, какая погода была,	You remember what a lovely day it was?
Как в праздник! И я выходил без пальто.	A holiday! I didn't need a coat.
Сегодня пришла, и устроили нам	You came today and it turned out
Какой-то особенно пасмурный день	A sullen, leaden day
И дождь, и особенно поздний час	And it was raining and somehow late,
И капли бегут по холодным ветвям.	And branches cold with running drops.
Ни словом унять. Ни платком утереть ...	Word cannot soothe, nor kerchief wipe away ...

Variants tried out and discarded (line by line):

Line 1:

> From morning on I waited yesterday
> I was waiting for you yesterday from morning on
> I waited for you yesterday all morning
> All day long I waited yesterday

Line 2:

> They knew you wouldn't come, they guessed
> They said all along you wouldn't come
> They were right when they said you wouldn't come
> They said you wouldn't come and they were right
> They had guessed that you weren't going to come

Line 3:

> Do you remember the wonderful weather?
> Do you remember how lovely the day was?
> You remember what a lovely day it was?

Line 4:

> A holiday! I didn't need a coat.
> Like a holiday! I went without my coat.

Line 5:

> You came today and it turned out
> Today you did arrive and it turned out
> Today you did arrive and we were given
> Today you came and we were given
> You only came today and we were given

Line 6:

> A sullen, leaden day
> A particularly gloomy sort of day
> A particularly sullen sort of day
> A specially heavy, overcast day
> A really sullen, overcast day
> A thoroughly sullen, dreary day

Line 7:

> It poured with rain and the hour was so late
> So much rain, and the hour was so late
> And it was raining, and somehow/thoroughly late
> Steady rain, the hour so very late
> Such rain, and the hour so very late

Line 8:

> And branches cold with running drops
> And drops trickling down chilly branches
> [The] chilled branches drenched in running drops
> And drops trickling down the cold branches

Line 9:

> Word cannot soothe, nor kerchief wipe away
> No word will soothe, no handkerchief wipe dry
> That/This no word can/will soothe, no cloth can/will wipe away

The poem is surprisingly elusive. The ridiculous number of changes comes of the attempt to preserve as far as possible rhythm and euphony, everyday diction, blurred outlines, sadness and bewilderment, and time frames. Even now I cannot be sure that the version included here will be my final one; and more felicitous renderings may well be found by other translators.

'Final' version:

> Yesterday from early on I waited,
> they had all guessed you wouldn't come,
> d'you remember how lovely yesterday was?
> Holiday weather! I went out with no coat.

Today you arrived, and we were given
a somehow specially sombre day,
it rained, and the hour was somehow late,
and drops trickled down cold branches.

This – no word can salve, no handkerchief wipe away.

The refrain of 'Now summer is gone' also went through many versions. It reads literally: 'Only of that [is] too little'. Russian uses a genitive with any expression of quantity (also with negatives), and therefore the subject of the sentence is an impersonal, and unstated, 'it'. *Sculpting in Time* has: 'But there has to be more'. When I returned to the poem after many years I felt this carried a demanding, or querulous, note absent from the original. I tried 'But/only that's not enough/cannot be all/ is too little/small' etc., none of which is satisfactory because both 'not' and 'too' destroy the oddly positive impact of the impersonal, subjectless Russian. Julia Dale (for whose insights I am endlessly grateful) suggested the bold solution, 'and yet …', which captures the openness, the blank quality, of the original, somehow conveyed in the genitive case – a feeling that perhaps there is more to be said, but no indication that anyone can know what it might be.

Then, above all as a result of listening to the poem in both Russian and English, I abandoned 'and yet …' because the shortened line and the sudden post-plosive silence after 'yet' seemed so far from the flow and beat of the Russian '*tol'ko etovo malo*'. I always try – with varying degrees of success – to reproduce rhythm, a living element of verse, and have therefore settled on 'And yet surely there's more'. I don't find this necessarily 'better' than 'And yet …', but I like the fact that it is much closer to the original beat. Both versions convey an unfocused yearning that seems to contain something of the longing often expressed in Andrei Tarkovsky's films and writing.

An insurmountable problem presented by this poem in Russian is that, with one exception, every line ends in '-*lo*', alternately stressed (as in 'hullo' pronounced in Scottish), and unstressed (as in 'hoopla'). The exception ends in '-*ly*'. There is clearly no possibility in English of reproducing this pattern, which can feel quite natural in an inflected language, where the same number and case endings recur so often. For obvious reasons such repetitions unify a poem rather in the way that patches of colour unify a painting or phrases a piece of music. One way of compensating for the loss is to use alliteration as and when one can do so satisfactorily. Here (and also, for instance, in 'The White Day') the fairly frequent 'n' sound has been useful.

Bibliography

Works by Arsenii and Andrei Tarkovsky

Andrei Tarkovsky, *Andrei Rublëv*, trans. by Kitty Hunter Blair, London 1991.

Andrei Tarkovsky, *Andrei Tarkovsky: Interviews*, ed. by John Gianvito, Jackson 2006.

Andrei Tarkovsky, *Bright, Bright Day*, London and Florence 2007.

Andrei Tarkovsky, *Collected Screenplays*, trans. by Natasha Synessios and William Powell, introduction by Natasha Synessios, London 1990.

Andrei Tarkovsky, *Sculpting in Time: Reflections on Cinema*, trans. by Kitty Hunter Blair, London 1986.

Andrei Tarkovsky, *Time within Time: The Diaries*, trans. by Kitty Hunter Blair, Calcutta 1991.

Arsenii Tarkovsky, 'Hope for the Future of Russian Poetry', interview, *Voprosy literatury*, no.6, 1979.

Arsenii Tarkovsky, 'Nauka i poezia', *Khimia i zhizn'*, no.7, 1982.

Arsenii Tarkovsky, 'Nobility of Spirit', *Literaturnaia gazeta*, no.7, 11 February 1987.

Arsenii Tarkovsky, *Sobranie sochinenii v trëkh tomakh [Works in 3 Volumes]*, Moscow 1991–3.

Arsenii Tarkovsky and Marina Tarkovskaia, *Sud'ba moia sgorela mezhdu strok [Between the Lines My Fate Had Burnt Up]*, ed. by V.A. Amikhranian; poetry by Tarkovksy with commentaries by Tarkovskaia, Moscow 2009.

References

Layla Alexander-Garrett, *Andrei Tarkovsky: The Collector of Dreams*, London 2012.

André Bazin, *What Is Cinema?*, trans. by Hugh Gray, Berkeley 2005.

Robert Bird, *Andrei Rublëv*, London 2004.

Robert Bird, *Andrei Tarkovsky, Elements of Cinema*, London 2008.

Robert Bresson, *Notes on the Cinematographer*, London 1986.

Michel Chion, *Audio-Vision*, New York 1994.

Michel Chion, *Voice in Cinema*, New York 1998.

Gilles Deleuze, *Cinema 1: The Movement Image*, trans. by Hugh Tomlinson and Robert Galeta, London and New York 1989.

Gilles Deleuze, *Cinema 2: The Time Image*, trans. by Hugh Tomlinson and Robert Galeta, London and New York 1989.

Geoff Dyer, *Zona*, Edinburgh and London 2012.

Igor Evlampiev, *Khudozhestvennaia filosofia Andreia Tarkovskogo [The Artistic Philosophy of Andrei Tarkovsky]*, Ufa 2012.

Jean-Luc Godard, *Interviews*, Jackson 1998.

Mikhail Iampolski, *The Memory of Tiresias: Intertextuality in Film*, Berkeley 1998.

G.A. Jonsson and T.A. Ottarsson (eds), *Through the Mirror, Reflections on the Films of Andrei Tarkovsky*, Newcastle upon Tyne 2006.

Arkadii Khvoroshchan, 'Derzhava knigi' ('The Realm of the Book', interview with

Arsenii Tarkovsky), *Almanakh bibliofila*, Moscow 1979, vol.7.

Mark Lefanu, *The Cinema of Andrey Tarkovsky*, London 1987.

Tony Mitchell, 'Andrei Tarkovsky and Nostalghia', *Film Criticism*, vol.8, no.3, 1984.

Terence McSweeney, 'Sculpting the Time Image: An Exploration of Tarkovsky's Film Theory from a Deleuzian Perspective', in G.A. Jonsson and T.A. Ottarsson (eds), *Through the Mirror, Reflections on the Films of Andrei Tarkovsky*, Newcastle upon Tyne 2006.

Thomas Redwood, *Andrei Tarkovsky's Poetics of Cinema*, Newcastle upon Tyne 2010.

Arkady and Boris Strugatsky, *Roadside Picnic*, London 2012.

Natasha Synessios, *Mirror*, London 2001.

Marina Tarkovskaia, *Oskol'ki zerkala [Fragments of a Mirror]*, Moscow 2006.

Evgenii Tsymbal and Viacheslav Okeanskii, *Fenomen Andreia Tarkovskogo v intellektual'noi i khudozhesvennoi kul'ture [The Phenomenon of Andrei Tarkovsky in Intellectual and Artistic Culture]*, Ivanovo 2008.

Maya Turovskaya, *Tarkovsky: Cinema as Poetry*, trans. by Natasha Ward, London 1989.

Dziga Vertov, *Kino-eye*, trans. by Kevin O'Brien, ed. and introduction by Annette Michelson, Los Angeles 1984.

General

Aeschylus, *Prometheus Bound*, Harmondsworth 1961.

Anna Akhmatova, *Sobrannye sochinenia v 6 tomakh [Works in 6 Volumes]*, Moscow 2007.

Anna Akhmatova, *Vospominania ob Anne Akhmatovoi [Anna Akhmatova Remembered]*, Moscow 1991.

Marc Augé, *Oblivion*, trans. by Margolin de Jager, Minneapolis 2004.

William Barrett, *Irrational Man*, London 1962.

Samuel Beckett, *Molloy, Malone dies, The Unnamable*, London 1959.

Henri Bergson, *Creative Evolution*, London 1911.

Henri Bergson, *The Creative Mind*, New York 2007.

Henri Bergson, *Matter and Memory*, trans. N.M. Paul and W. Scott Palmer, New York 2004.

Henri Bergson, *The World of Dreams*, New York 1958.

Maurice Blanchot, *The Gaze of Orpheus and Other Literary Essays*, New York 1981.

Piotr Chaadaev, *Philosophical Letters and An Apology of a Madman*, trans. and introduction by Mary Barbara Zeldin, Knoxville 1969.

Vitali Chentalinski, *Les surprises de la Loubianka*, Paris, 1996.

R.G. Collingwood, *Speculum Mentis*, Oxford 1924.

Gilles Deleuze, *Le Bergsonisme*, Paris 1966.

Mladen Dolar, 'Which Voice?' in *In the First Circle*, exhibition catalogue, Fundacio Tapies, Barcelona 2011.

F.M. Dostoyevsky, *Demons*, trans. and annotated by Richard Pevear and Larissa Volokhonsky, London 2006.

Hilary Fink, *Bergson and Russian Modernism, 1900–30*, Evanston 1999.

Pavel Florensky, *Ikonostasis*, trans. by Donald Sheehan and Olga Andreyev, New York 1996.

Ernst Gombrich, *Art and Illusion*, London 1960.

Vasily Grossman, *Life and Fate*, trans. by Robert Chandler, London 1985.

Georgii Ivanov, *Peterburgskie zimy*, New York 1952.

Viacheslav Ivanov, *Freedom and the Tragic Life*, London 1952.

Paul Klee, *Pedagogical Sketchbook*, London 1953.

Osip Mandelshtam, *Complete Critical Prose and Letters*, ed. by Jane Garry Harris, trans. and notes by Jane Garry Harris and Constance Link, Ann Arbor 1979.

David Nichol, *Triumphs of the Spirit in Russia*, London 1997.

Friedrich Nietzsche, *Thus Spoke Zarathustra*, Harmondsworth 1961.

Ovid, *Metamorphoses*, Harmondsworth 1961.

Kathleen F. Parthé, *Russia's Dangerous Texts*, New Haven and London 2004.

A.S. Pushkin, *Polnoie sobranie sochinenii v 10 tomakh*, Moscow 1962.

Raymond of Capua, *The Life of St Catherine of Siena*, London 1960.

St Augustine, *Confessions*, Harmondsworth 1961.

Paul Schrader, *Transcendental Style in Film: Ozu, Bresson, Dreyer*, Berkeley 1972.

Sergei Shumov and A. Andreev, *Skovoroda, Grigorii: Zhizneopisanie, sochinenia [Life and Works]*, Kiev and Moscow 2002.

Mary Warnock, *Time and Imagination*, Oxford 1994.

On translation

Walter Benjamin, *Illuminations*, London 1999.

Paul Ricoeur, *On Translation*, London and New York 2006.

Other relevant works

András Bálint Kovács and Ákos Szilágyi, *Les mondes d'Andrej Tarkovski*, Lausanne 1987.

Maria Belkina, *Skreshchenia sudeb [Intersecting Destinies]*, Moscow 2005.

Nathan Dunne (ed.), *Tarkovsky*, London 2008.

V.P. Filimonov, *Andrei Tarkovsky*, Moscow 2012.

Aleksandr Gordon, *Ne utolivshii zhazhdy [Unquenched Thirst]*, Moscow 2007.

Peter Green, *The Winding Quest*, London 1993.

Elizabeth Grosz, *The Nick of Time: Politics, Evolution and the Untimely*, Durham NC and London 2004.

Iaroslav Iaropolov (ed.), *Nostalgia po Tarkovskomu [Nostalgia for Tarkovsky]*, Moscow 2007.

Vida Johnson and Graham Petrie, *The Films of Andrei Tarkovsky: A Visual fugue*, Bloomington 1994.

Thomas Redwood, *Andrei Tarkovsky's Poetics of Cinema*, Newcastle upon Tyne 2010.

Vitaly Shentalinsky, *The KGB's Literary Archive*, London 1995.

George Steiner, *After Babel: Aspects of Language*, Oxford 1992.

Olga Surkova, *Tarkovskii i ia, dnevnik pionerki [Tarkovsky and I: A Pioneer's Diary]*, Moscow 2002.

Olga Surkova, *S Tarkovskim i o Tarkovskom [With Tarkovsky, About Tarkovsky]*, Moscow 2005.

Arsenii Tarkovsky: significant biographical dates

Some biographical details are included in the 'Notes to the Poems', but this brief chronological list may be helpful.

Born 1907	in Elisavetgrad, Kherson Province, in the Ukraine.
1916–25	With interruptions due to the 1917 revolution and subsequent civil war, attends the local gymnasium and then the technical college.
1919	Death in battle of his fifteen-year-old brother, Valerii.
1925	Moves to Moscow, attends Higher Course in Literature until its closure in 1929. Meets the poet Georgii Shengeli who becomes his friend and mentor, as a result starts to write for the newspaper, the *Hooter*.
1928	Marriage to Maria Vishniakova.
1931	Starts to writes for national radio.
1932	Birth of his son Andrei.
1933	Thanks to Shengeli, starts working as a translator of verse, principally by young poets of the Soviet republics.
1934	Publication of first book of translations. From this year until the Second World War, and again after the war, travels fairly frequently to the Caucasus and Central Asia in connection with his translation work.
1937	Leaves his family to live with Antonina Bokhonova, who becomes his second wife.
1940	Membership of the Soviet Union of Writers.
January 1942	Begins active service and becomes correspondent of army newspaper, *Battle Alert*. Awarded Red Star.
December 1943	Gravely wounded. Series of operations and leg amputation before life eventually saved by Moscow surgeon.
1946	Meets Anna Akhmatova.
1947	Leaves Antonina Bokhonova for Tatiana Ozerskaia, whom he marries in 1951.
1949	Given secret orders by Kremlin officials to translate lyrical poems written by Stalin in his youth; some months later the order is rescinded.
1962	Publication of first collection of poems, *On the Eve of Snowfall*.
1966	Visits France with a literary delegation; visits again in 1970.
1967	Visits London.
1970s–1980s	Further collections of poems are published and he wins literary awards.
1986	Andrei Tarkovsky dies in Paris.
1989	Arsenii dies in Moscow.

Index

Individual poems are listed alphabetically by title under Tarkovsky, Arsenii
Titles of films by Andrei Tarkovsky listed alphabetically under director's name

*film character
**literary character